The Glannon Guide to Evidence

The Glannon Guide to Evidence

Learning Evidence
Through Multiple-Choice
Questions and Analysis

Second Edition

Michael Avery
Professor Emeritus
Suffolk University School of Law

Introduction

This book provides a short, clear, and straightforward explanation of the Federal Rules of Evidence. The text illustrates the rules by analyzing multiple-choice questions—practical problems like those you will encounter in practice and those that your professors use in drafting exams. Some of the questions are based on real issues that arose in the civil and criminal cases that I tried. More significantly, the contextual approach in this book is based on my observations of the common mistakes people make about evidence law during four decades of trying cases and three decades of teaching evidence.

The three most important areas in evidence law are: (1) the rule against hearsay (Chapter 8); (2) character evidence (Chapter 4); and (3) impeaching witnesses (Chapter 6). Most of the evidence problems you will encounter in practice fall into one of those three areas, as do most of the questions on the bar exam and, probably, most of the questions on your law school exam. To prepare you for those challenges, this book spends more time on those issues than on all other issues combined. That is not to say you should ignore the other issues. You will need to know all the rules at one time or another. The chapters of this book correspond to each of the ten substantive articles of the Federal Rules of Evidence.

In order for an item of evidence to be admissible, it must be able to overcome all potential objections. You should think of the rules of evidence as a series of hurdles on a track. You must have a legal argument that gets you over each hurdle in order to run the track and get an item of evidence admitted. If you fail to master all the rules, you may trip over a hurdle and a crucial piece of evidence might be excluded. But not all the hurdles are raised for each item of evidence offered. The ones you will encounter most often are hearsay, character, and impeachment. It makes sense to spend most of your time on those topics.

Other than in academic discussions, you will rarely encounter the rules of evidence in the abstract. For example, you must learn and understand the elements of what makes something hearsay. But you will rarely be asked to enumerate the elements of hearsay outside of a classroom. You will be asked a more concrete question. A lawyer will ask a witness on the stand to relate what someone said outside the courtroom, the other lawyer will object to the question, and the lawyers will argue about whether the answer the witness would give to this specific question constitutes hearsay. We make decisions about the rules of evidence in response to the offer of a specific item of evidence in the context of a specific case.

You should thoughtfully read the rules and the explanations of what the rules mean. You should concentrate your studying, however, on the application of the rules to specific factual situations. That is what you need to master. This book is organized to assist you in doing just that. Each chapter or section begins with the definition and explanation of a given rule of evidence. The text that follows contains multiple-choice questions, in which the rules are applied to factual scenarios that commonly arise in the trial of cases. Each question is followed by an analysis in which I tell you the correct answer and explain why the others are wrong.

The questions in each chapter primarily relate to the rules under discussion in that chapter. From time to time, however, I include potential answers that refer to basic understandings from other chapters. As I've said, an item of evidence must satisfy all of the rules in order to be admissible. References to foundational material from different chapters will provide you with opportunities to review your overall knowledge of evidence law as you go along.

When you come to a multiple-choice question, cover up the analysis without looking at it. You should read the facts of the question carefully. Take note of what type of case is on trial, the procedural posture of the case (for example, whether the lawyer is conducting direct or cross-examination), and what the evidence in question is offered to prove. Then read the answers and select the best one. Spend some time thinking about it. You should be able to articulate a reason for rejecting each answer that you believe is wrong, and to explain why your selection of the best answer is correct. Then read the analysis and see how you did.

You can only increase your knowledge of Evidence (or any other subject) by becoming aware of what you don't know. If you skip the process of doing your own analysis and jump ahead to read my explanation of the answers, you will not discover gaps in your understanding. Such gaps are inevitable when you are learning anything new, so you shouldn't feel bad about them. You must, however, become aware of them so that you can fill them in. This book is designed to help you do that.

Acknowledgments

First I want to thank my friend and colleague Joe Glannon for encouraging me to contribute to his wonderful Glannon Guide series. Professor Glannon has been an inspiration to several generations of Suffolk Law students, to the countless number of students across the country who have used his books, and to his colleagues. It is an honor to be associated with him in this venture.

Second, I would like to thank very much the Suffolk law students who worked with me on this project as research assistants: Elyse Hershon, Danielle Simonetti, AlexaRae Wright, and Jessica K. Myer. They tested out the multiple-choice questions for me and reviewed the text for accuracy and clarity. Their many suggestions for changes were invaluable. Any errors or confusion that remain are my fault alone.

I also wish to thank the law professors who carefully reviewed the manuscript for Aspen. Their critiques and suggestions were extremely helpful. Again, any errors that remain are mine alone.

Finally I am indebted to the many students who have been in my Evidence classes over the years for their intelligent and enthusiastic participation. Many of the multiple-choice problems in this book have appeared in Microsoft PowerPoint presentations over the years and the students' critical responses to them have been exceedingly helpful.

Michael Avery

August 2018

The Glannon Guide
to Evidence

1

General Provisions

CHAPTER OVERVIEW
A. Scope and Applicability of the Rules
B. Rulings on Evidence
C. Preliminary Questions
D. Limited Admissibility
E. Rule of Completeness
✦ Avery's Picks

The Federal Rules of Evidence were first adopted in 1975 and have been amended several times since then. For the most part, the Advisory Committee on the Federal Rules of Evidence recommends rules, the Supreme Court approves them, and then Congress enacts them. Congress may enact rules on its own, without going through the Advisory Committee and the Supreme Court. Most states have adopted the Federal Rules of Evidence as their state rules of evidence, often with modifications to one or more rules. The state where you practice may have some rules that are significantly different from the Federal Rules, and you will have to know them when you practice in state court or when state rules govern an action in federal court.

A. Scope and Applicability of the Rules

The Federal Rules govern trials and proceedings in the federal courts, including bankruptcy and admiralty matters and proceedings before federal magistrates, with some exceptions. The rules do not apply to the determination of preliminary facts necessary to decisions by the court on the admissibility of evidence under Rule 104(a), grand jury proceedings, proceedings for extradition or rendition, preliminary examinations in criminal cases, sentencing, granting or revoking probation, issuance of warrants for arrest, criminal summonses, search warrants, and proceedings with respect to release on bail or otherwise. As a result, for example, hearsay may be admitted in such proceedings. The rules with respect to privilege, however, apply to all proceedings.

B.   Rulings on Evidence

Under Rule 103(a), the appellate courts will not reverse a trial court's erroneous rulings with respect to the admission or exclusion of evidence unless a substantial right of a party is affected. Whether substantial rights were affected is determined under the harmless error standard. An error is harmless where the reviewing court is confident that it did not affect the judgment. In order to preserve an evidentiary issue for appeal the party must object to the evidence at trial. If the trial judge sustains an objection, the evidence will not be admitted; if the judge overrules the objection, the evidence is admitted.

Where the trial judge admits evidence, in order to preserve the issue for appeal the opponent must make a timely objection or motion to strike, stating the specific ground of the objection unless the specific ground was apparent from the context. If a party fails to object or to make a motion to strike, evidence will be admitted and may be used by the jury for any purpose for which it is logically relevant, unless the judge on her own instructs the jury to consider the evidence only for a limited purpose.[1] Where the trial judge excludes evidence, in order to preserve the issue for appeal the proponent must make an offer of proof, unless the substance of the evidence was apparent from the context in which questions were asked.

Counsel must make an offer of proof outside the hearing of the jury. If the evidence consists of testimony by a witness, the witness may be examined outside the jury's presence, or counsel may represent to the judge what the expected testimony would have been. If the evidence in question is an exhibit, it may be marked for identification and it becomes part of the appellate record, but the trial jury does not see it.

Requests for rulings admitting or excluding evidence may be made before trial, by means of a motion in limine. Once the court makes a definitive ruling on the motion, a party does not have to renew its objection or offer of proof at trial in order to preserve the issue for appeal.

Appellate courts may take notice of "plain error" with respect to evidentiary matters where substantial rights of a party were affected, although the party failed to bring the error to the attention of the trial court. An appellate court may find plain error where the mistake was clear and obvious and prejudiced the substantial rights of a party. It is exceedingly rare for the appellate courts to find plain error in civil cases.

---

1.   See the discussion of Rule 105, *infra.*

C. Preliminary Questions

The trial judge decides preliminary questions of fact that must be resolved in order to rule on the admissibility of evidence. Under Rule 104(a) the judge is not constrained by the rules of evidence, except with regard to privileges, with respect to the material the judge may consider in order to decide preliminary questions.

> **Rule 104. Preliminary Questions**
> (a) **In General.** The court must decide any preliminary question about whether a witness is qualified, a privilege exists, or evidence is admissible. In so deciding, the court is not bound by evidence rules, except those on privilege.

The proponent of an item of evidence has the burden of convincing the court by a preponderance of the evidence that a necessary factual foundation for admissibility exists. Let's consider some examples to see how Rule 104(a) works in practice. Suppose a party in a personal injury case wishes to call an expert witness whose testimony relies upon certain scientific principles. Under Rule 702 the trial judge must find that the scientific principles are reliable before permitting the expert to testify.[2] Under Rule 104(a) the materials the judge looks at to determine reliability do not have to be admissible in evidence. So the court might take into account affidavits from other experts, articles in scientific journals, and representations by counsel, although such materials would be inadmissible in evidence. If the court determines by a preponderance of the evidence that the scientific principles are reliable, the court will allow the expert to testify.

Similarly, suppose a police officer is asked to testify to the statement of an eyewitness to a shooting, made to the officer during his investigation. The statement would be hearsay, but admissible under the hearsay exception for an excited utterance if the person made the statement while under the stress of a startling event.[3] The trial judge must decide whether the person was under the stress of witnessing the shooting when he made the statement in question. In making that determination, the judge may take into account information from a variety of sources (for example, affidavits of other witnesses), whether or not that information would be admissible in evidence.

Where the facts that establish the foundation for admissibility of an item of evidence are themselves admissible in evidence, a witness may testify to them in the presence of the jury in order to lay the foundation. If the material offered in support or opposition is inadmissible in evidence, the court reviews such material outside the presence of the jury. Once the judge has admitted something in evidence it is up to the jury to determine how much weight to give it.

---

2. Expert witnesses and scientific evidence are discussed in Chapter 7.
3. Hearsay and the exceptions to the hearsay rule are discussed in Chapter 8.

Rule 104(b) deals with a different type of preliminary question—one involving evidence that is conditionally relevant.

Rule 104. Preliminary Questions

(b) Relevance That Depends on a Fact. When the relevance of evidence depends on whether a fact exists, proof must be introduced sufficient to support a finding that the fact does exist. The court may admit the proposed evidence on the condition that the proof be introduced later.

This provision controls the situation where an item of evidence will be relevant only if a certain fact is proven. For example, ordinarily the state of mind of a homicide victim is not relevant.[4] Suppose the victim told her neighbor that she was going to take her children and move into a shelter because she feared that her husband would kill her. Her statement is hearsay and not admissible under the state of mind exception. However, if the husband was aware of her intention to leave with the children, it could provide him with a motive to kill her, and thus be relevant. The relevance of the victim's state of mind in this example depends upon the existence of a fact, namely, whether her husband knew of her intention to leave. The court would admit the victim's statement to her neighbor only upon the introduction of evidence sufficient to support a finding that the husband knew of her intention.

What does evidence "sufficient to support a finding" mean? It means evidence that would be sufficient to convince a reasonable jury of the fact by a preponderance of the evidence. The trial judge does not decide whether the fact existed. The judge decides only whether there is enough evidence in the record from which a jury could decide that the fact existed. If there is, the judge will admit the evidence in question and advise the jury it may consider the evidence only if the jury finds, by a preponderance of the evidence, that the necessary fact existed. In our example, if the judge concluded there was sufficient evidence to support the necessary finding, the judge would admit the victim's statement to the neighbor, and tell the jury it could take the statement into account only if the jury decided by a preponderance of the evidence that the husband knew of his wife's intention to leave.

QUESTION 1. The defendant is on trial for assault and battery against his girlfriend. The two of them live together. When a police officer arrived at their home on the night in question, the girlfriend told the officer that the defendant had hit and choked her, torn her dress, threw her on the ground and kicked her repeatedly. At the trial, however, she testified that she had fallen down the stairs and the defendant had not struck her. The prosecutor calls the officer as a witness to testify to the victim's earlier statements and argues they are admissible under the excited utterance

---

4.   The state of mind of homicide victims is discussed in greater detail in Chapter 8.

exception to the hearsay rule. The defendant objects. The prosecutor then offers to give the judge a copy of the police report, which includes statements by neighbors who witnessed the officer's interview of the victim in front of her home on the night in question. The neighbors said that she was crying, shaking, and bleeding while talking with the officer. The prosecutor also offers to show the court photos he says were taken by one of the neighbors, showing the victim talking to the officer with tears on her face and blood on her torn dress. The defendant objects to the court reviewing the police report and the photos. The court should:

A. Admit the evidence of the victim's statements to the officer, and advise the jury it may take the statements into account only if the jury finds the victim was under the stress of a startling event when she made them, based on the jury's review of the police report and the photos.
B. Decline to review the police report and the photos, because the report is hearsay and the photos have not been properly authenticated.
C. Review the police report and the photos without showing them to the jury, and admit the victim's statement to the officer if the judge is convinced by a preponderance of the evidence that the victim was under the stress of a startling event when she spoke to the officer.
D. Review the police report and the photos and show them to the jury, and admit the victim's statement to the officer if the judge is convinced by a preponderance of the evidence that the victim was under the stress of a startling event when she spoke to the officer.

ANALYSIS. The victim's statement is admissible under an exception to the hearsay rule if she made it while under the stress of a startling event. Under Rule 104(a) the judge determines questions of the admissibility of evidence and determines any preliminary factual questions that have to be resolved to decide the issue of admissibility. This problem should be decided under Rule 104(a) because it involves the *admissibility* of evidence, not the *conditional relevance* of evidence. There is no need to establish any given facts for the victim's statement to be relevant. Thus **A** is incorrect, because it describes the procedure for determining issues of conditional relevance. Choice **B** is incorrect because the judge is not bound by the rules of evidence with respect to what she may consider to determine the preliminary facts with respect to admissibility. That means that the judge may consider the hearsay police report and the photos that have not been authenticated[5] to determine whether the victim was under the stress of a startling event when she spoke to the officer. The judge should

5. The topic of authentication is discussed in Chapter 9.

not, however, allow the jury to see or hear any inadmissible evidence. Thus the correct answer is **C** and **D** is incorrect.

D.   Limited Admissibility

Often an item of evidence is admissible on one issue in a case, but not on others; for one purpose, but not for others; or against one party, but not against others. In such circumstances, Rule 105 provides that the judge, if requested to do so by a party, must give a limiting instruction to the jury, specifying the use to which the evidence may be put. A judge may also decide to give a limiting instruction on her own, but it is rare for judges to do so.

> **Rule 105. Limiting Evidence That Is Not Admissible Against Other Parties or for Other Purposes**
> If the court admits evidence that is admissible against a party or for a purpose—but not against another party or for another purpose—the court, on timely request, must restrict the evidence to its proper scope and instruct the jury accordingly.

The burden is on the party objecting to the evidence to request a limiting instruction. If the party does not make such a request and the court does not give a limiting instruction, then the evidence is admissible for any and all purposes for which it is logically relevant.

For example, Rule 609 provides that under certain circumstances previous criminal convictions may be used to impeach the credibility of a witness.[6] Under Rule 609 a conviction is admissible only for the light it sheds on whether the witness might testify falsely, not for any other purpose. Suppose that a defendant is charged in a criminal case with bank robbery, and he has a previous conviction for manslaughter, a felony. If the defendant testifies and the court permits the prosecutor to introduce the defendant's manslaughter conviction to impeach him, defense counsel can request a limiting instruction. The court would then advise the jury that the conviction may be considered only insofar as it reflects on the credibility of the defendant as a witness, and that the jury may not use it for any other purpose, such as drawing inferences about the likelihood that the defendant committed the bank robbery.[7]

Here is a second example. Plaintiff has sued Defendant 1 and Defendant 2 civilly for assault and battery. Plaintiff alleged that the two defendants beat him up because they did not like him. When he was arrested, Defendant 1 admitted to a police officer that he and Defendant 2 jumped the plaintiff on a

---

6.   Impeachment of witnesses through the use of criminal convictions is discussed in Chapter 6.

7.   If the prosecutor wanted to use the conviction for another purpose he would have to explicitly articulate a theory of admissibility under another rule. *See* Chapter 4.

dark street at night and beat him. At the trial, plaintiff calls the police officer to testify about Defendant 1's statement. Both Defendant 1 and Defendant 2 object. The plaintiff may introduce the statement against Defendant 1, under an exemption to the hearsay rule for statements by a party introduced by the opposing party.[8] Defendant 2 did not make the statement, however, and thus plaintiff may not introduce it against him under the hearsay rule. The court should overrule Defendant 1's objection, sustain Defendant 2's objection, and admit the statement with a limiting instruction that the jury may use it only in the case against Defendant 1, but may not consider it with respect to the liability of Defendant 2.

Under some circumstances, the judge may conclude that jurors will not be able to comply with a limiting instruction. In other words, the mental gymnastics required to use a piece of evidence for one purpose and put it out of mind for other purposes will be too difficult. Under these circumstances, the judge will have to determine whether the evidence should be excluded altogether in order to protect the rights of the party objecting to it. We will discuss this issue in Chapter 4 when we take up the exclusion of relevant evidence because the risk of unfair prejudice exceeds the probative value of the evidence.[9]

QUESTION 2. A Driver for the ABC Company crashed his truck into the plaintiff's car. Plaintiff sued the Driver and the ABC Company. During discovery, plaintiff obtained evidence that the Driver had three previous accidents, all his fault, while working for ABC. Plaintiff went to trial against both defendants and, in addition to the respondeat superior claim against ABC, also alleged a theory of negligent retention against the Company. At trial plaintiff sought to introduce the evidence of the three previous accidents. Defendants objected. The court should:

A. Admit the evidence against both parties.
B. Admit the evidence against neither party.
C. Admit the evidence against the company on the negligent retention claim only, with a limiting instruction that it cannot be used for any other purpose.
D. Admit the evidence against the company only on the respondeat superior claim, with a limiting instruction that it cannot be used for any other purpose.

---

8. The admissibility of statements by a party opponent is discussed in Chapter 8.
9. For example, the confession in the previous example by one defendant could not be introduced in a criminal case where the two defendants were tried jointly. The Supreme Court has ruled that the risk that the jury would use Defendant 1's confession against Defendant 2 is unacceptably high and violates Defendant 2's constitutional right to confront the witnesses against him. *See Bruton v. United States*, 391 U.S. 123 (1968). The Confrontation Clause is discussed in Chapter 8.

ANALYSIS.   The rule against using prior acts to prove character and thus how a person acted in a given instance would bar using the prior accidents to prove that the Driver was negligent in this instance.[10] **A** is therefore incorrect. The evidence of the accidents is admissible on the negligent retention claim to show that the Company had knowledge of the Driver's previous accidents. Thus **B** is incorrect. The evidence is only admissible against the Company and only on the negligent retention claim to show such knowledge. Plaintiff will have to introduce other evidence to prove that the Driver was negligent in this instance. **C** is the correct answer and **D** is incorrect.

E.   Rule of Completeness

A party may introduce only a portion of a writing or a recording. If the opponent believes there is a danger the jury may be misled by taking something out of context, Rule 106 provides a remedy.

> **Rule 106. Remainder of or Related Writings or Recorded Statements**
> If a party introduces all or part of a writing or recorded statement, an adverse party may require the introduction, at that time, of any other part—or any other writing or recorded statement—that in fairness ought to be considered at the same time.

The rule permits the opponent to request permission from the court to introduce any other part of the writing or recording, or any other writing or recording, immediately. In other words, the opponent will not have to wait until it is his or her turn to introduce evidence in order to put the matter in context. The rule does not require that the writing or recording in question be admitted in its entirety, but only that such portions be admitted that "ought in fairness" to be considered contemporaneously with the fragment initially offered. The rule by its terms is not applicable to oral statements, but many federal judges do apply it to oral statements.

QUESTION 3.   The Closer.   Plaintiff 1 and Plaintiff 2 sued the defendant for personal injuries sustained in an automobile accident. The plaintiffs alleged that the defendant ran a red light and collided with the vehicle in which they were riding. The defendant claimed that he had the green light at the intersection and that it was the car in which plaintiffs were riding that ran a red light. Two months after the accident, Plaintiff 1 gave a recorded statement to an investigator in which he described his injuries and admitted that there was a possibility that the plaintiffs' car had the red light. The defendant offers the portion of the statement containing

---

10.   We discuss the rules regarding character evidence and prior acts evidence in Chapter 4.

Plaintiff 1's admission in evidence. Plaintiff 1 and Plaintiff 2 object. The court should:

A. Admit the statement against both plaintiffs under the Rule of Completeness.
B. Admit the statement against both plaintiffs under the excited utterance exception to the hearsay rule.
C. Admit the statement against both plaintiffs if the jury finds that the recorded statement was authentic and Plaintiff 1 was not under duress when he gave the statement.
D. Admit the statement against Plaintiff 1, sustain Plaintiff 2's objection to the statement, and give the jury a limiting instruction.

ANALYSIS. We will discuss hearsay in much greater detail in Chapter 8, but you have learned so far that there is an exception to the hearsay rule for statements made while one is under the stress of a startling event. An automobile accident may qualify as a startling event, but here the statement was made two months later. Thus Plaintiff 1's statement is not admissible under the excited utterance exception and **B** is incorrect. It is the trial judge's function to determine the admissibility of evidence, including whether a recording is authentic and, when pertinent, whether the person who made the statement was under duress. Thus **C** is incorrect. The Rule of Completeness permits a party to request that additional portions of a recorded statement be admitted when the opposing party has offered only a portion of the statement and there is a risk the jury will be misled by taking something out of context. It does not allow a statement to be introduced against additional parties when it is only admissible against one party. Thus **A** is incorrect. In this problem the defendant may introduce the statement against Plaintiff 1 under the exemption from the hearsay rule for statements by a party opponent. Plaintiff 2 did not make the statement, however, and therefore the statement is not admissible against Plaintiff 2. Given that, the judge should admit the statement with a limiting instruction that the jury may only consider it with respect to Plaintiff 1. Thus **D** is the correct answer.

Avery's Picks

1. Question 1   **C**
2. Question 2   **C**
3. Question 3   **D**

2

Judicial Notice

CHAPTER OVERVIEW
A. When the Court May Take Judicial Notice of a Fact
B. The Effect of Judicial Notice
✵ Avery's Picks

Judicial notice is a method of establishing adjudicative facts at trial without the necessity of calling witnesses or introducing other evidence. When a fact cannot reasonably be disputed, the trial judge takes judicial notice of it and no further proof is necessary to establish the fact.

A. When the Court May Take Judicial Notice of a Fact

Judicial notice is controlled by Rule 201.

> **Rule 201. Judicial Notice of Adjudicative Facts**
>   **(a) Scope.** This rule governs judicial notice of an adjudicative fact only, not a legislative fact.
>   **(b) Kinds of Facts That May Be Judicially Noticed.** The court may judicially notice a fact that is not subject to reasonable dispute because it:
>   **(1)** is generally known within the trial court's territorial jurisdiction; or
>   **(2)** can be accurately and readily determined from sources whose accuracy cannot reasonably be questioned.

The rule concerns judicial notice of adjudicative facts, that is, the facts in the case before the court. For example, whether the street where an accident occurred was a one-way street is an adjudicative fact. It does not govern judicial notice of legislative facts, such as those that appellate courts may assume to be true for the purpose of making policy decisions. For example, in interpreting the breadth of a fair housing ordinance, assessing the negative social effects of housing discrimination involves legislative facts.

There are two circumstances under which a judge may take judicial notice of an adjudicative fact. First, the court may take judicial notice of facts that are not capable of dispute because they are generally known within the jurisdiction of the trial court. For example, a judge in Boston could take judicial notice of the fact that the Boston Red Sox play baseball in Fenway Park, that a given street in the City of Boston is one-way, or that Cambridge and Boston are on opposite sides of the Charles River. Sometimes facts are generally known everywhere; for example, that water boils at 212 degrees Fahrenheit and freezes at 32 degrees. Second, the court may take judicial notice of facts that are capable of accurate and ready determination by resort to sources whose accuracy cannot reasonably be questioned. For example, after consulting the text *Gray's Anatomy*, a court could take judicial notice that the tibia is the larger of two bones below the knee in human beings, and that it connects the knee with the ankle bones. After consulting the *Farmer's Almanac*, the court could take judicial notice of the time of sunset or high tide on a given day.

The court may not take judicial notice of facts that might reasonably be disputed. For example, it would be inappropriate to take judicial notice of whether the fracture of an ankle can give rise to varicose veins and shortness of breath, whether a terrazzo floor becomes dangerously slippery when wet, or the extent to which angina pectoris tends to shorten life.

The court has discretion to take judicial notice of facts, whether or not the parties request it to do so. If a party requests the court to take judicial notice of a fact and supplies the court with the necessary information, it is mandatory that the court take judicial notice of the fact. The court may take judicial notice of facts at any stage of the proceeding. It is not necessary for a party to give the opposing party advance notice that it will request the court to take judicial notice, but the opposing party must be given an opportunity to be heard on the issue. The Advisory Committee Note to Rule 201 states that once judicial notice has been taken, no contrary proof is admissible.

B.   The Effect of Judicial Notice

Rule 201 provides that the effect of a court taking judicial notice is different in civil and criminal cases.

Rule 201. Judicial Notice of Adjudicative Facts
(f) **Instructing the Jury.** In a civil case, the court must instruct the jury to accept the noticed fact as conclusive. In a criminal case, the court must instruct the jury that it may or may not accept the noticed fact as conclusive.

In a civil case, the judge instructs the jury that it must find the facts that the court has judicially noticed to be conclusively proven. In a criminal case, however, the judge instructs the jury only that it may accept judicially noticed facts as conclusively proven, but it is not required to do so. The reason for the difference is the constitutional right of the defendant in a criminal case to have the facts determined by the jury.

QUESTION 1. In a trial in Boston, plaintiff seeks to prove that the Arno River flows through Florence, Italy. The trial judge may:

A. Take judicial notice of the fact because it is generally known in the jurisdiction of the trial court.
B. Take judicial notice of the fact if the fact can readily be ascertained by resort to a source the accuracy of which cannot reasonably be questioned.
C. Take judicial notice of the fact if the judge has been to Florence and seen the Arno River.
D. Not take judicial notice of the fact.

ANALYSIS.   Let's begin with choice **C**. It is not appropriate for a judge to take judicial notice of a fact merely because the judge personally knows the fact to be true. The question is not what the judge knows, but what is generally known and indisputable. Thus **C** is incorrect. Choice **A** is incorrect because it is not generally known in Boston that the Arno River flows through Florence, Italy. It is, however, indisputable that the Arno River flows through Florence, and this can be ascertained by looking at any reliable world atlas. Thus **B** is the correct answer and **D** is incorrect.

QUESTION 2. Assuming the fact in question is relevant to the case, which of the following facts is inappropriate for judicial notice:

A. That the Boston Red Sox are the best team in major league baseball.
B. That the Declaration of Independence was signed in 1776.
C. That a normal body temperature reading for a human being is 98.6 degrees Farenheit.
D. That Ecuador is located in South America.

ANALYSIS.   Historical facts may be so familiar that they are generally known in the jurisdiction of the trial court. In any event, they may be ascertained through recourse to authoritative sources. Thus **B** may be judicially noticed. Well-established scientific or medical facts may be ascertained through recourse to authoritative sources. Thus **C** may be judicially noticed. Controversial statements about science or medicine, for example, the specific benefits of medical marijuana, require proof. Geographical facts can be established through reliable sources, and **D** may be judicially noticed. Statements that are contro-versial, or that reflect values or judgment, require proof. Thus, **A** may not be judicially noticed.

QUESTION 3. The Closer. The defendant is on trial for negligent homicide. The state alleges that the defendant drove the wrong way on Tremont Street, a well-travelled one-way street in downtown Boston, and struck a messenger who was pedaling the proper direction on his bicycle. Before trial the prosecutor asks the court to take judicial notice that Tremont is a one-way street from East to West. The defendant objects. The court should:

A. Decline to take judicial notice because the prosecutor's request was pre-trial, rather than during the trial.
B. Decline to take judicial notice because the state should be required to prove the fact through witnesses, given its crucial importance in the case.
C. Take judicial notice that Tremont Street is one-way from East to West, and advise the jury that it is bound by the court's ruling.
D. Take judicial notice that Tremont Street is one-way from East to West, and advise the jury that it may accept the court's ruling as conclusive, but that it is not required to do so.

ANALYSIS. The court may take judicial notice of facts at any point in the proceedings. If the court takes judicial notice of a fact on a pretrial motion, it will inform the jury at some appropriate point during the trial of its ruling. Thus **A** is incorrect. There is nothing in Rule 201 that limits judicial notice to facts of minor importance, and there is no impediment to taking judicial notice of a fact that bears directly on the guilt of the defendant. It is well known in the City of Boston that Tremont Street is a one-way street that runs East to West, and the fact is an appropriate one for judicial notice. Thus **B** is incorrect. In a criminal case the judge may not require the jury to find as conclusive a fact that the court has judicially noticed. The defendant is entitled to have the jury find the facts, even where the judge has concluded that a fact cannot rea-sonably be disputed. Thus **C** is incorrect and the correct answer is **D**.

 Avery's Picks

1. Question 1   **B**
2. Question 2   **A**
3. Question 3   **D**

3

Burden of Proof and Presumptions

CHAPTER OVERVIEW
A. Burden of Proof
B. Presumptions
C. Irrebuttable Presumptions
D. Presumptions in Criminal Cases
✧ Avery's Picks

Presumptions can be a confusing topic, made more so by commentators who like to rehearse the historic debates among leading professors about the appropriate effect of presumptions on the burdens placed on each side at trial. Here we set forth a simple and straightforward understanding of Rule 301, which governs presumptions in federal trials where federal law supplies the rule of decision. Rule 301 governs all such cases unless there is a specific statute that supplies the rules for a particular presumption. In order to understand presumptions, we must begin with the burden of proof.

A. Burden of Proof

The expression "burden of proof" encompasses two distinct burdens that are imposed on the parties to a trial: the burden of production, and the burden of persuasion. The burden of production refers to the burden on a party of going forward with evidence on an issue. For example, at the outset of a civil case, the burden of production is on the plaintiff to produce evidence sufficient to support a finding in his favor on each element of the claim. If the plaintiff fails to do so, the court will grant a directed verdict for the defendant. The burden of production may shift to the opposing party during a trial, imposing on that party the requirement of coming forward with evidence in order to avoid a directed verdict.

The burden of persuasion refers to which party has the burden of convincing the jury of its version of events under the appropriate standard after all the evidence is in. As a general rule, the burden of persuasion does not shift between the parties during the course of a trial, but remains on the party who had it initially.

Discrimination in employment litigation is an example of an area in which the burden of production shifts. The plaintiff has the initial burden of production to introduce evidence sufficient to support a finding of discrimination, typically evidence that: (1) the plaintiff is a member of a protected class; (2) the plaintiff was qualified for the position in question; (3) the plaintiff suffered an adverse employment action, for example, was fired or not hired or promoted; and (4) the employer filled the position with a person of similar qualifications who was not a member of the protected class. Once the plaintiff has introduced such evidence, the burden of production shifts to the employer to introduce evidence that there was a lawful explanation for the adverse treatment of the plaintiff. If the employer fails to meet its burden of production, the plaintiff is entitled to judgment. If the employer does introduce evidence of a non-discriminatory reason for its actions with respect to the plaintiff, it has met its burden of production. In that event, the fact finder must decide based on all the evidence in the case whether the employer subjected the plaintiff to an adverse employment action as a result of intentional discrimination. On that ultimate issue, the plaintiff has the burden of persuasion.

There are three different standards for the burden of persuasion, depending on what sort of case is being tried. In most civil cases the rule is the preponderance of the evidence standard. The party with the burden of persuasion must convince the finder of fact by a preponderance of the evidence that it is entitled to a verdict. If based on all the evidence the finder of fact is uncertain who has the stronger case, or believes the opponent has the stronger case, the party with the burden of persuasion will lose. In some civil cases the standard is clear and convincing evidence, which requires evidence sufficient to demonstrate a high degree of probability that the proposition to be proved is true. In criminal cases the government must convince the finder of fact beyond a reasonable doubt of each element of the charged offense to justify a verdict of guilty.

In civil cases, the plaintiff has the burden of production and the burden of persuasion with respect to the elements of the plaintiff's claim. The defendant has the burden of production with respect to affirmative defenses. In civil cases, substantive law determines which party has the burden of persuasion with respect to affirmative defenses. In criminal cases, the prosecution has the burden of production and the burden of persuasion with respect to the elements of the crime. The defendant has the burden of production with respect to affirmative defenses, and may have the burden of persuasion with respect to them as well.[1]

B.   Presumptions

Presumptions establish that once the finder of fact has determined that a basic fact exists, the finder of fact may presume that a second fact exists (the presumed fact). For example, if the jury has determined that a letter has been mailed, it may presume that it has been received. If the jury finds that a person has been missing and there has been no word of his whereabouts for more than seven years, it may presume that he is dead. Unless the rules respecting a particular presumption are set out in other statutes or rules, Rule 301 governs presumptions in civil actions where federal law provides the rule of decision.

> **Rule 301. Presumptions in Civil Cases Generally**
> In a civil case, unless a federal statute or these rules provide otherwise, the party against whom a presumption is directed has the burden of producing evidence to rebut the presumption. But this rule does not shift the burden of persuasion, which remains on the party who had it originally.

Rule 302 provides that where state law provides the rule of decision with respect to a claim or defense, state law provides the effect to be given to presumptions. In civil actions filed in federal court due to diversity of citizenship between the parties, state law will control the effect the court will give to presumptions.

Under Rule 301, where there is a presumption, once the proponent has introduced evidence of a basic fact, the burden of production shifts to the opponent to introduce evidence to contest the presumed fact. If the opponent does not introduce such evidence, the court will instruct the jury that if it finds the basic fact to be proven, it may presume that the second fact has been established. For example, if the plaintiff introduces evidence that a letter has been mailed, and the defendant does not introduce any evidence to contradict the fact of receipt, the judge will instruct the jury that if it finds the letter was mailed, it may presume that it was received.

If the opponent meets its burden of production and offers evidence to controvert the existence of the presumed fact, then the presumption has no legal effect in the case. It "disappears" as a legal matter.[2] There is some controversy among the lower federal courts and the commentators about what it means to say that the presumption disappears. Some say that once evidence

---

1. The law of the jurisdiction where the case is tried determines which party has the burden of persuasion. The general rules articulated in the text may vary with respect to specific claims, and the rules in a given state may vary from the federal rules.

2. This is often referred to as the "bursting bubble" theory of presumptions. The idea is that the presumption is like a soap bubble floating in the air, but once it is pricked by evidence that the presumed fact does not exist, it disappears.

contesting the presumed fact is admitted the presumption completely disappears and the trial judge should say nothing to the jury about the presumption. Others say that the judge has discretion to give some effect to the presumption by treating it as a permissive inference and advising the jury that if it believes that the basic fact has been proven, it may "infer" (rather than "presume") that the second fact existed. The latter position has strong support in the language of the Conference Committee, which reported out the final language of Rule 301 after there were different versions drafted by the Advisory Committee, the House of Representatives, and the Senate. The Conference Committee stated:

> If the adverse party offers no evidence contradicting the presumed fact, the court will instruct the jury that if it finds the basic facts, it may presume the existence of the presumed fact. If the adverse party does offer evidence contradicting the presumed fact, the court cannot instruct the jury that it may *presume* the existence of the presumed fact from proof of the basic facts. The court may, however, instruct the jury that it may infer the existence of the presumed fact from proof of the basic facts.[3]

The debate may not be of great moment with respect to those presumptions that are based on common sense and logic, for example, whether a letter that has been mailed has been received, or whether a person missing for seven years has died. On those issues jurors will probably treat proof of the basic fact as a strong indication that the second fact existed, whether or not the judge instructs them that the inference is permissible.

Rule 301 clearly establishes that a presumption shifts only the burden of production, and the burden of persuasion as to any issue remains on the party on whom it was originally placed.

QUESTION 1. The plaintiff in Connecticut ordered merchandise from a manufacturer in California. The plaintiff received the merchandise in damaged condition. The goods passed through the hands of two common carriers before delivery to the plaintiff. Plaintiff sued the manufacturer and both carriers. The manufacturer introduced evidence that the merchandise was in good condition when it placed it in the hands of the first carrier, and the plaintiff testified that when she received the merchandise it was damaged. There is a common law presumption that when merchandise in good condition was placed in the hands of connecting carriers and delivered to the recipient in damaged condition, the last carrier caused the damage. Assume that all relevant jurisdictions have adopted Rule 301 and that it governs the case. Which of the following statements is true?

---

3. NOTES OF CONFERENCE COMMITTEE, HOUSE REPORT No. 93–1597.

A. The judge should instruct the jury that it must presume that the last carrier damaged the goods.

B. If the last carrier introduces evidence that the merchandise was damaged when it received it from the first carrier, the judge is not allowed to instruct the jury that it may presume that the damage was caused by the last carrier.

C. If the last carrier introduces no evidence that the merchandise was damaged when it received the goods from the first carrier, the judge should instruct the jury that it may presume the damage was caused by the last carrier.

D. The presumption shifts the burden of persuasion to the last carrier to prove that it did not damage the merchandise.

ANALYSIS.   Let's begin with **D**. Rule 301 states explicitly that presumptions only affect the burden of production, not the burden of persuasion. In this case the plaintiff has the burden of persuasion and must persuade the jury by a preponderance of the evidence that a particular defendant damaged the goods in order to find that defendant liable. Thus **D** is incorrect. Choice **A** would give the presumption legal effect regardless of whether or not the last carrier defendant offers any evidence rebutting the fact that it caused the damage to the merchandise. That would create an irrebuttable presumption that the last carrier is always liable for damage to merchandise. The common law presumption here, however, is rebuttable and thus **A** is incorrect.

The statement in **C** is missing a very important step. Even though the opponent offers no evidence to contradict the presumed fact, the jury may presume the existence of the presumed fact only where it has found that the basic fact existed. Merely introducing evidence of the basic facts is not enough to give rise to the presumption—the jury must be convinced by a preponderance of the evidence that the basic facts existed. In this problem in order to presume that the last carrier caused the damage, the jury must find that the merchandise was in good condition when the manufacturer delivered it to the first carrier and damaged when the plaintiff received it. If the last carrier introduces no evidence that the goods were damaged when it received them, the judge would instruct the jury: "If you find, by a preponderance of the evidence, that the merchandise was in good condition when the manufacturer delivered it to the first carrier and was damaged when delivered to the plaintiff, you may presume that the damage was caused by the last carrier." Thus **C** is incorrect.

Choice **B** is a correct statement of the law. If the last carrier offers evidence that the goods were damaged when it received them it has met its burden of production by contradicting the presumed fact (that it caused the damage). Under those circumstances the presumption loses its effect and the judge is not permitted to instruct the jury that it may presume the last carrier caused the damage.

QUESTION 2. Defendant rented an apartment from Landlord on a month-to-month basis. Under the law in their state, the lease renewed automatically unless the tenant gave the landlord written notice that he wanted to terminate the rental. Landlord died and Defendant stopped paying rent and moved out the first of the next month. Landlord's Estate sued Defendant for the ongoing rent. Defendant claimed that he mailed a notice of termination to Landlord a month in advance of when he moved out. The Estate offered no evidence as to whether the Landlord received the notice, but called a witness who testified that Defendant admitted to her that he had never sent a notice of termination. Defendant has requested the court to advise the jury that if it finds by a preponderance of the evidence that Defendant mailed a notice, it may presume that the Landlord received it. Should the court give the requested instruction to the jury?

A. Yes.
B. No.

ANALYSIS. The plaintiff has not offered any evidence on the existence of the presumed fact, whether the Landlord received the notice. It has contested only the basic fact, whether the Defendant mailed the notice. If the jury concludes by a preponderance of the evidence, despite the testimony of the Estate's witness, that the Defendant did mail the notice, then Defendant is entitled to the benefit of the presumption that the Landlord received the notice. The correct answer is **A**.

C.   Irrebuttable Presumptions

"Irrebuttable" or "conclusive" presumptions are actually substantive rules of law. They may be common law rules, or may be enacted by statute. For example, a statute may provide that there is an irrebuttable presumption that a child under the age of seven acts with due care. In other words, there is a substantive rule that a child under age seven cannot be found to be negligent. Or a jurisdiction may recognize the rule that a child under the age of eighteen is conclusively presumed to be incapable of consenting to sexual relations. In that jurisdiction a defendant charged with the rape of a child under the age of eighteen would not be permitted to raise consent as a defense. Irrebuttable or conclusive presumptions do not operate like the rebuttable presumptions we discussed under Rule 301. They do not shift the burden of production from one party to another. They simply remove certain issues from evidence and proof and substitute definitive rules in their place.

D.   Presumptions in Criminal Cases

Rule 301 governs presumptions in civil cases only. The Federal Rules have no provisions that control the use of presumptions in criminal cases. Presumptions are rare and given limited effect in criminal cases because they may be deemed to unconstitutionally interfere with the right of a criminal defendant to have the facts determined by a jury. The use of presumptions in criminal cases is controlled by constitutional law and criminal procedure and is outside the scope of the present text.

QUESTION 3. The Closer. The committee of the legislature charged with family law matters is considering how to protect children born to parents who are married and living together from claims that another man is actually their biological father. The committee is of the view that any litigation of the question of biological fatherhood for such children is so painfully intrusive and destabilizing of family relations that it causes irreparable harm to the children. Assume that the state in question has adopted Rule 301 and that the committee has asked you, its counsel, to draft an appropriate statute. Which of the following will provide the sort of statute that the committee is looking for?

A. A Rule 301 presumption that if a child is born to a woman who is married at the time of the child's birth, her husband is presumed to be the father of the child.

B. An irrebuttable presumption that the husband of a woman who has a child during their marriage is the father of the child.

ANALYSIS.   First, we are not discussing the wisdom of what the legislature is trying to do. You may agree or disagree with its goals. The issue here is what sort of presumption will be most effective in achieving those goals. The question the committee has put to its counsel is how to most securely limit the ability to litigate of a man claiming to be the father of a child born to a woman while she is married to another man.

Suppose the plaintiff seeking to prove his paternity has had sufficient access to a child to obtain DNA evidence that creates a very high probability that he is the child's father. If the legislature had adopted the Rule 301 presumption described in **A**, how could he use that evidence? For the presumption in **A** the basic fact is that the child was born to the mother while she was married to her husband. The presumed fact is that the husband is the child's father, and the burden of production is on the plaintiff to introduce evidence to contest the presumed fact. The DNA evidence would do so, and under Rule 301 the plaintiff would be allowed to introduce such evidence. With that, the presumption would disappear from the case as a legal matter, and the finder of fact would have to determine paternity from all the evidence in the case. The presumption in **A** would provide very little protection from litigation of the paternity issue.

On the other hand, the irrebuttable presumption in **B** would prohibit the plaintiff from introducing any evidence that he is the biological father of the child. Setting issues of the constitutionality of the statute aside, the suit would be dismissed soon after it was filed.[4] Choice **B** is the answer that better achieves the goal of the legislature.

 ## Avery's Picks

1. Question 1   **B**
2. Question 2   **A**
3. Question 3   **B**

---

4.   If you are interested in the constitutional issues, which have to do with the constitutional rights of parents, see *Michael H. v. Gerald D.*, 491 U.S. 110 (1989).

4

Relevance and Its Limits

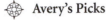
The first question you should ask yourself about a proposed piece of evidence is whether it is relevant. All evidence must at the very least be relevant in order to be admissible. Not all relevant evidence is admissible, because it may be excluded under one of the other rules. But if evidence is not relevant, it is inadmissible. The Rules provide the definition of relevance.

A.   Definition of Relevance

Rule 401. Test for Relevant Evidence
Evidence is relevant if:
>   (a) it has any tendency to make a fact more or less probable than it would
be without the evidence; and
>   (b) the fact is of consequence in determining the action.

Notice that there are two requirements that must be met for evidence to
be considered relevant. Under (**a**), evidence must have a tendency to make a
fact more or less probable than it would be without that evidence in order
to be relevant. Under (**b**), the fact to be proved must be "of consequence" in
deciding the case in order to be relevant. Both requirements must be met for
evidence to be relevant.

The inquiry under (**a**) is a question of logic and of fact. The standard is a
generous one. Rule 401 does not require that evidence make a fact *more probable than not* in order to be relevant, it merely requires that the evidence *has
any tendency* to make the fact *more or less probable than it would be without the
evidence*. The issue under (**b**) is a question of substantive law. We look to the
underlying law that applies to the case (e.g., torts, contracts, criminal law) to
determine what facts are of consequence to the claim being litigated.

As an example, let's consider an automobile accident case, where plaintiff
claims he was injured when defendant's car ran into him when he was in the
crosswalk. Plaintiff offers evidence from a police officer who investigated the
accident. The officer would testify that she observed a substantial amount of
fresh blood in the crosswalk when she arrived at the scene a few moments after
the accident. Are the observations of the officer relevant? Take the question
under part (**b**) first. Is whether the plaintiff was in the crosswalk when he was
struck "of consequence in determining the action?" Yes, in most jurisdictions
if not all, the substantive law provides that drivers of vehicles owe a duty of
care to a pedestrian in a crosswalk. The question under part (**a**) is whether the
fact that the officer observed fresh blood in the crosswalk makes it more likely
than it would be in the absence of such evidence that the plaintiff was in the
crosswalk when he was struck. Common sense tells us that the answer is yes.
Because we have answered both questions in the affirmative, the evidence of
the officer's observations regarding the blood is relevant.

Let's consider an example in which a criminal defendant's evidence is
challenged on relevance grounds. Suppose the defendant is charged with first
degree murder (premeditated murder) and offers a witness to testify that he
drank most of a bottle of vodka and a bottle of wine in the two hours before he
killed the victim. The prosecution objects on relevance grounds. Under section
(**a**) the question is whether evidence that the defendant drank the vodka and
the wine has any tendency to prove that he was so intoxicated that he did not
have the ability to premeditate killing the victim. One might find as a matter

of fact and logic that the large quantity of liquor could so dull the senses that the defendant was unable to form a plan to commit murder. The question under section (**b**) is whether voluntary intoxication is a legally permissible factor to take into account in determining whether the defendant engaged in premeditation. The state's criminal law would determine that issue. Some states allow voluntary intoxication to be taken into account in determining whether a defendant possessed the requisite mental state to commit first degree murder and some do not. If state law provided that voluntary intoxication could not be taken into account, the defendant's intoxication would not be of consequence in determining the action, and thus would not be relevant. Evidence has to satisfy the requirements of both sections (**a**) and (**b**) to be relevant.

In considering issues under section (**a**) you should be careful not to confuse the standard for determining the relevance of a piece of evidence with the standard for deciding the case. To be relevant, a piece of evidence does not have to establish liability by a preponderance of the evidence in a civil case, or guilt beyond a reasonable doubt in a criminal case. Those are the standards that are applied to the whole body of evidence that a party introduces, to determine if all the evidence taken together is sufficient to justify a verdict. Rule 401 is about a narrower issue—whether a single piece of evidence is qualified on relevance grounds to be a part of the case. Professor McCormick famously put it this way, "A brick is not a wall." To be relevant, an item of evidence does not have to construct a whole wall; it simply has to be one of the bricks out of which a wall can be made.

Evidence that is not relevant is inadmissible. The mere fact that evidence is relevant, however, does not guarantee that it is admissible. Relevance is merely one hurdle that evidence must overcome. As we will see, several rules provide for the exclusion of relevant evidence on a variety of grounds.

QUESTION 1. Defendant is charged with murder. The perpetrator slit the victim's throat and the pathologist has testified that in her expert opinion, based on the nature of the wound and other factors, the perpetrator was probably right-handed. The prosecutor offers to call a witness who knows the defendant well and who would testify that defendant is right-handed. Is the evidence relevant?

A. No, because the majority of people are right-handed and thus the evidence cannot prove that the defendant was the killer.
B. No, because the killer might have wielded the knife with his right hand, even if he was left-handed.
C. No, because it doesn't matter what hand the killer used – slitting someone's throat is still murder.
D. Yes.

ANALYSIS.   Imagine that you are a member of the jury in this case. After you hear the pathologist's testimony, the first thing that will cross your mind is probably the question of whether the defendant is right-handed. Why? Because if he is, that puts him in the universe of people who are more likely to have been the killer. Conversely, if he is left-handed, it is less likely that he is the person who killed the victim. That is all the evidence has to show in order to make it more likely that the defendant was the killer than it would be in the absence of evidence about which is his master hand. Because the question of who killed the victim is of consequence in determining whether the defendant is guilty of murder, this evidence is relevant.

Of course it is true, as answer **A** suggests, that millions of people are right-handed. And it is also true, as **B** indicates, that the killer may not have used his master hand to attack the victim. But those arguments demonstrate that this evidence alone will not be enough to justify a conviction. Of course the fact that the defendant is right-handed alone does not prove his guilt beyond a reasonable doubt. It does not have to, however, in order to be relevant. Answer **C** suggests that we can somehow leap to the final question of guilt or innocence without establishing facts that add up to our conclusion. That is not how cases are built. They are built like walls out of individual bricks, as Professor McCormick suggested, and we determine whether an item of evidence is relevant by asking whether it constitutes a brick that might eventually form part of a wall. The correct answer here is **D**, because knowing whether the defendant is right-handed makes it more likely that he is the killer than if we didn't know that, and if there is enough other evidence of guilt, it may help build a successful case against him.

QUESTION 2. The pathologist's evidence in a murder case has shown that the victim was killed in a manner that was likely to get the victim's blood onto the body and/or clothing of the killer. The crime lab has tested the jacket that defendant was wearing when he was arrested shortly after the killing and has found traces of blood on it. The lab is not able to say, however, whether the blood is that of the victim, or even whether the blood is human blood. Is evidence from a scientist at the lab that there was blood on the defendant's jacket relevant?

A. Yes.
B. No, because unless the blood can be shown to be that of the victim, it does not prove anything.
C. No, because unless the blood is human blood, it does not prove anything.
D. No, because there is no evidence as to how this blood got onto the jacket.

ANALYSIS. The prosecution offers the blood evidence to prove that the defendant was the killer. Whether the defendant was the killer may not fully answer the question of whether he is guilty of murder, but it is clearly "of consequence."

The logical question is whether the evidence of blood on defendant's jacket has any tendency to make it more probable that he was the killer than it would be without that evidence. That we do not know how this blood got onto the defendant's jacket, whether it is the victim's blood, or whether it is even human blood, are all good arguments why this evidence, standing alone, would not be sufficient to conclude beyond a reasonable doubt that the defendant was the killer. That, however, is the standard for determining guilt, not the standard for determining relevance.

Does the presence of blood make it more likely that defendant was the killer than it would be if he had no blood on his clothing? It may be helpful in answering this question to imagine you are an investigator of this crime. Does the fact that the defendant has some kind of blood on his jacket make you want to investigate him further, to find out if there is other evidence that points toward his guilt? Of course it does. The blood on the jacket, at a minimum, puts him in the universe of people that, according to the pathologist, are more likely to have killed the victim than people with no blood on their clothing. The correct answer is **A**, the evidence is relevant.

QUESTION 3. Defendant is charged with the murder of a victim who was stabbed to death. The pathologist has testified that the wounds were inflicted with a serrated knife. The police searched the defendant's home and found the following items: a paring knife, a chef's knife, and a receipt dated the day before the murder for the purchase of a serrated bread knife. No serrated knives were found in the home. Which of these items are relevant?

A. All of them, because they demonstrate the defendant's interest in knives and a knife was used to stab the victim.

B. The receipt for the bread knife.

C. None of them, because there is no evidence that either the knives found in the home or the bread knife that was purchased were actually used to commit the murder.

ANALYSIS. The prosecution offers these items to prove that the defendant was the killer, which is of consequence in determining whether he is guilty of murder. Evidence that a defendant had an instrument that could have been used to kill the victim makes it more likely that he was the killer than it would be in the absence of such evidence. Possession of common items such as kitchen knives of a type other than the type used on the victim, however, does not make it more likely that the defendant was the killer, thus **A** is incorrect. Choice **C** is incorrect because the evidence does not have to definitively prove that the knife was used in the murder in order to make the evidence regarding the serrated knife relevant. The fact that the defendant purchased a serrated knife shortly before a murder committed with a serrated knife, and no longer has the serrated knife in his home, does make it more likely that he was the killer than if we had no such evidence. This is true even though there is no other evidence linking the knife the defendant purchased to the murder. Thus **B** is the correct answer.

1. Rule with Respect to Evidence of Similar Events

In accident cases and products liability cases, a plaintiff may seek to prove that a place or a product were unreasonably dangerous by showing that other accidents occurred at that place or while people were using that product. In such cases the law requires that the plaintiff demonstrate that the other accidents occurred under substantially similar conditions in order for them to be relevant and admissible.

QUESTION 4. Plaintiff's decedent suffered fatal injuries when his car went off the road and over a cliff at a curve in a hilly roadway, on a sunny afternoon in July. His estate is suing the highway department for negligence in the design of the road, arguing that it was unreasonably dangerous. Plaintiff's attorney wants to offer evidence at trial that five other drivers died at the same curve when their cars went off the road and over the cliff on snowy days during the previous December and January, in order to prove that the location was unreasonably dangerous. Is the evidence of the other accidents relevant?

A. Yes, the fact that a lot of people have been killed in the same spot makes it more likely that the road is unsafe than if only one person had died there.
B. No, because what happened on other occasions can never prove what happened on a particular occasion.
C. No, because the conditions under which the other accidents occurred were not substantially similar to the conditions under which this accident occurred.

ANALYSIS. Plaintiff wants to offer evidence of other accidents to prove that the road was unreasonably dangerous. Whether the road was unreasonably dangerous is a fact of consequence in determining the liability of the defendant in this tort suit.

The logical question is whether the existence of other accidents makes it more likely that an unsafe road caused this accident than if we knew of no other accidents. We must begin by recognizing that many factors may cause a motor vehicle accident, including, for example, speed, driver inattention, automobile equipment failure, actions by other drivers, and weather conditions, in addition to whether the road was safely designed. In order to determine with confidence whether unsafe road design caused the other accidents, we have to know something about the circumstances under which they occurred. If those accidents were caused by other factors, they may not tell us anything about whether the road itself was safely designed. For that reason, **A** is incorrect—the mere existence of the other accidents is not sufficient to prove that the road was unsafe. Choice **B** says that evidence of other accidents can never be relevant, but that is not the case. Sometimes the existence of other accidents does tell us something about the nature of the place where a particular accident occurred.

The correct answer is **C**. Evidence of other accidents is relevant to prove a dangerous condition caused the present accident if, and only if, those accidents occurred under substantially similar conditions to the present accident. If there are multiple accidents in the same place under substantially similar conditions, it is more probable that a danger inherent in the place itself was a contributing cause of the accidents than if there was only one accident.

B.   Exclusion of Relevant Evidence on Grounds of Unfair Prejudice, Confusion, and Misleading the Jury

Evidence must be relevant to be admissible, but not all relevant evidence is admissible. Rule 403 describes some of the circumstances under which the trial judge may exclude relevant evidence.

> **Rule 403. Excluding Relevant Evidence for Prejudice, Confusion, Waste of Time, or Other Reasons**
> The court may exclude relevant evidence if its probative value is substantially outweighed by a danger of one or more of the following: unfair prejudice, confusing the issues, misleading the jury, undue delay, wasting time, or needlessly presenting cumulative evidence.

The rule gives the trial judge discretion to exclude relevant evidence if its probative value is *substantially outweighed* by one of the factors mentioned. The rule is tilted toward admissibility. The burden of showing that relevant evidence should be excluded is on the opponent. In practice, a judge has considerable discretion under the rule to exclude evidence in whole or in part, to limit or change the method of presentation, or to condition the admissibility of the evidence on specific factors. This gives a judge the ability to maximize the extent to which the jury receives necessary information, while limiting the risk of unfair prejudice or the unnecessary consumption of time.

Undue delay, wasting time, and needlessly presenting cumulative evidence are straightforward considerations of judicial economy and we need not discuss them at any length. Here is an example from a case the author tried several years ago. In a murder case, the defendant pleaded not guilty by reason of insanity, claiming that before the killing he had suffered from hallucinations. He had come to believe creatures that tormented him inhabited a tree outside his window, and he made a videotape of the tree to prove to his friends that the creatures were there. To prove the defendant was hallucinating, his counsel offered to play the ninety-minute video, which in reality simply showed a tree with nothing in it. The judge admitted the tape, but allowed defense to show it to the jury for only five minutes. Rule 403 gives a judge discretion to limit a party's time for presentation, exhibits, or witnesses for the sake of the efficient use of the court's time.

By far the most common reason parties invoke Rule 403 is the claim that the risk of unfair prejudice substantially outweighs the probative value of an item of evidence. It is essential to understand what "unfair prejudice" means in the context of Rule 403. Here is a simple definition: *evidence is unfairly prejudicial if it invites the jury to make a decision on an improper ground.*

A common example of evidence that may be unfairly prejudicial is something that elicits a strong emotional response by jurors, creating a danger they will render a verdict based on sympathy or anger, rather than the facts of the case. In a murder case, for example, colored photographs of a bloody crime scene or close-ups of the injuries to the victim may have a powerful emotional influence on the jury. There is a danger jurors will become so upset that they will not afford the defendant the full benefit of the reasonable doubt standard before concluding he is guilty. On the other hand, such evidence may be highly probative in demonstrating how the crime took place, or showing precisely what caused the death of the victim. If the defendant objects to the evidence, the judge must determine whether the risk of unfair prejudice, the emotional impact it will have on the jury, substantially outweighs the legitimate significance of the evidence in proving the prosecution's case. In making this determination, the judge should take into account whether giving the jury a limiting instruction, cautioning them to view the evidence dispassionately, can control the risk of prejudice.

Another common example of the use of Rule 403 is when an item of evidence may be admissible for one purpose, but not another, and the risk that the jury will use the evidence for the improper purpose is so great that limiting instructions by the judge may not control it. Again, the evidence invites a decision on an improper ground. The judge must decide whether the risk the jury will use the evidence for an improper purpose substantially outweighs the probative value of the evidence for the legitimate purpose for which a party has offered it.

A common mistake that students and young lawyers make is to believe that evidence is unfairly prejudicial merely because it is powerful. We do not consider evidence to be unfairly prejudicial, however, merely because it damages the opposing party's case, or because it "strikes a hard blow," as Justice Souter once put it. As long as the purpose for which the jury will use the evidence is a proper one, evidence is not unfairly prejudicial no matter how powerful it may be.

Balancing the risk of unfair prejudice against probative value requires the parties to articulate *specifically* both what the value of the evidence is in proving the proponent's case and how the evidence may cause the jury to return a verdict on an improper ground. In assessing probative value, the judge should consider how central the fact to be proved is to the claim or defense it is offered to support, weigh the significance of this evidence in the context of all the available evidence in the case, and take into account whether there are alternate means of proving the fact in question. In measuring the risk of prejudice, the judge should determine precisely how the jurors might use the evidence improperly, assess how tempting, compelling, or inflammatory the improper use is, and consider how effective a limiting instruction would be in controlling the risk of prejudice. Trial judges have wide discretion in making these determinations, and appellate courts seldom reverse rulings trial judges make under Rule 403.

QUESTION 5. In a freakish coincidence, the deceased was accidentally shot by a hunter at the same moment a contract killer drilled him. The gangster claims that his shot was not fatal, and that the victim was killed by the hunter's bullet. At the trial of the gangster, the prosecution offers in evidence colored photographs of the victim's internal organs taken during the autopsy. The pathologist would use the photos to trace the path of both bullets through the victim's body in order to support her conclusion that the fatal wound was inflicted by the gangster's bullet. The defendant objects to the photos on the ground that the risk of unfair prejudice outweighs probative value. How should the court rule?

A. Sustain the objection because the jurors will be so inflamed by emotion when subjected to the gory autopsy photos that they could not dispassionately weigh the evidence in the case.
B. Overrule the objection because there is no risk of unfair prejudice.
C. Overrule the objection because the risk of unfair prejudice does not substantially outweigh the probative value of the evidence.
D. There isn't enough information to answer the question.

ANALYSIS. There is no doubt that autopsy photographs in color, showing the human body in an altered state, have the potential to be inflammatory and to unfairly influence a jury's verdict. There is a risk of unfair prejudice, thus **B** is incorrect. At the same time, such photographs are often necessary to illustrate or explain the cause or manner of death. Trial judges frequently admit autopsy photographs where the proponent can show a legitimate need for them, and appellate courts almost never reverse such rulings. In this case, the judge would have to determine how necessary the photos are to explaining and supporting the pathologist's conclusions. If the hunter's bullet only passed through the victim's leg, and the gangster's shot went through his heart, the photos may not be very important. However, if both shots were through the torso, it may be difficult to follow or credit the pathologist's testimony without the pictures. Whether **A** or **C** is the correct answer will depend upon such factors. The question does not supply that information, and so the correct answer is **D**. If the judge admits the photos, she should give a limiting instruction cautioning the jurors not to be swayed by any emotion they might engender.

QUESTION 6. Plaintiff's decedent was killed in an automobile accident when his car was struck by a truck that defendant was driving. Defendant was also injured and his blood was drawn at the emergency room shortly after the accident. Analysis of the blood demonstrated a blood alcohol level of 0.24%, which is three times the level at which a driver is presumptively considered to be intoxicated in the state where the accident occurred. At the wrongful death trial, plaintiff offers evidence of the defendant's blood alcohol level as measured in the hospital. Defendant objects on the ground that the risk of unfair prejudice exceeds the probative value of the evidence. How should the court rule?

A. Overrule the objection because the risk of unfair prejudice does not substantially outweigh the probative value of the evidence.
B. Overrule the objection because there is no risk of unfair prejudice.
C. Sustain the defense objection because many people have such strong feelings about drunk driving that the jury is likely to rule against the defendant regardless of what the other evidence shows about who caused the accident.

ANALYSIS.   The evidence of severe intoxication on the part of the truck driver is likely to be highly probative in determining who caused the accident. It would not be correct, however, to say there is no risk of unfair prejudice posed by this evidence. The jurors could feel so strongly about drunk driving that they might return a verdict against the defendant to punish him, even though they were not convinced by a preponderance of the evidence that his intoxication caused the accident. Nonetheless, unless it could be shown that there was no possibility that the defendant's intoxication caused the accident, a judge would be very unlikely to find that the risk of unfair prejudice outweighed the probative value of the evidence. Choice **A** is the correct answer.

> **QUESTION 7.** Plaintiff is a twelve-year-old girl who sustained permanent brain injuries when struck by an automobile when she was crossing the street. The brain injuries have seriously impaired her ability to walk and to talk. In the suit against the driver of the car, plaintiff's counsel proposes to call the girl to the stand. She would be able to walk from her seat to the witness stand only very awkwardly, with great difficulty, and slowly. She would be able to answer only very simple questions concerning her name, age, and the special school she attends, and would speak with great hesitation and in an unnatural voice that is difficult to understand. She has no memory of the accident itself. Defendant objects on the ground that the unfair prejudice her appearance would cause substantially outweighs the probative value of her testimony. How should the court rule?
>
> **A.** Exclude the plaintiff as a witness because her disabilities are likely to cause the jurors to return a verdict based on sympathy for her, rather than the facts of the case, and the probative value of her evidence is low because everything she could say could be proved through other witnesses or exhibits.
> **B.** Overrule the defense objection because any unfair prejudice caused by the plaintiff's appearance would not substantially outweigh its probative value.
> **C.** Overrule the defense objection because the plaintiff's appearance would not cause any unfair prejudice.

ANALYSIS. We need to begin by determining the probative value of plaintiff's appearance and testimony and whether there is any risk of unfair prejudice. Plaintiff's testimony can provide no evidence regarding the liability issues in the case, but her appearance as a witness is very significant with respect to the extent of her damages. Plaintiff could call expert witnesses and introduce medical reports to describe her condition, but they would not provide a complete substitute for seeing firsthand the difficulties that plaintiff has in walking and speaking. Observing the plaintiff is crucially important in assessing the extent of her injuries, and the probative value of this evidence is high.

There is some risk of unfair prejudice, and therefore **C** is incorrect. Arguably the jurors might be so emotionally affected by the plaintiff's plight that they would want to provide for her, even if there was little evidence of negligence on the part of the defendant driver. The risk that the jury may effectively lower the bar on the burden of proof is one of the common risks of evidence that has a significant emotional impact. The question is whether the risk substantially outweighs the probative value of the evidence.

Trial judges have great discretion when it comes to balancing the risk of unfair prejudice against probative value under Rule 403. There are many cases where it is possible to imagine one judge ruling one way and another judge the opposite way on the same set of facts. But in this example, the vast majority of judges would find **B** to be the correct answer. In personal injury cases involving serious injuries there is always a risk that jurors may be motivated by sympathy toward the injured plaintiff. In this case there really is no substitute for allowing jurors to see firsthand the extent of plaintiff's disability. Any risk of prejudice should be addressed by the routine instruction that judges give that the jury verdict should not be based on sympathy, but should be firmly grounded on the facts of the case.

Rule 403 also provides that the judge may exclude evidence if the risk that it will be misleading or confusing substantially outweighs its probative value. Evidence is misleading or confusing if it distracts jurors by requiring them to spend time on side issues that are not material to the dispute between the parties, or because the manner of presentation makes it unnecessarily difficult for jurors to see the point of the evidence. In determining whether to admit such evidence, the judge must decide whether the risk of misleading or confusing the jury substantially outweighs its probative value.

We will return to Rule 403 frequently throughout this book as we discuss the other rules of evidence. Rather than working through additional multiple-choice problems now, it makes more sense to explore additional examples of how the rule is applied in the context of those rules.

C.   Exclusion of Relevant Evidence on Policy Grounds

There are several rules that exclude particular types of evidence on policy grounds, even though such evidence might be logically relevant. In the ordinary course, the court makes determinations on an ad hoc basis about whether a piece of evidence is relevant, whether it poses a risk of unfair prejudice that outweighs its probative value, and whether it should be admitted. The rules we are about to discuss, however, make these decisions for whole categories of evidence. These rules are similar to each other in terms of their structure. Typically they make a given type of evidence inadmissible for specific purposes, but indicate that such evidence may be admissible if offered for other purposes. We will discuss each rule in turn.

1.   *Subsequent Remedial Measures*

Rule 407. Subsequent Remedial Measures
When measures are taken that would have made an earlier injury or harm less likely to occur, evidence of the subsequent measures is not admissible to prove:

- negligence;
- culpable conduct;

- a defect in a product or its design; or
- a need for a warning or instruction.

But the court may admit this evidence for another purpose, such as impeachment or—if disputed—proving ownership, control, or the feasibility of precautionary measures.

Sometimes, after someone has suffered an injury, the party in control of the person, place, or thing that caused it will take steps to minimize the risk of such injuries in the future. Suppose, for example, that a child drowns in a neighbor's backyard swimming pool. After the drowning, the neighbor builds a high fence with a locked gate, so that outsiders cannot have access to the pool. The parents of the child who drowned sue the neighbor for negligence in maintaining the pool at the time their child died, and want to introduce evidence of the subsequent erection of the fence to prove that the neighbor's pool was unreasonably dangerous without such a fence. Rule 407 establishes that evidence that the neighbor built the fence after the drowning is not admissible to prove that the premises were dangerous without it.

Evidence of such measures may be relevant both to show that there was a less dangerous alternative to what the defendant had originally done, and to show that the defendant has admitted that greater safety was possible by choosing to take the remedial measure. Nonetheless the law excludes the evidence in order to encourage people to take remedial measures to limit the risk of future accidents.

Notice that the rule uses very broad language to describe what sort of evidence is prohibited: "subsequent remedial measures." The intent is to exclude evidence of any sort of action that would minimize the risk of injuries in the future. Examples include fences, repairs or replacement of equipment, adoption of new procedures, discharging employees who caused the injury, retraining employees, recall of products, and any other measure of a remedial nature. The rule applies to measures that were taken after the injury or harm that is the subject of the case on trial.

Evidence of subsequent remedial measures is excluded, however, only if offered to prove negligence, culpable conduct, a defect in a product or its design, or a need for a warning or an instruction. If the evidence is offered for any other purpose, it is admissible. Rule 407 gives the most common examples of such purposes, but the list is illustrative and not exhaustive. Evidence of a subsequent remedial measure is admissible to impeach the testimony of a witness who has stated something that is inconsistent with the remedial measure taken. The opposing party may also offer evidence of remedial measures to contradict a claim by a defendant that it did not own or control the person, place, or thing that caused the injury, or to contradict a claim that the measure in question is not feasible.

QUESTION 8. Plaintiff was injured while spreading sand on a cranberry bog in the winter when his hand was caught on a rotating rod that was used to break up the sand in a hopper pulled by a tractor. He sued the company that designed the hopper and the rod, claiming the design was unreasonably dangerous without a guard to prevent workers from getting their hands too near the rotating rod. The lead designer claimed at the trial that he had chosen the "safest" available design. Plaintiff offered to introduce evidence that following his injury, the designer had changed the design of the hopper to add a guard over the rod, and that this design had been available at the time of the original design of the machine on which he was injured. Is the evidence admissible?

A. Yes, to impeach the testimony of the designer.
B. No, because the evidence of what the company may have done after the plaintiff's accident is not relevant to whether it was negligent in causing the injury to the plaintiff.
C. No, because it is evidence of a remedial measure taken subsequent to the injury to the plaintiff.
D. Yes, to prove that it was feasible to build the machine with a guard.

ANALYSIS. Evidence that a machine was redesigned after an injury to include a guard is precisely the sort of evidence contemplated by Rule 407. The evidence is relevant on the question of whether the original design was reasonably safe, and therefore **B** is not correct. The evidence should be excluded if offered to prove that the original design was not reasonably safe, and in that event, **C** would be the correct answer.

The evidence is admissible if offered for another purpose, however. May it be offered here, as **D** suggests, in order to prove that installing a guard was feasible? Not in this case, because the defendant has not contested feasibility. If the defendant had argued, for example, that adding a guard would make the machine too expensive to produce, or that adding a guard would interfere with the proper functioning of the machine, then plaintiff could introduce the fact that the defendant had redesigned the machine with a guard to prove that it was possible to do so. Evidence of subsequent remedial measures is admissible to prove feasibility, or to prove that the defendant owned or controlled the person, place, or thing that caused the injury, only when the defendant contests those issues. Here it did not, and **D** is incorrect.

The correct answer in this case is **A**. The designer has testified that he originally chose the "safest" available design. Yet after the accident he switched to a different design that had been available previously, one with a guard. That change is inconsistent with and impeaches his testimony that the original design was the safest one.

If a trial judge permits evidence of a subsequent remedial measure to impeach a defense witness, or to prove ownership, control, or feasibility if the defendant contests such matters, the judge should give a limiting instruction. The court should explain to the jury that the evidence cannot be used to prove negligence, and that the jury can only use the evidence for the specific purpose for which it is admitted.

2. *Evidence of Settlement Discussions*

Rule 408. Compromise Offers and Negotiations

(a) Prohibited Uses. Evidence of the following is not admissible—on behalf of any party—either to prove or disprove the validity or amount of a disputed claim or to impeach by a prior inconsistent statement or a contradiction:

(1) furnishing, promising, or offering—or accepting, promising to accept, or offering to accept—a valuable consideration in compromising or attempting to compromise the claim; and

(2) conduct or a statement made during compromise negotiations about the claim—except when offered in a criminal case and when the negotiations related to a claim by a public office in the exercise of its regulatory, investigative, or enforcement authority.

(b) Exceptions. The court may admit this evidence for another purpose, such as proving a witness's bias or prejudice, negating a contention of undue delay, or proving an effort to obstruct a criminal investigation or prosecution.

If every case filed in court had to go to trial to be resolved, the judicial system would come to a screeching halt. Most cases are settled. The rules of evidence encourage settlements by making evidence of compromises, settlement offers, and statements made during negotiations generally inadmissible. Such evidence cannot be admitted to prove the validity or amount of a disputed claim, or to impeach a witness with a prior inconsistent statement or a contradiction. As with Rule 407, such evidence is admissible for purposes other than the proscribed ones.

First, notice that the rule only comes into play when there is a "disputed claim." This means that one party is making a claim, and the opposing party is contesting it in some manner. The contest can be either about liability or damages (the amount of the claim). A case does not have to be filed in court in order for there to be a claim. But Rule 408 covers only statements made by one who is aware that an opposing party is making or denying some type of claim. Imagine that a driver jumps out of his car after an auto accident and runs to the other car shouting, "The accident was my fault, so I'll pay all your damages." The people in the other car haven't done anything yet to suggest they will make a claim; hence Rule 408 does not bar the statement. In the event of a later lawsuit by the folks in the second car, they would be able to offer the first driver's admission of fault against him at the trial. If *A* has loaned *B* money and *B* has not paid it back, *A* has a claim for the money. If *B* acknowledges that he owes *A* the amount in question but has not paid it, there is no dispute about the claim.

Once there is some kind of disputed claim, Rule 408 renders inadmissible a broad swath of evidence. The rule covers completed settlements, offers to settle, and conduct or statements made during negotiations. It covers statements both by a party proposing a settlement, and by a party who indicates it would be willing to accept a settlement. Such evidence is inadmissible to prove the validity or amount of the claim, and to impeach or contradict a trial witness's testimony with inconsistent or contrary statements made during negotiations.

QUESTION 9. Plaintiff has sued Defendant over an auto accident that resulted in damage to the vehicles but not in personal injury. In Plaintiff's lawsuit against Defendant, Plaintiff would testify that as soon as he got out of his car, Defendant said to Plaintiff: "Would you take a check for $5000 to settle all this?"

Defendant's objection to this testimony should be:

A. Sustained, because the statement was made in the course of attempting to settle a claim.
B. Sustained, because Defendant's offer to pay for Plaintiff's damages does not conclusively prove that Defendant believed himself to be at fault for the accident.
C. Overruled, admissible to show Defendant's consciousness of his own negligence.

ANALYSIS.   In order for Rule 408 to apply, there must be a claim. Offers made to compromise a claim are inadmissible to prove fault. Here, however, there was no claim. The Defendant spontaneously offered money before the Plaintiff had even made a claim. Thus, **A** is incorrect. **B** suggests there may be reasons other than consciousness of liability for Defendant to have made the offer. That may be true, but his offer to settle makes it more likely that he believed he was at fault than if he made no such offer. Conclusive proof is not required for relevance. Thus **B** is incorrect and the correct answer is **C**.

QUESTION 10. Defendant's car collided with two pedestrians in the street, causing each of them physical injuries. Plaintiff 1 settled his claim against the defendant before trial for $100,000. Plaintiff 2 offered to accept a settlement of $40,000, but the defendant refused to offer any more than $10,000. At the settlement conference, plaintiff 2 admitted that he was crossing the street outside the crosswalk, but produced a video of the accident from a surveillance camera that showed that defendant's car entered the intersection against a red light. At the trial of plaintiff 2 against the defendant, which of the following evidence is admissible?

A. Plaintiff 2 offers to prove that defendant settled with plaintiff 1 in order to prove that defendant was driving negligently at the time of the accident.
B. Defendant offers evidence that plaintiff 2 was willing to accept a settlement of $40,000 in order to prove that the claim was not worth any more than that.
C. Plaintiff 2 offers to introduce the videotape he showed at the settlement conference in order to prove that defendant negligently entered the intersection against a red light.
D. Defendant offers to prove that plaintiff 2 admitted at the settlement conference that he was outside the crosswalk.

ANALYSIS. Plaintiff 2 cannot offer to prove that defendant settled with plaintiff 1. The language of Rule 408 covers evidence of a compromise settlement between the defendant and another party, and plaintiff is offering it for the impermissible purpose of establishing the validity of a claim. The defendant cannot offer plaintiff 2's offer to accept a settlement of $40,000, because Rule 408 covers that as well and the defendant is offering the evidence to put a ceiling on the amount of plaintiff 2's damages. Defendant also cannot introduce plaintiff 2's admission made at the settlement conference that he was outside the crosswalk. Rule 408 covers not only settlements and offers, but also all statements made by the parties during negotiations. This serves the purpose of encouraging the parties to talk candidly about the strengths and weaknesses of their positions during settlement. Here defendant wants to offer plaintiff 2's statement to undermine the validity of plaintiff 2's claim, an impermissible purpose under the rule. Choices **A**, **B**, and **D** are incorrect answers.

What about the video of defendant's car running the red light? Is it inadmissible because it was used at the settlement conference? No, because the video is evidence that existed independent of settlement proceedings. Rule 408 would prohibit the parties from introducing any statements that either party made about the video at the settlement conference, but the fact that the video was used at the conference does not render the video itself inadmissible in evidence. Parties frequently use pre-existing documents, photographs, and other exhibits in settlement conferences. What they say about them during negotiations is inadmissible in evidence, but Rule 408 does not bar the pre-existing materials themselves from evidence at trial. Choice **C** is the correct answer.

There is an exception in section (a)(2) of Rule 408 for evidence offered in criminal cases with respect to statements made during negotiations in a related civil claim, where the claim is one by a public office in the exercise of its regulatory, investigative, or enforcement authority. The rationale is that a party should expect that self-incriminating statements made to government agents could later be used against him in a criminal case.

Section (b) of Rule 408 provides that if evidence of settlements, offers to settle, and statements made during negotiations are offered for a purpose other than to establish the validity or amount of a claim, they are admissible. The rule provides examples of such purposes, but is not intended to be exhaustive. Notice that the rule refers to purposes "such as" the examples given, which are, "proving a witness's bias or prejudice, negating a contention of undue delay, or proving an effort to obstruct a criminal investigation or prosecution." A witness might be biased or prejudiced, for example, if he has previously accepted a settlement from the party on whose behalf he testifies at a trial. Settlement negotiations may delay performance with respect to contractual obligations, and it would be unfair to allow a jury to conclude a party engaged in culpable delay when the delay was in fact caused by time the parties agreed to take to explore a settlement. On the other hand, if a party engages in bogus settlement talks merely in order to obstruct a criminal investigation, the government is allowed to prove the obstruction by introducing evidence of the bogus settlement behavior.

3. *Offers to Pay Medical and Similar Expenses*

Rule 409. Offers to Pay Medical and Similar Expenses
Evidence of furnishing, promising to pay, or offering to pay medical, hospital, or similar expenses resulting from an injury is not admissible to prove liability for the injury.

Defendants or potential defendants may offer to pay an injured person's medical or similar expenses (e.g., ambulance and hospital bills) before there has been any determination of liability. The defendant may offer to do so for humane reasons, or to limit damages by providing prompt medical assistance, or for other reasons. Rule 409 encourages such payments by making them inadmissible in evidence.

This rule is similar to Rule 408, but there is one very important distinction. Statements that accompany an offer to pay medical expenses are admissible under Rule 409, as compared with Rule 408 under which all statements made during settlement negotiations are excluded from evidence. Suppose that a defendant says to the injured party, "I was at fault in the accident, so I will pay your medical expenses." The offer to pay the medical expenses is inadmissible, but the injured party can introduce the defendant's statement, "I was at fault in the accident."

4. *Pleas, Plea Discussions, and Related Statements in Criminal Cases*

Rule 410 provides somewhat similar protections in criminal cases for settlement discussions that Rule 408 provides in the civil context. The purpose is to encourage plea-bargaining. An important distinction between the rules, however, is that Rule 408 excludes the proscribed evidence regardless of which party offers it, whereas Rule 410 excludes settlement evidence only when the government offers it against the defendant.

Rule 410. Pleas, Plea Discussions, and Related Statements

(a) Prohibited Uses. In a civil or criminal case, evidence of the following is not admissible against the defendant who made the plea or participated in the plea discussions:

(1) a guilty plea that was later withdrawn;

(2) a nolo contendere plea;

(3) a statement made during a proceeding on either of those pleas under Federal Rule of Criminal Procedure 11 or a comparable state procedure; or

(4) a statement made during plea discussions with an attorney for the prosecuting authority if the discussions did not result in a guilty plea or they resulted in a later-withdrawn guilty plea.

(b) Exceptions. The court may admit a statement described in Rule 410(a)(3) or (4):

(1) in any proceeding in which another statement made during the same plea or plea discussions has been introduced, if in fairness the statements ought to be considered together; or

(2) in a criminal proceeding for perjury or false statement, if the defendant made the statement under oath, on the record, and with counsel present.

The rule provides that the prosecution may not offer evidence against the defendant regarding guilty pleas that were later withdrawn, nolo contendere (no contest) pleas, and statements made during proceedings on such pleas. A variety of circumstances may justify a court in allowing a defendant who pleaded guilty to withdraw the plea. It would defeat the purpose of allowing a defendant to withdraw a plea of guilty and go to trial, however, if the court were to allow the previous guilty plea in evidence. The rule thus makes such evidence inadmissible against the defendant. A nolo contendere plea does not constitute an admission of guilt by a defendant, and so the rule also excludes it from evidence in a later trial.

When a criminal defendant offers to plead guilty, the court must conduct an examination of the defendant to make sure that he is voluntarily waiving his right to a trial, and to insure that there is a factual basis for finding the defendant guilty. Typically the judge will put the defendant under oath and ask him a series of questions. At some point the court will ask the prosecutor to state the facts that the government believes it will be able to prove at trial. The court will then ask the defendant if those facts are true. During this process the defendant may make a variety of incriminating statements. Rule 410 provides that if the plea is later withdrawn, or if the plea was a nolo contendere plea, the statements made by the defendant during this colloquy with the court are inadmissible against him in a later trial.

The rule also covers statements a defendant makes in plea discussions with the prosecuting attorney. To determine whether to accept a plea of guilty to a reduced charge, or whether to allow a defendant to become a cooperating witness for the government, federal prosecutors typically meet with the defendant and his attorney. At this conference the prosecutor will ask the defendant to relate his version of the case. This is known as a "proffer" of what the defendant would testify to if he were called as a government witness. If the discussions do not lead to a guilty plea, or a guilty plea is later withdrawn, Rule 410 renders such statements inadmissible against the defendant. The purpose is to encourage the defendant to be truthful with the prosecutor by protecting him from self-incrimination if he does not end up pleading guilty.

The language of the rule provides just two exceptions, although the case law has developed a third. First, there is a rule of completeness that provides that if some statement made during a plea or plea discussions has already been admitted into evidence in a proceeding, other statements are admissible that fairness requires be considered together. Second, if the defendant makes a statement on the record (for example, during the plea colloquy), under oath, and while represented by counsel, and is later prosecuted for perjury for making a false statement, the statement is admissible in evidence. Those are the only exceptions the rule provides.

The third exception was recognized in *United States v Mezzanatto*, 513 U.S. 196 (1995). The defendant had met with the prosecutor to discuss a possible plea. The prosecutor required the defendant to sign a "proffer letter" before talking with him. The letter spelled out the conditions under which the discussion would take place. It included a provision that if the discussion did not result in a guilty plea, and the defendant testified at trial, he could be impeached with any inconsistent statements he made during the proffer. The defendant signed the letter, and was later impeached with inconsistent statements from the proffer during his testimony at trial. Although this did not fall within the exceptions Rule 410 provided, the Supreme Court upheld the practice. It is now routine practice for federal prosecutors to insist on this provision in proffer letters, and as a result whenever there is such an agreement, statements made during pleas discussions may be introduced in evidence if they are inconsistent with a defendant's trial testimony.

QUESTION 11. After his arrest, federal law enforcement officers came to the defendant's jail cell and talked with him. They told him they could help him and would speak to the prosecutor on his behalf, if he would admit to his participation in the crime and identify the others who were involved. The defendant signed a waiver of his *Miranda* rights, and confessed to the officers. The prosecutor refused to give the defendant any special consideration and when the case went to trial, the prosecutor offered the defendant's statements to the officers in evidence. Is the evidence admissible?

A. No, because Rule 410 bars evidence of plea-bargaining.
B. No, because the officers said they would talk with the prosecutor.
C. No, because the defendant's constitutional rights were violated.
D. Yes.

ANALYSIS. It is true that the purpose of Rule 410 is to encourage plea-bargaining. The terms of the rule, however, apply only to "a statement made during plea discussions with an attorney for the prosecuting authority." The prosecutor must be present for the rule to apply, or at a minimum, the prosecutor must explicitly authorize someone else to negotiate on his or her behalf. The rule does not cover discussions with law enforcement officers acting on their own, and thus **A** is incorrect. The officers here merely promised the defendant they would speak to the prosecutor, which they did, but that did not make their conversation with the defendant a discussion with the prosecutor. Choice **B** is incorrect. A person in custody has the right not to speak with officers, and must be advised of that right in the Miranda warnings. The defendant may waive his right to remain silent, however, and since there is a signed waiver here, there is no violation of constitutional rights and **C** is incorrect. The correct answer is **D** and the statements to the officers are admissible.

5. *Evidence of Liability Insurance*

Rule 411. Liability Insurance
Evidence that a person was or was not insured against liability is not admissible to prove whether the person acted negligently or otherwise wrongfully. But the court may admit this evidence for another purpose, such as proving a witness's bias or prejudice or proving agency, ownership, or control.

The last of the bars against certain categories of evidence covers evidence of liability insurance. A party may not introduce evidence that the opposing party either had or did not have insurance in order to prove that the other party was negligent or acted wrongfully. Evidence of liability insurance may be offered for other purposes, however. Rule 411 provides some examples, but as with Rules 407 and 408, the words "such as" indicate that the list of exceptions provided in the rule is illustrative and not exhaustive.

The rule notes that evidence of insurance may be admitted to prove a witness's bias or prejudice, or to prove agency, ownership, or control. An investigator for the company that provides liability insurance to the defendant may testify as a witness at trial. In that event, the plaintiff may on cross-examination elicit the fact that the investigator works for the defendant's insurance company, to impeach the witness on the ground of bias. A defendant may deny that it owned or controlled the person, place, or thing that caused the plaintiff's injury. In that event, plaintiff can offer evidence that the defendant paid for the insurance on the person, place, or thing in order to prove that there was ownership or control. In the event that the court admits evidence of insurance for these purposes, the judge should give a limiting instruction to the jury that the proponent cannot use the evidence to prove negligence or wrongdoing by the defendant.

QUESTION 12. Plaintiff's husband, a professional basketball player, died suddenly from heart problems while playing basketball with friends. Before his death, the decedent had been receiving treatment

from a doctor for a previous episode when he had collapsed during a
basketball game. Plaintiff sued the doctor for malpractice. The doctor
claimed historical cocaine use had contributed to the patient's death, but
that the patient had denied such use for the first ten weeks of medical
treatment, admitting it only shortly before his death. Plaintiff denied
that her husband had ever used cocaine and denied he had ever told the
doctor he had done so. At trial the defendant doctor offered to introduce
in evidence life insurance policies that the player's team had purchased
on his behalf, which contained provisions that the policies would be
canceled in the event of illicit drug use. The plaintiff objected to the
insurance policies. The court should:

A. Exclude the policies because they have no relevance to the
   malpractice issues.
B. Exclude the policies under rule 411.
C. Admit the policies with a limiting instruction that they can only be
   considered on the issue of the credibility of the plaintiff and her
   husband with respect to cocaine use.
D. Conduct a balancing test under Rule 403 to determine whether the
   probative value of the evidence on credibility issues is substantially
   outweighed by the risk of unfair prejudice.

ANALYSIS.   This problem presents the judge with a difficult decision. Rule
411 excludes evidence of insurance only when offered to prove that a person
acted negligently or otherwise wrongfully. If the evidence is offered for any
other relevant purpose, Rule 411 does not bar it. The first inquiry in solv-
ing this problem should be to ask for what purpose this evidence might be
relevant.

The cancelation provision in the life insurance policies could have provided the player with a motive to deny cocaine use to the doctor, and a motive
for the plaintiff to continue to deny it after her husband's death. The policies
are relevant with respect to credibility, thus **A** is incorrect. Because the evidence is relevant on an issue other than proof of whether the defendant acted
negligently, Rule 411 would not bar the evidence and thus **B** is incorrect.

Before admitting the policies, however, the court must determine whether
the risk of unfair prejudice substantially outweighs their probative value. The
correct answer is **D**. It would not be proper to admit the evidence without
conducting a 403 analysis, and so **C** is incorrect. The risk of unfair prejudice
includes the risk that a jury might conclude that the plaintiff is attempting to
secure an unjust double recovery for her husband's death, by collecting both
insurance and a damages award from the doctor. On the other hand, the policies have considerable probative value in demonstrating a financial incentive
to lie about cocaine use. We needn't attempt to resolve this difficult issue for
our purposes here, but it is important that you appreciate the significance of
the Rule 403 issue.

D.   Character Evidence

The Federal Rules put significant limits on the use of character evidence. By character evidence we mean evidence that a person has a propensity to act in accord with a particular character trait, offered to prove that he behaved that way on a specific occasion. For example, the prosecution might like to offer evidence that a defendant has robbed several banks in the past, suggesting that he is a thief by nature, to prove that he committed the bank robbery for which he is on trial. Evidence of character and character traits offered for that purpose is generally not admissible. There are different rules for cases in which the defendant is accused of a sexual assault, which we discuss below. We begin, however, by discussing the rules for all other cases.

Rule 404 defines the circumstances under which a party may offer character evidence, and Rule 405 provides for the form in which one may present character evidence. In circumstances where character evidence is admissible, a character witness may only give her opinion of someone's character, or state what she knows to be the reputation of that person with respect to a given character trait. The character witness may not relate any conduct of the person in question in order to suggest what his character is, except in a small number of cases, which we describe below.

In our ordinary lives, we do rely on character evidence. We usually do so, however, to predict how others will behave in the future. For example, a prospective employer consults references, asking about a job applicant's character, in order to predict whether the person will be a good employee in the future. In trials, however, we are attempting to reconstruct the past. Evidence of a character trait is much more reliable in predicting behavior at an indefinite time in the future than in determining what happened on a specific occasion in the past. For example, someone who is a thief by nature is likely to steal again at some point in the future. However, it is much harder to conclude that a given person is the one who stole something on a specific occasion in the past merely because he is a thief by nature. We prefer to resolve historical disputes on the basis of case-specific evidence, rather than generalities about someone's character.

1.   When Character Evidence Is Admissible

Rule 404(a) provides the basic rules about when one may offer character evidence:

> **Rule 404. Character Evidence; Crimes Or Other Acts**
>   (a) Character Evidence.
>   (1) Prohibited Uses. Evidence of a person's character or character trait is not admissible to prove that on a particular occasion the person acted in accordance with the character or trait.
>   (2) Exceptions for a Defendant or Victim in a Criminal Case. The following exceptions apply in a criminal case:

(A) a defendant may offer evidence of the defendant's pertinent trait, and if the evidence is admitted, the prosecutor may offer evidence to rebut it;

(B) subject to the limitations in Rule 412, a defendant may offer evidence of an alleged victim's pertinent trait, and if the evidence is admitted, the prosecutor may:

(i) offer evidence to rebut it; and

(ii) offer evidence of the defendant's same trait; and

(C) in a homicide case, the prosecutor may offer evidence of the alleged victim's trait of peacefulness to rebut evidence that the victim was the first aggressor.

(3) Exceptions for a Witness. Evidence of a witness's character may be admitted under Rules 607, 608, and 609.

As we said above, evidence that a person has a propensity to act in a certain way is generally not admissible to prove that he acted that way on a specific occasion. There are some exceptions in criminal cases, however. The defendant is allowed to offer evidence of a pertinent trait of good character in order to show that he was unlikely to have committed the crime. The character trait must be relevant to the crime charged. For example, if the defendant is charged with assault and battery, he can offer evidence that he has a peaceful, nonviolent character. Evidence that he is honest, however, would not be admissible. If the defendant offers good character evidence, the prosecution is allowed to rebut with evidence that the defendant had bad character with respect to the trait in question.

The defendant in a criminal case is also permitted to offer evidence of a pertinent trait of the alleged victim of the crime. This is most commonly done in cases where a defendant is charged with using violence against another person. If the defendant pleads self-defense, he may offer evidence of the alleged victim's character for violence, to suggest that the victim was the first aggressor. If he does so, the prosecution may rebut with evidence that the alleged victim had good character with respect to the trait at issue. The prosecution may also rebut evidence of the alleged victim's bad character with evidence of the bad character of the defendant with respect to the same trait. The defendant can open the door to bad character evidence regarding himself either by offering evidence of his good character, or by offering evidence of the victim's bad character.

In criminal cases the "on-off switch" for character evidence is in the hands of the defendant. The prosecution may not offer character evidence unless the defendant does so first, either by offering evidence of his own good character or the bad character of the alleged victim. The only exception is in homicide cases where the defendant pleads self-defense. In such cases, the prosecution may offer evidence that the alleged victim had a peaceful character, whether or not the defendant has offered any character evidence.

There are no similar exceptions in civil cases. Character evidence is inadmissible in civil cases, except for a few cases that meet the requirements of

Rule 405(b), claims for sexual assaults under Rule 415, and the character of witnesses for truthfulness, all of which are discussed below.

2. What Form Character Evidence May Take

Federal Rule 405 defines the permissible form of character evidence. In almost all cases proof of character is limited to the testimony of a witness who supplies her opinion of the subject's character, or her knowledge of the subject's reputation with respect to character.

> **Rule 405. Methods Of Proving Character**
> (a) By Reputation or Opinion. When evidence of a person's character or character trait is admissible, it may be proved by testimony about the person's reputation or by testimony in the form of an opinion. On cross-examination of the character witness, the court may allow an inquiry into relevant specific instances of the person's conduct.
> (b) By Specific Instances of Conduct. When a person's character or character trait is an essential element of a charge, claim, or defense, the character or trait may also be proved by relevant specific instances of the person's conduct.

Most cases fall within Rule 405(a), and proof of character is limited to opinion or reputation evidence. To establish a foundation for opinion evidence, the proponent must elicit facts to show that the character witness knows the subject well enough to have an opinion about the character trait in question. With respect to reputation evidence, the proponent must show that the character witness is familiar with what people in a given community say about the subject's character. The community may be geographical, or a work, school, or other relevant environment. (Reputation evidence with respect to character is an exception to the hearsay rule under Rule 803(21).)

Suppose the defendant is charged with embezzling money from his employer. The defense may call a respected member of the community to testify that he has known the defendant for many years, has worked with him raising money for community organizations, and has socialized with him several times per month for a long time. This witness would be allowed to testify, "In my opinion, the defendant is honest and trustworthy in financial matters."

The general rule is that a party may not prove the character of a person by eliciting testimony about specific conduct of the person in the past that demonstrates a character trait. Rule 405(b), however, defines a limited exception under which a party may offer evidence of previous specific conduct in order to prove the existence of a character trait. The exception is confined to cases where character is an element of a charge, claim, or defense.

The cases where character constitutes such an element are limited to defamation, negligent entrustment, negligent hiring or retention, child custody, and criminal cases in which the defense is entrapment. In a defamation case, the defamatory words must be false and truth is a defense. For example, if the defendant has stated that the plaintiff is a thief, the fact that the plaintiff has in fact committed thefts is admissible to establish the truth of the defendant's statement. In a negligent entrustment, hiring, or retention case, the fact that the defendant has entrusted responsibility to someone with inappropriate character demonstrates negligence. In a child custody case, the character of the parties seeking custody is of obvious importance. In a criminal case where the defense is entrapment, the defendant must show that he had no predisposition to commit the offense and only did so under pressure or unreasonable entreaties by a government agent. A party may not use specific acts to prove character other than in those narrow circumstances.

QUESTION 13. Defendant is charged with murder, by stabbing the victim with a Bowie knife. The prosecution offers to call a witness in its case in chief to testify that the defendant has a reputation in his neighborhood as a violent person. Defendant's objection should be:

A. Sustained, improper character evidence.
B. Overruled, the evidence is in the proper form under Rule 405(a).
C. Overruled, such evidence is admissible in a homicide case.
D. Overruled, the evidence is relevant because it makes it more likely than it would be in the absence of the evidence that the defendant committed the murder.

ANALYSIS. The prosecution offers evidence that the defendant is violent in order to prove that he may have killed the victim. This is evidence of character to prove how a person probably acted on a given occasion. Such evidence is often logically relevant, but we exclude it because jurors might give it too much weight. Choice **D** is incorrect. The reputation evidence in this instance is in the proper form, but the form alone will not make it admissible, so **B** is incorrect. Choice **C** is incorrect because the only special rule for homicide cases is one that allows peaceful character evidence with respect to the victim when the defendant pleads self-defense. Choice **A** is the correct answer because the prosecution is offering character evidence before the defendant has done anything to make character evidence admissible.

QUESTION 14. Defendant is on trial for embezzlement. In his defense, he offers evidence from his minister that he has kept the books for the church for the past ten years and there has never been a penny missing. The prosecution's objection to this evidence should be:

A. Sustained, relevance.
B. Sustained, improper form of character evidence.
C. Sustained, religion may not be taken into account in assessing credibility.
D. Overruled, the defendant is allowed to present evidence of his good character.

ANALYSIS. First, **A** is incorrect because the evidence is relevant, as we discussed in the last question. **C** correctly states a proposition of evidence law, namely, that religious beliefs may not be used to attack or support a witness's credibility. That does not mean, however, that a minister may never testify, and thus **C** would be an incorrect basis for sustaining the objection to this testimony. Choice **D** also states a correct proposition: that the defendant is permitted to offer character evidence. He must do so in the proper form, however. Here the minister is testifying to specific conduct of the defendant—honestly maintaining the church's books for ten years—which violates Rule 405(a). This example is similar to the embezzlement example given earlier in the text, but with a very important difference. In the earlier example, the witness testified to his *opinion* that the defendant was honest, not to specific conduct. Choice **B** is the correct answer. To be admissible, character evidence must satisfy both Rules 404 and 405.

QUESTION 15. Plaintiff sues the defendant corporation under respondeat superior, alleging that a driver for the company ran a red light, causing an accident in which plaintiff sustained serious injuries. The defendant company offers evidence that the driver has been with the company for 20 years and has an accident-free driving record. The plaintiff's objection should be:

A. Overruled, the defendant in a civil case is permitted to offer good character evidence to show that its driver is not the sort of person who would have run a red light.
B. Overruled, the driver is not a defendant in the case and the rule against character evidence applies only to parties.
C. Overruled, but the plaintiff can rebut with evidence that the driver was careless on other occasions, even though his driving may not have caused accidents.
D. Sustained.

ANALYSIS. There is no rule allowing a defendant in a civil case to use good character evidence similar to the rule permitting such evidence by criminal defendants. Choice **A** is incorrect. With respect to **B**, let's look again at the language of Rule 404(a), which states, "Evidence of a person's character or character trait is not admissible to prove that on a particular occasion the person acted in accordance with the character or trait." The proscription is not limited to evidence concerning the *parties*, but renders character evidence inadmissible with respect to any *person*. Choice **B** is incorrect. Choice **C** is incorrect for the reasons **A** and **B** are incorrect. Moreover, **C** demonstrates one of the reasons for the character evidence bar. If the defendant could introduce evidence of the driver's good record, and the plaintiff could rebut with evidence of previous instances of careless driving in the past, the trial would be about this driver's entire life on the road. This would prolong the trial, and distract the jury from the real issue of what happened in this accident. Choice **D** is the correct answer—the evidence is inadmissible.

QUESTION 16. Plaintiff sues the defendant Highway Department because his car slid off the road at a curve and went over a cliff, causing him serious injuries. Plaintiff sues the defendant for negligent design of the roadway and the failure to have a guardrail. Plaintiff offers evidence that six other cars had slid at that curve under substantially similar circumstances and gone over the cliff within the previous six months. The defendant's objection should be:

A. Sustained, the evidence is not relevant.
B. Sustained, it violates the bar against character evidence.
C. Overruled.

ANALYSIS.   This question requires you to understand the difference between evidence of similar events and character evidence. We talked about evidence of similar events in the relevance section above. Here the defendant is offering evidence about the dangerous nature of a location, not the character of any person. The rules concerning character evidence are not at issue here, and therefore **B** is incorrect. As we said in the relevance section, evidence of similar events is relevant in a tort case if other accidents occurred under substantially similar circumstances. The question specifies that they did, and so **C** is the correct answer and **A** is incorrect because this evidence is relevant.

QUESTION 17. Husband and wife are getting divorced and wife seeks sole custody of the children on the ground that the husband physically abused her and the children and thus is an unfit parent. Which of the following types of evidence would the wife's lawyer be able to introduce to prove her case?

A. The opinion of a neighbor, who knew the family well, that the husband was violent and abusive.
B. The testimony of a neighbor, who had discussed the husband with many other people in the neighborhood, that the husband had a reputation for being violent and abusive.
C. The testimony of a neighbor who saw the husband strike the children on several specific occasions.
D. All of the above.
E. None of the above.

ANALYSIS. The correct answer is **D**, all of the above. This child custody case falls within the small group of cases in which character is an element of the claim. In such cases, it is permissible to prove character through opinion evidence, reputation evidence, and evidence of specific acts.

E.   Cross-Examination of a Character Witness

As we have said, when character evidence is admissible, with very few exceptions, it must be in the form of opinion or reputation evidence by a witness with sufficient familiarity with the subject or his reputation to give such testimony. The direct examination of the character witness is limited to laying the foundation for his testimony and eliciting his opinion or information about the subject's reputation. The cross-examiner, however, may ask questions about specific acts. The last sentence of Rule 405(a) states, "On cross-examination of the character witness, the court may allow an inquiry into relevant specific instances of the person's conduct."

Suppose, for example, a defendant charged with a violent assault calls a character witness who testifies that in her opinion the defendant is peaceful and non-violent. The prosecutor may ask this witness on cross-examination, "Do you know that the defendant beat his brother so badly last year that he was hospitalized?"

In order to ask such a question, the cross-examiner must have a good faith basis in fact for the question. The cross-examiner may not make things up to make the defendant look bad. The specific act in question must be pertinent to the character trait the witness has testified about. For example, the cross-examiner could not ask a character witness who testified about the defendant's non-violent character about incidents of theft. Moreover, the cross-examiner is limited to asking questions of the character witness and cannot prove the incident with the brother by calling other witnesses or offering exhibits or documents.

The theory of permitting such questions is that they reflect on the weight the jury may give the testimony of the character witness. If the witness has not heard of the incident, perhaps she does not know the defendant that well and her opinion should be discounted. Or if she has heard about the incident and nonetheless believes the defendant is peaceful, perhaps the character witness has bad judgment. In practice, the cross-examiner gets an opportunity for the jury to hear about bad behavior on the part of the defendant. The judge will instruct the jury that the evidence is admissible for the limited purpose of assessing the value of the character witness's testimony, but there is a risk that jurors will use it substantively against the defendant. Where such evidence is available, the defendant must consider whether the risk outweighs the value of using good character witnesses.

> **QUESTION 18.** Defendant is charged with assault and battery. Defendant claims misidentification. Defendant calls his pastor as a witness. The pastor testifies that he has known defendant for most of his life, and that in his opinion defendant is a peaceful and nonviolent person who is not capable of committing the type of act with which he is charged.
>
> The prosecutor has credible evidence that defendant once attacked and severely beat a former employer. The prosecutor:
>
> **A.** May not ask the pastor whether he has heard about the prior attack and may not introduce any other evidence that the attack occurred.
> **B.** May ask the pastor whether he has heard that defendant once attacked a former employer, and, if the pastor denies having heard this, may call another witness to testify to the prior attack.
> **C.** May ask the pastor whether he has heard that defendant once attacked a former employer, but may not introduce other evidence of the attack.
> **D.** May not ask the pastor about the former attack unless criminal charges were brought against defendant for that attack.

ANALYSIS.   Rule 405 (a) allows the cross-examiner to ask a character witness about specific incidents, and so **A** is incorrect. **D** is also incorrect, because there is no requirement that a prior incident led to criminal charges. The cross-examiner must have a good faith basis for asking the question, but there are other ways of establishing a good faith basis that do not involve criminal charges. The cross-examiner may not, however, introduce independent evidence that the incident in question occurred. Therefore, **B** is incorrect. The correct answer is **C**.

F.   Proof of Other Crimes, Wrongs, or Acts

As we have discussed, except for the few cases covered by Rule 405(b), it is not permissible to offer evidence of specific acts by a person to prove a character trait in order to prove the person acted in accord with his character on a particular occasion. This rule is reiterated in Rule 404(b). Rule 404(b), however, also establishes that proof of other conduct may be admissible for other purposes.

> **Rule 404. Character Evidence; Crimes Or Other Acts**
>   (b) Crimes, Wrongs, or Other Acts.
>   (1) Prohibited Uses. Evidence of a crime, wrong, or other act is not admissible to prove a person's character in order to show that on a particular occasion the person acted in accordance with the character.
>   (2) Permitted Uses; Notice in a Criminal Case. This evidence may be admissible for another purpose, such as proving motive, opportunity,

intent, preparation, plan, knowledge, identity, absence of mistake, or lack of accident. On request by a defendant in a criminal case, the prosecutor must:

> (A) provide reasonable notice of the general nature of any such evidence that the prosecutor intends to offer at trial; and
>
> (B) do so before trial—or during trial if the court, for good cause, excuses lack of pretrial notice.

Rule 404(b) embodies the rule against propensity evidence. Evidence of other crimes, wrongs, or acts is not admissible to prove a person had a *propensity* to behave in a given way, and therefore probably behaved that way during the incident in question. Evidence of other crimes, wrongs, or acts, however, may be admissible if offered for any other purpose. The rule lists the most common examples of other purposes, but it is not intended to be exhaustive. If such evidence is offered for any purpose other than the propensity purpose, it is arguably admissible.

Why do we say it is "arguably" admissible? Because in virtually all cases under Rule 404(b), the judge will have to make a decision about whether the risk of unfair prejudice substantially outweighs the probative value of the evidence. The risk of unfair prejudice is the risk that the jury will use the evidence for the propensity purpose, as character evidence. The probative value is the significance of the evidence when used for the non-propensity purpose.

Let's look at an example to clarify how this rule works. Suppose the defendant is charged with the murder of his neighbor. The prosecution has evidence that a month before the murder, a witness saw the defendant kill the victim's dog in an unprovoked attack on the animal. This evidence tends to show that the defendant was violent, and the fact that he had a propensity to be violent suggests that he may be guilty of killing his neighbor. The evidence is inadmissible when used as character evidence in that way. The fact that the defendant killed the dog, however, also suggests that he disliked the neighbor, and thus shows that he had a motive for killing him. Motive is a permissible use of other acts evidence under Rule 404(b) and evidence of killing the dog would be admissible if offered for that purpose. The question remains, however, whether the risk that the jury will use the evidence as improper character evidence substantially outweighs the probative value of the evidence to prove motive.

When evidence of other crimes, wrongs, or acts is offered under Rule 404(b) there are always four questions that you must answer:

1. Is there a risk that the evidence leads to an inference that the person had a propensity to behave in a certain way as a result of his character?
2. Is there another purpose for which the evidence could be offered, other than the propensity inference?
3. How effective will a limiting instruction be in containing the risk of unfair prejudice?
4. Will the risk of unfair prejudice substantially outweigh the probative value of the evidence?

The use of other acts evidence *for purposes other than character evidence* is very common, particularly in criminal cases. In practice it is almost always possible to come up with an argument that evidence is admissible for some purpose other than the propensity inference. The contested issue in most cases is whether the risk of unfair prejudice substantially outweighs the probative value of the evidence. We will return to that issue below, but for now, let's look at some questions to explore some of the other purposes for which other acts evidence might be offered.

QUESTION 19. Defendant is charged with murder. The cause of death was a gaping wound that the pathologist testified was caused by a machete. The prosecutor has a witness who would testify that the defendant threatened the witness with a machete a month before the murder took place. The prosecution's best argument for the admissibility of this evidence is:

A. The evidence is not capable of a propensity inference.
B. The evidence demonstrates that the defendant had a motive to kill the victim.
C. The evidence proves that the defendant had the means to kill the victim.
D. The evidence proves that the defendant did not kill the victim by accident.

ANALYSIS.   Choice **A** is not correct. The evidence is capable of a propensity inference, namely, that the defendant is violent because he threatened the witness with a machete. Unlike the example above in the text, here the evidence does not tell us anything about the defendant's motive to kill the victim, because his previous threat was against the witness, not the victim. Thus **B** is incorrect. The fact that the defendant previously threatened someone else with the machete does not tell us anything about whether the unrelated killing of the victim was an accident. Thus **D** is not correct. The evidence does show, however, that the defendant had a machete, and therefore had the means, or the opportunity, to commit this crime. For that purpose the evidence would be admissible and thus **C** is the correct answer.

The defendant might argue that the risk of unfair prejudice from this evidence exceeds its probative value, under Rule 403. The defendant might ask the court to limit the testimony to the fact that the witness saw the defendant with a machete, and exclude the fact that the defendant threatened him with it. The judge would have discretion under Rule 403 to limit the testimony in this way in order to minimize the risk that the jury would use the evidence to conclude the defendant had a propensity to be violent.

QUESTION 20. Defendant is on trial for murder. He is accused of setting fire to the victim's house while she was sleeping, which he denies. Defendant offers court records to prove that the victim's landlord has been convicted of three counts of arson on other buildings he owned, as well as fraud in obtaining the insurance proceeds from the buildings. The landlord made an insurance claim on this building as well. The prosecution's objection to this evidence should be:

A. Sustained, only the prosecution can offer evidence of other crimes under Rule 404(b).
B. Overruled, the evidence shows a common scheme or plan of arson and fraud by the landlord.
C. Overruled, the evidence shows that the landlord had the knowledge of how to burn a building.
D. Sustained, this is improper character evidence regarding the landlord.

ANALYSIS. Rule 404(b) by its terms does not restrict a defendant from offering evidence of other acts, as long as the evidence is not offered for a propensity purpose, thus **A** is incorrect. The evidence here would be improper character evidence (**D**), if there were no purpose for it other than to suggest the landlord is an arsonist by nature. The argument that the evidence shows the landlord knows how to burn a building is weak in the absence of something that shows particular skill was required, thus a judge is not likely to admit this evidence under **C**. The evidence does show, however, that the landlord has an ongoing scheme or plan to burn his property for the insurance proceeds. A judge is likely to admit the evidence under **B**. The judge would have to consider, however, whether the risk of unfair prejudice substantially outweighs the probative value of the evidence. In this example, the risks of unfair prejudice are reduced (but not entirely eliminated) because the person against whom the propensity inference would run is not a party to the case.

QUESTION 21. Defendant is charged with bank robbery. He was arrested after paint, identified as coming from the exploding packet in the money taken from the bank, was found on his clothing. The bank was robbed by someone wearing a President Obama mask, who gave the teller a note saying, "I have a gun, I want the money in the drawer, and I don't want change." There were three previous robberies in which the perpetrator wore an Obama mask, said he had a gun, and said, "I don't want change." The mask slipped during those robberies and the tellers saw the robber's face, but no one was arrested for them. Those tellers have now identified this defendant as the one who robbed their banks. Which of the following statements is correct?

A. The evidence is not capable of a propensity inference.
B. The tellers' testimony would be improper character evidence.
C. The evidence is not relevant.
D. The evidence is arguably admissible on the issue of identity.

ANALYSIS.   The evidence here is capable of a propensity inference, namely, the defendant is a thief by nature, so **A** is incorrect. It would be improper character evidence, under **B**, if there were no other purpose for which it could be offered. Here the evidence shows that there is a bank robber with a very idiosyncratic modus operandi. He wears a mask of President Obama, claims to have a gun, and makes a joke about the president's slogan in his first campaign for the White House. The prosecution's theory is that there is one "Obama robber" and that he is the defendant, as identified by the tellers from the other banks. The evidence is relevant on that theory, so **C** is incorrect. The evidence is arguably admissible because the distinctive modus operandi establishes the identity of the robber. Choice **D** is the correct answer. In order for modus operandi evidence to be admissible to prove identity, the M.O. must be truly idiosyncratic. For example, evidence that the robber wore a plain mask, claimed to have a gun, and escaped in a stolen car would not be sufficient to establish a unique modus operandi—most bank robbers operate in that fashion. In order to determine whether the evidence should be admitted, the court would have to determine under Rule 403 whether the risk of unfair prejudice (propensity use of the evidence) substantially outweighed the probative value of the evidence.

QUESTION 22. Defendant is charged with grand larceny in connection with the theft of diamond tennis bracelets ordered by a hacker who penetrated a jewelry store's computer and had the bracelets delivered to a post office box without paying for them. The defendant was previously charged with stealing diamond necklaces from another jewelry store by hacking into its computer in the same manner and having the necklaces delivered to a post office box without paying for them. In the first trial there was evidence from a computer expert who testified that the instructions to ship the necklaces came from the defendant's computer, and the necklaces were later recovered in the defendant's apartment. Nonetheless, the defendant was found not guilty in the first case. May the prosecution offer that evidence from the first trial in the defendant's trial on the theft of the tennis bracelets?

A. Arguably yes, because it proves that the defendant had the requisite knowledge to hack into the jewelry store's computer.
B. No, because the defendant was found not guilty of the first crime.
C. No, because the evidence is not relevant.
D. No, it is improper character evidence.

ANALYSIS. You may be surprised at the answer to this question. First, let's ignore the fact that the defendant was found not guilty of the first crime and analyze this problem in the same way we have looked at the last few questions. Knowledge of how to hack into a commercial computer and have products delivered without paying for them is relatively rare. If the defendant did the theft of the necklaces it would demonstrate such knowledge, and that would make it more likely than it would be without such evidence that he was the person who stole the tennis bracelets. The evidence would be relevant for a purpose other than the propensity inference, and choices **C** and **D** would be incorrect. But does it matter that the defendant was found not guilty in the first trial?

Even where a defendant has been charged with and found not guilty of other acts, those acts may be introduced against him in a later trial as long as there is enough evidence that he did them to satisfy the preponderance of the evidence standard. It is the preponderance of the evidence standard that governs whether there is sufficient evidence that the defendant committed the other acts for them to be admissible. When the defendant was found not guilty in the first trial, it meant that the jury had concluded there was insufficient evidence to conclude that he was guilty *beyond a reasonable doubt*. The reasonable doubt standard is higher than the preponderance of the evidence standard, however, and the fact that there was not enough evidence to satisfy the jury beyond a reasonable doubt does not mean that the evidence does not satisfy the preponderance standard.

The evidence of the computer expert coupled with the fact that the necklaces were found in the defendant's apartment is sufficient to establish by a preponderance of the evidence that the defendant stole them, so that evidence is arguably admissible in this trial for the theft of the tennis bracelets. Choice **A** is the correct answer. In order to determine whether the evidence should be admitted, the court would have to determine under Rule 403 whether the risk of unfair prejudice (propensity use of the evidence) substantially outweighed the probative value of the evidence.

1. Balancing the Risk of Unfair Prejudice Against Probative Value

A defendant's initial objection to proof of other acts will be that it constitutes improper character evidence and invites a propensity inference. The prosecutor will usually articulate another purpose for the evidence, similar to those we have discussed in the above questions. Then the defendant will make the objection that the risk of unfair prejudice, namely the risk that the jury will use the evidence as evidence of his bad character, substantially outweighs the probative value of the evidence for the alternative purpose.

A trial judge has substantial discretion in resolving Rule 403 questions and an appellate court will rarely reverse her decisions. These discretionary decisions do not lend themselves to the sorts of correct and incorrect answers that we usually give to multiple-choice questions.

It is important for lawyers arguing prejudice vs. probative value objections to be as precise as possible about the nature of the unfair prejudice and the significance of the proof for a legitimate purpose. In assessing the risk of prejudice of other act evidence, one must analyze how blameworthy the character trait in question is, how negatively the jury may view the defendant given the culpability of the other acts, how likely it is that the jury will infer the defendant's guilt of the crime charged from the character evidence presented, and whether a limiting instruction will be sufficient to control the risk. Evidence that a defendant has smoked marijuana, for example, is not likely to lead to the conclusion that he is a murderer. On the other hand, evidence that a defendant gratuitously killed a neighbor's pet dog, as in one of our earlier examples, might turn the jury so far against him that he would not be afforded the full measure of the reasonable doubt standard on the murder charge. With respect to probative value, one must analyze how central the purpose to be served is to the claim it is offered to support, weigh the significance of this evidence in the context of all the available evidence in the case, and take into account whether there are alternate means of proving the fact in question.

G.   Habit

The Federal Rules permit evidence of habit or routine practice to prove how a person or organization acted on a given occasion.

> **Rule 406. Habit; Routine Practice**
> Evidence of a person's habit or an organization's routine practice may be admitted to prove that on a particular occasion the person or organization acted in accordance with the habit or routine practice. The court may admit this evidence regardless of whether it is corroborated or whether there was an eyewitness.

A "habit" is a person's regular response to a specific situation that he or she frequently encounters. For example, if the engineer on a train always blows the train whistle when approaching a particular road, we can say it is his habit to do so. If a driver always immediately puts on her seat belt when sitting down behind the wheel of a car, that is a habit. If a ballistics expert always opens the chamber every time he picks up a revolver in order to check if the gun is loaded, and empties it of any bullets before further examining it, that qualifies as a habit. In these examples, the person frequently encounters the same particular situation and invariably does the same thing in response. To qualify as habit evidence, there must be numerous instances of the same specific situation, and the person must regularly make the same response.

Habit evidence is different from character evidence. Character evidence is about a general trait of a person. For example, we might say that an individual is honest, peaceful, or careful. Those character traits affect how the person behaves in a wide variety of circumstances. Habit evidence does not relate to a general characteristic of a person, but to specific behavior in a particular, often repeated, situation. If we say that a person is a careful driver, we imply that he or she is generally careful when operating a motor vehicle. The fact that someone habitually wears her seat belt does not necessarily imply that she is a careful driver, but is merely evidence that on a particular occasion she probably had her seat belt on. Evidence that the train engineer always blows the train whistle when approaching a particular road is competent proof that he blew it on a specific occasion when he was approaching that road, but it is not evidence that he was otherwise operating the train safely. Character evidence frequently involves moral overtones; habit evidence usually does not.

Frequently the behavior that qualifies as habit evidence appears to be instinctive, semi-automatic, or unconscious. It is an ingrained response to a specific, frequently encountered situation, and the person makes the same response each time without really thinking about it.

Under the Federal Rules we do not use the term *habit* the way we often do in ordinary conversation. For example, one might say about another person, "He has a habit of not telling the truth." Under the Federal Rules that would be character evidence. The person is described as generally dishonest or deceitful. The same is true of an expression like, "he has a habit of drinking too much." The person is described as one who generally abuses alcohol. In neither of the examples are we dealing with a specific situation, and neither would qualify as habit evidence under the rules.

The rules also permit evidence of the routine practice of an organization, to prove that something was done on a specific occasion. For example, suppose we have evidence that in a particular office the person who receives the mail regularly stamps each envelope with a device that prints the word "received" and the date on the envelope. This evidence can be introduced to prove that an envelope in the office with a given date stamped on it was received on that date. As a different example, we could introduce evidence that bartenders at a given tavern always ask patrons for identification before serving them liquor, regardless of their apparent age, to prove that on a specific occasion the bartender asked a customer for his identification before serving him.

Any witness with personal knowledge may testify to the habit of another person or the routine practice of an organization. The rule specifically notes that the witness does not have to be an eyewitness, but the witness must have personal knowledge. Corroboration is not required for habit evidence to be admissible.

QUESTION 23. Suppose there is a question during a trial about whether Mr. Jones was in the Big Ten Bar and Grill at 5:30 PM on Friday, September 25, three years before the year in which the trial takes place. The party who wants to prove that Jones was present offers evidence from the bartender that he cannot specifically recall that date, but for years it was Mr. Jones's invariable practice on Fridays to stop by the bar for a couple of beers after he left work at 5:00 PM before catching the bus to his home. The opponent's objection to this evidence should be:

A. Sustained, because the bartender has no memory of this specific date.
B. Sustained, because what Mr. Jones did on other days is not relevant to what he did on this particular day.
C. Sustained, because drinking is an inappropriate subject matter for habit evidence.
D. Overruled, this is proper habit evidence.

ANALYSIS.   This situation meets the requirements for habit evidence and the correct answer is **D**. We are dealing with a specific and repeated situation, what Mr. Jones does after leaving work on Fridays. The bartender's evidence that he invariably stopped at the bar for a couple of beers before heading home on Friday is, under Rule 406, relevant and admissible to prove that he did so on a particular occasion, even though the bartender cannot remember that occasion. Thus **A** and **B** are incorrect. This example is different from the one in the text above. Here the evidence is not that Jones "has a habit of drinking too much," or that he abuses alcohol. The evidence is not about his general character when it comes to alcohol, but specifically about what he does on Fridays. Choice **C** is incorrect, and the evidence is admissible.

H.   Propensity Evidence in Sexual Assault Cases

The rules we have discussed above with respect to character evidence apply in all cases except criminal and civil cases in which there is an alleged sexual assault. In sexual assault cases the rules are different, both with respect to what evidence is admissible with respect to the character of the victim, and what is admissible with respect to the character of the defendant. With some exceptions, the rules preclude admitting any evidence concerning the character of an alleged victim of a sexual assault with respect to sexual matters. With respect to the defendant in a sexual assault case, the rules make admissible certain evidence that reflects on his character.

1.   *Evidence Regarding the Alleged Victim of a Sexual Assault*

Before the advent of rules protecting the alleged victim of a sexual assault, the experience of making a complaint and appearing in court to testify for the prosecution was most often a further torment for female victims. A common defense was to put the character of the complainant on trial, suggesting that she was promiscuous, unchaste, unstable, and in some way to blame for the assault. It is appalling to read the judicial decisions which for many years approved of this practice. In order to bring an end to the abuse of alleged victims during the judicial process, and in order to encourage greater reporting of sexual assaults, Congress enacted Rule 412 to the Federal Rules of Evidence. All states have a similar provision in their evidence law.

Rule 412. Sex-Offense Cases: The Victim

(a) Prohibited Uses. The following evidence is not admissible in a civil or criminal proceeding involving alleged sexual misconduct:

(1) evidence offered to prove that a victim engaged in other sexual behavior; or

(2) evidence offered to prove a victim's sexual predisposition.

(b) Exceptions.

(1) Criminal Cases. The court may admit the following evidence in a criminal case:

(A) evidence of specific instances of a victim's sexual behavior, if offered to prove that someone other than the defendant was the source of semen, injury, or other physical evidence;

(B) evidence of specific instances of a victim's sexual behavior with respect to the person accused of the sexual misconduct, if offered by the defendant to prove consent or if offered by the prosecutor; and

(C) evidence whose exclusion would violate the defendant's constitutional rights.

(2) Civil Cases. In a civil case, the court may admit evidence offered to prove a victim's sexual behavior or sexual predisposition if its probative value substantially outweighs the danger of harm to any victim and of unfair prejudice to any party. The court may admit evidence of a victim's reputation only if the victim has placed it in controversy.

(c) Procedure to Determine Admissibility.

(1) Motion. If a party intends to offer evidence under Rule 412(b), the party must:

(A) file a motion that specifically describes the evidence and states the purpose for which it is to be offered;

(B) do so at least 14 days before trial unless the court, for good cause, sets a different time;

(C) serve the motion on all parties; and

(D) notify the victim or, when appropriate, the victim's guardian or representative.

(2) Hearing. Before admitting evidence under this rule, the court must conduct an in camera hearing and give the victim and parties a right to attend and be heard. Unless the court orders otherwise, the motion, related materials, and the record of the hearing must be and remain sealed.

(d) Definition of "Victim." In this rule, "victim" includes an alleged victim.

In criminal cases, the rule excludes all evidence of an alleged victim's other sexual behavior and/or sexual predisposition and provides only limited exceptions. In civil cases, the rule allows such evidence only if its probative value substantially outweighs the danger of harm to any alleged victim and of unfair prejudice to any party, but permits evidence of an alleged victim's reputation only if she has placed it in controversy. The rule provides a procedure requiring notice and a hearing for resolving issues of admissibility.

The rule excludes evidence of other sexual behavior and sexual predisposition whether offered through cross-examination, exhibits, or other witnesses. It excludes such evidence whether it is offered directly or through innuendo. For example, evidence that the alleged victim wore provocative clothing, used off-color language, or told risqué jokes is not admissible.

There are narrow exceptions to this rule of exclusion. Two of the exceptions in criminal cases are straightforward. The rule gives the court discretion to permit evidence of other specific instances of an alleged victim's sexual behavior, if the defendant offers it to prove that someone else was the source of semen, injury, or other physical evidence. For example, the court may permit a defendant to offer evidence that the alleged victim had sexual intercourse with someone else, to prove that the other person caused injuries that were observed when she was examined after the alleged assault by the defendant. The rule also gives the court discretion to permit the defendant to offer evidence of the alleged victim's other sexual behavior with him, if his defense to the charge against him is that the alleged victim consented to sexual activity. The rule gives the court discretion to permit the prosecutor to offer evidence of the alleged victim's other sexual behavior with the defendant in any case where such evidence would be relevant.

The third exception is less well defined. The rule gives the court discretion to permit evidence the exclusion of which would violate the defendant's constitutional rights. Due process requires that a criminal defendant have the constitutional right to introduce evidence in support of his theory of defense, and the Sixth Amendment specifically guarantees him the right to confront the witnesses against him through cross-examination. This does not mean, however, that whenever the person accused of a sexual assault makes a consent defense, he can offer evidence of the alleged victim's other sexual behavior or predisposition. That is precisely what the rule is designed to prohibit.

Exactly what evidence a criminal defendant does have the right to present is not well defined by the case law. The Supreme Court has held, however, that the Confrontation Clause may require a court to permit a defendant to cross-examine the alleged victim of a rape about matters that would provide a motive for her to falsely accuse the defendant.[1] In that case, the defense claimed the alleged victim had concocted the rape allegation because she feared that the man with whom she was having an extra-marital affair would break it off

---

1.   *Olden v. Kentucky*, 488 U.S. 227 (1988).

if he suspected she had consented to sex with another man. The Court held that, under all the circumstances of the case, it had been an error to restrict the defendant's right to cross-examine the complainant about the affair. Whether the Constitution requires permitting a defendant to introduce evidence of an alleged victim's other sexual behavior or predisposition in a given case is heavily dependent on the factual circumstances of that case.

QUESTION 24. The defendant is on trial for the crime of rape. He and the alleged victim had been in a sexual relationship for four years and then broke up. A year later they ran into each other at a conference and went to the alleged victim's hotel room to talk. She claims the defendant raped her. He admits that they had intercourse, but says it was consensual. The defendant has given notice that he intends to offer evidence that the alleged victim has had consensual sexual relations with a dozen different men in the past year. After a hearing, how should the court rule?

A. The court should exclude the evidence.
B. The court should admit the evidence because it is necessary to protect the constitutional rights of the defendant.
C. The court should admit the evidence because the defendant and the alleged victim have previously been sexually intimate.
D. The court should admit the evidence if its probative value on the issue of consent substantially outweighs the danger of harm to the victim.

ANALYSIS. Evidence that the alleged victim had consensual relations with other men falls squarely within the prohibition of Rule 412. The issue is whether it falls within any of the exceptions to the rule. Choice **D** is the exception that applies in civil cases. This is not a civil case and thus **D** is incorrect. If we were to say that admissibility here was required to protect the constitutional rights of the defendant, the exception would swallow the rule. The defense of consent does not automatically render admissible evidence that the alleged victim has consented to sexual relations with other men, and **B** is incorrect. Choice **C** is also incorrect, because the evidence the defendant seeks to offer goes beyond what the exception for a former sexual partner allows. Exception (b)(1)(B) permits only evidence of previous sexual activity between the defendant and the alleged victim, not sexual activity between the alleged victim and others. The correct answer is **A**.

2. Evidence Regarding the Defendant in a Sexual Assault Case

Federal Rules of Evidence 413, 414, and 415 provide that certain propensity evidence is admissible against defendants in different types of sexual assault and child molestation cases. Rule 413 provides that in criminal cases where the defendant is accused of a sexual assault, the prosecution may introduce evidence that the defendant committed other sexual assaults.

> **Rule 413. Similar Crimes in Sexual-Assault Cases**
>
> **(a) Permitted Uses.** In a criminal case in which a defendant is accused of a sexual assault, the court may admit evidence that the defendant committed any other sexual assault. The evidence may be considered on any matter to which it is relevant.
>
> **(b) Disclosure to the Defendant.** If the prosecutor intends to offer this evidence, the prosecutor must disclose it to the defendant, including witnesses' statements or a summary of the expected testimony. The prosecutor must do so at least 15 days before trial or at a later time that the court allows for good cause.
>
> **(c) Effect on Other Rules.** This rule does not limit the admission or consideration of evidence under any other rule.
>
> **(d) Definition of "Sexual Assault."** In this rule and Rule 415, "sexual assault" means a crime under federal law or under state law (as "state" is defined in 18 U.S.C. §513) involving: **(1)** any conduct prohibited by 18 U.S.C. chapter 109A; **(2)** contact, without consent, between any part of the defendant's body—or an object—and another person's genitals or anus; **(3)** contact, without consent, between the defendant's genitals or anus and any part of another person's body; **(4)** deriving sexual pleasure or gratification from inflicting death, bodily injury, or physical pain on another person; or **(5)** an attempt or conspiracy to engage in conduct described in subparagraphs (1)–(4).

Rule 414 provides in a similar fashion that in any criminal case where the defendant is accused of child molestation, evidence is admissible that he committed other acts of child molestation. The rule defines a child as a person below the age of fourteen and defines the nature of the acts that constitute child molestation. Rule 415 provides that the same evidence is available as under Rules 413 and 414 in civil cases where sexual assault or child molestation is alleged. All three of the rules require the proponent to give the defendant fifteen days' notice of intent to introduce such evidence.

We have not set forth the full text of the Rules 414 and 415, but all three rules operate in a fashion similar to Rule 413, and we can focus our discussion on it. The most important aspect of the rule is that it permits the prosecution to introduce evidence that the defendant is a sexual predator by nature, in order to demonstrate that it is more likely that he committed the crime charged than it would be the absence of such evidence regarding his character. The rule specifically permits evidence of other acts of the defendant to show that he has a *propensity* to commit sexual assaults. This is the exact opposite of how Rule 404(b) operates in all other criminal cases, where it excludes the use of other act evidence for propensity purposes.

It is important to note that Rule 413 does not make all evidence respecting the defendant's character with respect to sexual matters admissible. Unlike character evidence in other cases, opinion and reputation evidence is not admissible to prove the defendant's character. Only evidence that the defendant has committed other acts that fit the definition of criminal sexual assaults is admissible.

For example, suppose the defendant is charged with the rape of the victim. The prosecutor may call other women to testify that the defendant sexually assaulted them. Evidence of such assaults is admissible whether they took place before or after the assault alleged in the present case. It is not necessary to show that the defendant was convicted of the previous assaults. The standard of proof for admissibility is proof sufficient to establish by a preponderance of the evidence that the defendant committed the other sexual assaults in question. As we noted above with respect to other act evidence under Rule 404(b), even if the defendant was acquitted of the other acts, they may be admissible in this case as long as there is evidence sufficient to satisfy the preponderance of the evidence standard.

The defendant may argue that evidence of other sexual assaults is inadmissible under Rule 403, because the risk of unfair prejudice substantially outweighs probative value, or because the evidence is confusing, misleading, causes undue delay, wastes time or is needlessly cumulative. The argument that there is a risk of unfair prejudice, however, must be different here than in cases of other act evidence under Rule 404(b). Remember, with respect to evidence that is admissible under Rule 404(b) to prove motive, intent, and the other matters allowed under the rule, the risk of unfair prejudice is the risk that the jury will use the evidence for propensity purposes. The risk of unfair prejudice in those cases is the risk the jury will conclude that the defendant is the sort of person who commits a given type of crime by his very nature. That is not something that would qualify as unfair prejudice under Rule 413, because the intent of the rule is to permit evidence of other sexual assaults to be introduced to establish the defendant's propensity to commit such acts.

To argue that evidence of other sexual assaults creates an unacceptable risk of unfair prejudice under Rule 403, a defendant must argue that there is something other than the propensity inference that is prejudicial. There might be something, for example, about the circumstances of the crime or the victim that would cause such a strong emotional response by jurors that they would be unable to fairly and objectively assess the evidence of the defendant's guilt.

QUESTION 25. The defendant is charged with the rape of an adult woman. He denies any contact with the woman and argues that it is a case of mistaken identification. Which of the following items of evidence may the prosecutor introduce at trial?

A. Testimony by a close friend of the defendant that in his opinion that defendant is a sexual predator.

B. Testimony by someone from the defendant's neighborhood that he is familiar with the defendant's reputation in the neighborhood, and he has a reputation for groping women at parties.

C. Testimony by a woman who worked for the defendant that he refused to promote her because she would not have intercourse with him.

D. Testimony by a woman who says that the defendant took her out on a date and forced her to have sexual relations with him against her will.

E. All of the above.

F. None of the above.

ANALYSIS.   Choices **A** and **B** constitute opinion and reputation evidence, respectively, which is generally admissible to prove character under the Federal Rules, but not under Rules 413–415. Thus **A** and **B** are incorrect. **C** is evidence of sexual harassment and discrimination for which the defendant might be liable civilly, but the conduct described does not constitute a criminal sexual assault under Rule 413. Thus **C** is incorrect. Choice **D** is precisely the sort of evidence contemplated by Rule 413, evidence of another criminal sexual assault, and it would be admissible. Choice **D** is the correct answer.

QUESTION 26. The Closer.   The defendant is charged with lewd and lascivious behavior. The prosecution claims that he exhibited his private parts to a young girl as she walked along a path through a park in the afternoon. The girl has testified that the defendant came out from behind a tree carrying what appeared to be a pornographic magazine, that he dropped his pants and undershorts, and said to her, "Have you ever seen anything like this before?" She screamed and ran away. She has identified the defendant as the perpetrator in the courtroom. The prosecution has disclosed to the defendant that three other girls of approximately the same age were accosted on three different days on the same path, at about the same time of day, by an individual carrying what appeared to be a pornographic magazine who dropped his pants and undershorts and asked them, "Have you ever seen anything like this before?" Those three girls were shown a photo spread that contained the defendant's picture, but they did not identify him as the perpetrator. The defendant proposes to call the three girls as witnesses to testify that he is not the man who accosted them. How should the court rule on the prosecution's objection?

A. Sustained, the evidence is not relevant.

B. Sustained, the evidence is not permitted under the character rules.

C. Overruled.

ANALYSIS. If the three other girls had identified the defendant in this case as the perpetrator who accosted them, could the prosecution have called them as witnesses against the defendant? Yes, the evidence would have been relevant and admissible under Rule 404(b). Under that rule it would not have been admissible to prove that the defendant had a propensity to expose himself, but it would have been admissible on the issue of identity, assuming the court found that the risk of unfair prejudice did not substantially outweigh the probative value of the evidence. There was a series of crimes committed by a person with an idiosyncratic modus operandi, suggesting that the same person committed all of them. Had the other girls identified the defendant, this case would have been similar to the Obama bank robber case in Question 19.

Here, however, the other girls would testify that the defendant was not the man who accosted them, and the defendant wishes to call them as witnesses. Is the evidence relevant? Yes, evidence that the defendant is not the person who has committed a series of crimes with an idiosyncratic modus operandi is just as relevant as evidence that he is that person. Thus **A** is incorrect. Rules 404 and 405 do not bar the evidence because the defendant is not offering it for propensity purposes. He is offering it on the issue of identity, and it would be permissible under Rule 404(b) to do so. Thus **B** is incorrect. The correct answer is **C**—the prosecution's objection should be overruled. Notice that there is very little risk, if any, of unfair prejudice here because there is no particular person for the propensity inference to run against. On the other hand, the evidence is highly probative to establish that the perpetrator of these crimes was not the defendant.

✦ Avery's Picks

1.	Question 1	D
2.	Question 2	A
3.	Question 3	B
4.	Question 4	C
5.	Question 5	D
6.	Question 6	A
7.	Question 7	B
8.	Question 8	A
9.	Question 9	C
10.	Question 10	C
11.	Question 11	D
12.	Question 12	D
13.	Question 13	A
14.	Question 14	B
15.	Question 15	D
16.	Question 16	C
17.	Question 17	D

18. Question 18   **C**
19. Question 19   **C**
20. Question 20   **B**
21. Question 21   **D**
22. Question 22   **A**
23. Question 23   **D**
24. Question 24   **A**
25. Question 25   **D**
26. Question 26   **C**

5

Privileges

When Congress first adopted the Federal Rules of Evidence it had before it a detailed set of privileges. Many of them proved to be so controversial, however, that debate over them posed a risk to the adoption of the entire evidence code. Congress then abandoned specific privilege rules and passed only Rule 501, which leaves the law of privilege to the common law.

> **Rule 501. Privilege in General**
> The common law—as interpreted by United States courts in the light of reason and experience—governs a claim of privilege unless any of the following provides otherwise:
>
> • the United States Constitution;
> • a federal statute; or
> • rules prescribed by the Supreme Court.
>
> But in a civil case, state law governs privilege regarding a claim or defense for which state law supplies the rule of decision.

State law governs privilege claims in civil cases where state law provides the rule of decision. Federal common law controls privilege claims in other federal cases, unless there is a specific rule prescribed by constitutional law, a statute, or a rule of the Supreme Court. In 2008 Congress added Rule 502, discussed below, which addresses questions of waiver. In all other respects federal common law continues to control questions of privilege.

In this chapter we will discuss the most common privileges under federal common law: attorney-client and work product, spousal, psychotherapist-patient, and spiritual advisor. We will also review basic issues concerning the constitutional privilege against self-incrimination.

Privileges run against the basic demands the law places on every person in our society. Ordinarily a person has no right to refuse to be a witness, to refuse to disclose information sought during court proceedings, or to refuse to produce documents or things subpoenaed by a court. Privileges, however, protect certain relationships that society deems it important to foster. The protection of confidential communications is considered essential to promote these relationships.

Whenever a witness makes any assertion of privilege we must address certain basic questions. These include whether the witness is being asked about *confidential communications*; who is the *holder* of the privilege; whether the privilege has been *waived*; and whether the inquiry falls within any *exceptions* to the privilege. The witness who asserts a privilege has the burden of establishing her entitlement to the privilege. Whether a particular matter is privileged is for the court to decide under Rule 104(a). We will take these issues up as we discuss specific privileges below.

It is important to distinguish between privileges and the confidentiality rules that govern several professions. Physicians, psychotherapists, and attorneys, for example, are governed by ethical rules that require them to keep communications between them and their clients or patients and information regarding the clients and patients confidential. Professional associations, licensing boards, and in some instances state laws enforce these rules and professionals may be punished and/or sued for breaking them. These rules, however, do not themselves protect information from being subpoenaed and disclosed in court. The rules of privilege govern whether information is insulated from disclosure in court. If something is not privileged, a court may compel its production even if it is confidential.

A.   Attorney-Client Privilege and Work Product Protection

Naturally the privilege that you will invoke most often after you begin practicing law is the attorney-client privilege. The privilege protects confidential communications between a client and lawyer, and applies when the client has consulted the lawyer for the purpose of obtaining legal advice or discussing the possibility of representation. A "client" is a person, public officer, corporation, association, or other organization or entity, public or private, who consults an attorney. An "attorney" is anyone licensed to practice law, or anyone the client reasonably believes is licensed to practice law. It is not necessary that the client pay a fee to the lawyer, or for the lawyer to undertake the representation of the client, for the privilege to attach. It is enough that the client has consulted the lawyer with the purpose of discussing the possibility of representation or for the purpose of obtaining legal advice. Where a conversation with a lawyer is not for those purposes, however, it is not privileged merely because one of the participants happens to be a lawyer. Social conversation between a lawyer and client are not privileged. Where the lawyer is giving another type of advice, for example, investment advice or business advice, the communications are not privileged.

The client is the holder of the privilege. The attorney is ethically bound to assert the privilege on behalf of the client, but may not waive the privilege without the client's permission. The privilege survives the death of the client.

1. *Corporate Employees*

When the attorney-client privilege is asserted to protect the confidentiality of communications between corporate employees and the corporation's lawyer, it may be difficult to determine whether the corporate employees in question should be treated as "clients" for determining whether the communications were privileged. The leading Supreme Court case is *Upjohn v. United States*, 449 U.S. 383 (1981). The Court determined that communications between managers of Upjohn's foreign offices and the company lawyer were privileged. The Court took into account that the managers supplied information to the company's counsel to help the company secure legal advice, that they did so at the direction of their corporate superiors, that the communications concerned matters within the scope of the managers' corporate duties, and that the managers were responding to questions from the lawyer and were aware that they were being questioned so that the company could obtain legal advice. The Court did not establish any bright line test for determining when communications between corporate employees and the company counsel would be considered privileged. It did, however, reject the "control group" test employed in some states, under which the privilege attaches only to communications between the lawyer and senior management.

2. *Confidential Communications*

The privilege protects only *communications* between the lawyer and client that are *confidential*. In other words, the lawyer's observations of the client are not protected by the privilege. If a client consulted a lawyer for legal advice after committing a robbery, the client's statement to the lawyer that he had just committed a robbery would be privileged. If the lawyer observed that the client was wearing a disguise at the time, the lawyer could be compelled to testify about the client's disguised appearance. The attorney and client must take care to preserve the confidentiality of their communications for the privilege to be recognized. If they have a discussion about the client's legal matters in a public place and are overheard by others they know are present, the communications are not privileged. If the lawyer and client reasonably believe their conversation is private, but a third person eavesdrops on the conversation without their knowledge, the communication will be privileged.

The privilege will attach to consultations held in the presence of a third person if the presence of that person is essential to the relationship. For example, an interpreter may be necessary if the client does not speak English as her native language, or an accountant may be a necessary party to a consultation about tax matters. The privilege also attaches to communications between the client and necessary agents of the lawyer; for example, assistants, paralegals, investigators, or jury consultants.

The privilege does not extend to pre-existing documents, or to documents created independently of the attorney-client relationship, even though the lawyer and client may discuss such documents. For example, if a client brings documents from her business to the lawyer's office to obtain legal advice about them, the discussion between the lawyer and client about the documents is privileged, but the documents themselves are not. The privilege does not extend to facts, but does protect discussions between the client and the lawyer about facts. The client may be required to disclose facts within her knowledge, but not what she said to her attorney about them.

3. Work Product Protection

Federal common law also protects as privileged attorney work product. This includes material prepared by the lawyer in anticipation of litigation; for example, notes, memoranda, and analytical materials. The privilege for work product may be overcome if the opponent shows a "substantial need of the materials in the preparation of his case and that he is unable without undue hardship to obtain the substantial equivalent of the materials by other means."[1] Courts will generally order the disclosure only of materials that consist of facts about the dispute, and will protect the mental impressions, conclusions, opinions, or legal theories of counsel.

4. Exceptions

There are several exceptions to the attorney-client privilege. Perhaps the most common is the crime-fraud exception. Statements by the client to the lawyer

---

1. Fed. R. Civ. P. 26(b)(3).

about crimes the client has committed in the past are privileged, but if the client tells the lawyer about criminal or fraudulent activity he intends to commit in the future, those statements are not privileged. Also, if the client and the lawyer discuss fraudulent or criminal activities that they engage in jointly, their conversations are not privileged. Another exception is litigation between the lawyer and the client. For example, if the client does not pay the bill, or the client sues the lawyer for malpractice, then communications that are pertinent to those issues will not be privileged. In addition, the identity of the client is generally not privileged and the lawyer may be forced to disclose it, unless disclosure of the client's identity will disclose other privileged matters. Fee arrangements between the lawyer and the client are not privileged.

The joint client exception applies when two or more clients have conversations together with their attorney, and then later have a falling out and are in litigation against each other. A court will not consider their earlier communications with the lawyer to be privileged. Joint clients may protect against this, however, by agreeing in advance that joint communications will retain their privileged character even in the event of later litigation between them.

5. *Waiver*

Failure to assert a privilege in a timely fashion usually constitutes a waiver of the privilege. A client does not waive the attorney-client privilege merely by testifying about events that have been the topic of privileged communications with the lawyer. If the client testifies about the contents of the communications with the lawyer, however, that will constitute a waiver of the privilege.

The disclosure of attorney-client communications may constitute a waiver. Rule 502 controls the extent of a waiver that results from disclosures under various circumstances. The full text of Rule 502 is set out below. Generally, the rule provides that a waiver as the result of the disclosure of privileged material in federal proceedings or to federal officers or agencies will extend to undisclosed communications only if the waiver was intentional, the disclosed and undisclosed information concern the same subject matter, and they ought in fairness to be considered together. If disclosure in such proceedings or to such parties was inadvertent it will not operate as a waiver if the holder of the privilege took reasonable steps to prevent disclosure and promptly took reasonable steps to rectify the error. If the disclosure was in a state proceeding and is not the subject of a state court order concerning waiver, it will not operate as a waiver in a federal proceeding if it would not be a waiver under the rule if made in a federal proceeding or is not a waiver under the law of the state where disclosure occurred.

> **Rule 502. Attorney-Client Privilege and Work Product; Limitations on Waiver**
>
> The following provisions apply, in the circumstances set out, to disclosure of a communication or information covered by the attorney-client privilege or work-product protection.

(a) **Disclosure Made in a Federal Proceeding or to a Federal Office or Agency; Scope of a Waiver.** When the disclosure is made in a federal proceeding or to a federal office or agency and waives the attorney-client privilege or work-product protection, the waiver extends to an undisclosed communication or information in a federal or state proceeding only if:

(1) the waiver is intentional;

(2) the disclosed and undisclosed communications or information concern the same subject matter; and

(3) they ought in fairness to be considered together.

(b) **Inadvertent Disclosure.** When made in a federal proceeding or to a federal office or agency, the disclosure does not operate as a waiver in a federal or state proceeding if:

(1) the disclosure is inadvertent;

(2) the holder of the privilege or protection took reasonable steps to prevent disclosure; and

(3) the holder promptly took reasonable steps to rectify the error, including (if applicable) following Federal Rule of Civil Procedure 26 (b)(5)(B).

(c) **Disclosure Made in a State Proceeding.** When the disclosure is made in a state proceeding and is not the subject of a state-court order concerning waiver, the disclosure does not operate as a waiver in a federal proceeding if the disclosure:

(1) would not be a waiver under this rule if it had been made in a federal proceeding; or

(2) is not a waiver under the law of the state where the disclosure occurred.

(d) **Controlling Effect of a Court Order.** A federal court may order that the privilege or protection is not waived by disclosure connected with the litigation pending before the court—in which event the disclosure is also not a waiver in any other federal or state proceeding.

(e) **Controlling Effect of a Party Agreement.** An agreement on the effect of disclosure in a federal proceeding is binding only on the parties to the agreement, unless it is incorporated into a court order.

(f) **Controlling Effect of this Rule.** Notwithstanding Rules 101 and 1101, this rule applies to state proceedings and to federal court-annexed and federal court-mandated arbitration proceedings, in the circumstances set out in the rule. And notwithstanding Rule 501, this rule applies even if state law provides the rule of decision.

(g) **Definitions.** In this rule:

(1) "attorney-client privilege" means the protection that applicable law provides for confidential attorney-client communications; and

(2) "work-product protection" means the protection that applicable law provides for tangible material (or its intangible equivalent) prepared in anticipation of litigation or for trial.

QUESTION 1. The prosecutor has subpoenaed a witness to testify in a murder trial. The subpoena directed the witness to bring with him any correspondence he had with anyone concerning the death of the victim. Which of the following statements is true?

A. If the witness claims that any correspondence is protected by the attorney-client privilege, the judge will read the correspondence in question to determine whether the privilege applies.

B. The witness will not have to produce correspondence that the witness had with the defendant and which the witness discussed with his own lawyer, whom he consulted to determine if there was any risk that he could be arrested in connection with the victim's death.

C. The witness will not have to produce correspondence that he had with his own lawyer, whom he consulted to determine if there was any risk that he could be arrested in connection with the victim's death.

D. The witness will not have the attorney-client privilege for conversations he had with his own lawyer if the conversations were overheard on an electronic surveillance device the police had secretly installed in the lawyer's office.

ANALYSIS. Let's begin with **A**. The judge is the one who decides whether communications are protected by the attorney-client privilege, under Rule 104(a). Although the judge is not bound by any other rules of evidence when deciding questions under Rule 104(a), the rules with respect to privilege do apply. The judge will decide whether correspondence is protected by the attorney-client privilege by determining whether the communications were between a client and a lawyer, whether they were confidential, and whether the client had consulted the lawyer for the purpose of obtaining legal advice or discussing the possibility of representation. The judge will not, however, read the correspondence in question in order to determine whether it is privileged. If the communications were privileged, it would violate the privilege for the judge to read them. Thus **A** is incorrect.

Correspondence that the witness had with the defendant does not become privileged merely because the witness discussed the correspondence with his attorney. The discussions between the client and the lawyer would be privileged, but the pre-existing correspondence with the defendant is not. Thus **B** is incorrect.

Communications must be confidential in order to be privileged. Where the attorney and the client have taken reasonable steps to maintain confidentiality, such as having a conversation in the lawyer's office, secret eavesdropping will not destroy the privilege. Thus **D** is incorrect.

The correct answer is **C**. Correspondence between the client and the lawyer, given that the lawyer was consulted for legal advice, is protected by the attorney-client privilege.

B.   Spousal Privileges

There are two separate privileges that protect the marital relationship. One is testimonial and the other protects confidential communications between spouses. The United States Supreme Court has so far had no occasion to rule on the question of whether the spousal privileges apply to same sex marriages. Given recent changes in the case law it would be prudent for counsel to assert the privilege where it would protect a client's interests and litigate the issue.

1. *Testimonial Privilege*

A spouse has a privilege not to testify before the grand jury or at trial in a criminal case against the other spouse. The witness spouse is the holder of the privilege. In other words, a spouse called as a witness against his or her spouse may refuse to testify, but the defendant spouse has no right to keep the witness spouse from testifying if the witness chooses to do so. The privilege from testifying applies to communications between the spouses and observations made by the witness spouse, whether or not the communications or events witnessed were confidential. In short, the privilege allows the witness spouse to avoid giving any testimony against the other spouse. In order for the privilege to apply, the witness and the defendant must be married *at the time of the trial.* If they are, this privilege applies to any testimony that the witness might give, whether or not the witness and defendant were married at the time of the events or communications in question. The purpose of the privilege is to protect the marital relationship that exists at the time of the trial.

There are exceptions to the testimonial privilege. It does not apply if the defendant spouse is accused of committing a crime against the other spouse or a child in their custody. The privilege also does not apply where the spouses are accused of jointly committing a crime.

2. *Confidential Communications Between Spouses*

The second type of spousal privilege protects confidential communications between spouses during the marriage, and applies in both civil and criminal cases. Both spouses are holders of the privilege and may object to the introduction of evidence that would violate it. If either spouse objects the evidence may not be admitted. The privilege protects only *confidential communications*, not observations or other knowledge the witness spouse might have.

In order for communications to be privileged, the spouses must have taken reasonable care to protect their privacy and confidentiality. If spouses knowingly have conversations in the presence of other people, including children old enough to understand and repeat their words, the conversations are not privileged. If a third person eavesdrops on a private conversation between spouses without their knowledge, the conversation will be privileged.

The purpose of this privilege is to protect and further the marital relationship that exists at the time of the communications. The spouses must have been married at the time of the communications in question. If the spouses have divorced before the proceeding in question, confidential communications that occurred during their marriage will still be privileged, although any communications between them subsequent to the divorce will not. Communications that predated the marriage are not privileged.

The marital communications privilege does not apply when one spouse is charged with committing a crime against the other spouse (including crimes against property) or against a child in their custody; when the communications are in connection with the joint commission of a crime by the spouses; or in suits brought by one spouse against the other.

QUESTION 2. The defendant is on trial on a charge of importing cocaine. The prosecution has subpoenaed the defendant's former wife as a witness. They divorced two months before trial. While they were married, the wife overheard her husband talking on the telephone with his source in Colombia, placing an order for a delivery of cocaine. Alone in the room with her husband, she asked him whether he was dealing in drugs. He admitted that he was. On another occasion she saw him hand a small valise containing bundles of hundred dollar bills to a man who came to their home late at night. Which of the following statements is not true?

A. The husband may object to his wife testifying about his admission that he was dealing drugs because it was a privileged conversation.
B. The husband may successfully object to his wife testifying about his conversation with the source in Colombia, because it was a privileged conversation that took place in the marital home.
C. The judge should overrule the husband's objection on privilege grounds to the wife's observation of the cash payment.
D. If the case had come to trial three months previously the wife could have refused to be a witness against her husband.

ANALYSIS. The testimonial privilege permits a spouse to refuse to testify against her spouse in a criminal case. So if the trial had taken place before the divorce the wife could have refused to testify against her husband. Thus **D** is true. Note, however, that if the trial had taken place while they were married and she was willing to testify against her husband, he could not have objected to her taking the stand. The testimonial privilege belongs to the witness spouse, not the defendant spouse.

The marital communications privilege protects confidential communications between spouses that occur during the marriage. The husband's objection on privilege grounds to testimony from the wife about his admission that he was dealing drugs would be sustained. Thus **A** is true. The wife's observation of the husband's cash payment to the late-night visitor was not a confidential communication between the spouses, but merely an observation she made. Observations are not protected by the privilege for confidential communications, and thus the husband's privilege objection to her testimony about that event should be overruled. Choice **C** is a true statement.

The husband's conversation with his source in Colombia was not a confidential communication between the spouses. The fact that it occurred in the marital home is irrelevant. This also was merely an observation on the part of the wife. His objection on privilege grounds to her testimony about this should be overruled. Thus **B** is the incorrect statement.

C.   Psychotherapist-Patient Privilege

Federal common law does not recognize a general physician-patient privilege. Most states do have such a privilege. In civil actions tried in federal court in which state law applies the rule of decision, the court will honor the physician-patient privilege if it exists in the controlling state law.

Federal common law does recognize a psychotherapist-patient privilege.[2] The privilege protects confidential communications from patients to psychiatrists, psychologists, licensed social workers, mental health specialists, and marriage counselors for the purpose of seeking diagnosis or treatment for a mental or emotional condition. The privilege does not apply to communications with educational and vocational counselors. The privilege may not protect against disclosure of the therapist's diagnosis.

There are exceptions to this privilege for statements made during commitment proceedings and statements made during court-ordered examinations. In addition, if the patient has placed his mental condition at issue in a case, pertinent communications with therapists will not be protected by the privilege. If a plaintiff in a personal injury case claims to be suffering from clinically significant medical conditions, for example, post-traumatic stress disorder (PTSD), as a result of his injuries, relevant communications with therapists must be disclosed. On the other hand, if a plaintiff complains only of "garden variety emotional distress," courts will usually not order disclosure of communications with psychotherapists.

Under some circumstances courts will hold that the psychotherapist-patient privilege of a witness must give way to protect the constitutional rights of a criminal defendant. A defendant may have a constitutional right, for example, to obtain pertinent information from the treatment records of a complaining witness where such information is essential to the defense.

---

2.   The Supreme Court held that this privilege exists in *Jaffee v. Redmond*, 518 U.S. 1 (1996).

If a patient tells his psychotherapist about crimes or frauds he has committed in the past, the communications are privileged. If a patient tells the therapist about crimes or frauds he intends to commit in the future, the therapist has a duty to disclose the information in order to protect the potential victim. The lower federal courts are split on the question of whether the duty to warn potential victims destroys the psychotherapist-privilege for such communications in proceedings against the patient.[3] The Supreme Court has not yet ruled on this issue.

D.   Spiritual Advisor Privilege

This privilege protects confidential communications to a member of the clergy in order to seek spiritual or religious counseling. The privilege applies to the clergy of any religion. The holder of the privilege is the person who sought counseling, but the spiritual advisor may assert the privilege on her behalf. There are no exceptions to this privilege.

E.   Fifth Amendment Privilege

The Federal Rules of Evidence do not regulate the right to avoid self-incrimination. The Fifth Amendment privilege is a constitutional right. The Fifth Amendment to the United States Constitution provides that no person "shall be compelled in any criminal case to be a witness against himself." Similar provisions exist in state constitutions. The federal constitutional right applies to federal and state proceedings.

The full range of the protections provided by the Fifth Amendment privilege is beyond the scope of this volume. The law is complex with respect to the effect of the Fifth Amendment on police interrogations. The case law has made multiple permutations on the original decision in *Miranda* regarding the need for and effect of warnings to the defendant concerning his Fifth Amendment rights. You should consult constitutional law and criminal procedure texts to review these issues. Here we deal primarily with the Fifth Amendment privilege during criminal proceedings.

---

3. Compare, for example, *United States v. Auster*, 517 F.3d 312 (5th Cir. 2008) (where patient knew that threats of violence would be communicated to potential victims, he lacked a reasonable expectation of confidentiality in his communications and thus they were not privileged), with *United States v. Hayes*, 227 F.3d 578 (6th Cir. 2000) (the issues of the therapist's duty to warn potential victims of threats and the privileged nature of patient-psychotherapist communications are separate issues, thus the privilege was not destroyed by the fact that the potential victim was warned).

The Fifth Amendment privilege applies only to testimonial evidence. Testimonial evidence consists of oral or written statements that reflect a person's ideas or thought processes. The Fifth Amendment does not protect a person's external manifestations. Thus, for example, a witness may be required to stand in a line-up, show scars and tattoos, speak a given set of words, give blood and saliva samples, and provide handwriting exemplars.

A defendant has an absolute right not to take the stand in a criminal case. The prosecutor may not comment on the defendant's election not to testify. Witnesses other than a criminal defendant must take the stand and exercise their Fifth Amendment rights in response to questions. In civil cases the fact that a witness or a party has taken the Fifth Amendment with respect to an issue in the case is admissible in evidence, and the opposing party may comment on the exercise of the privilege.

The accused in a criminal case may testify at a preliminary hearing to suppress evidence on constitutional grounds without waiving his right not to take the stand at the trial. For example, a defendant may testify on a motion to suppress evidence seized during a search, in order to establish standing to challenge the search. The defendant may testify that he was the owner or occupant of the premises searched, in order to show that he had a reasonable expectation of privacy in those premises. The defendant's testimony from the motion to suppress hearing is inadmissible at trial and the prosecutor may not comment on it at trial. His appearance on the stand at the motion to suppress does not constitute a waiver of his right not to testify at trial.

A person waives his Fifth Amendment privilege not to incriminate himself by testifying. The waiver, however, is limited to the subject matter of the testimony and does not constitute a waiver with respect to other matters.

If the court has given a witness immunity from prosecution the witness cannot claim the Fifth Amendment privilege with regard to the matters for which he has immunity. If a witness refuses to testify after having been given immunity the court may hold him in civil contempt. The court may order the witness incarcerated until he is willing to testify or the termination of the proceeding to which he has been subpoenaed. There are two types of immunity. Transactional immunity means that the witness cannot be prosecuted at all with respect to the events that are the subject of the grant of immunity. It is rare for the prosecution to request transactional immunity for a witness. More common is use immunity. The government may still prosecute a witness who has received use immunity. But in such a prosecution the government cannot use the testimony the witness has given or any evidence derived from that testimony. Sometimes this is referred to as "use plus fruits" immunity, because it protects a witness from the use of his testimony or any fruits of his testimony.

QUESTION 3. The Defendant is charged with extortion. Part of the evidence against him is a handwritten note that the Victim received. The prosecution wants to prove it was written by the Defendant and obtains an order from the judge requiring the Defendant to produce handwriting exemplars at the police station. The officer conducting the procedure wants the Defendant to copy out the alphabet and a series of words typed on a form. He also wants to dictate the contents of the extortion note and have the Defendant write it out. Which of the following statements is true?

A. The Defendant may refuse to write out the dictated note because it would violate his Fifth Amendment rights.

B. The Defendant may refuse to provide any handwriting exemplars because it would violate his Fifth Amendment rights.

C. The Defendant must produce all the exemplars the officer requested.

ANALYSIS. The key to this problem is that the Fifth Amendment privilege against self-incrimination protects only testimonial statements, those that reflect a person's ideas or thought processes. Handwriting does not do that by itself, it's only the content that could be considered testimonial. Where one is simply copying letters or words on a form, the content is provided by the officer and therefore there is no Fifth Amendment privilege. Hence, **B** is incorrect. When one is taking dictation, however, choices the person makes about spelling do reflect his ideas and thus are testimonial. **A** is the correct answer.

QUESTION 4. The Closer. A wife has sued her husband for divorce, alleging intolerable cruelty resulting from the husband's extra-marital affairs. Adultery is a criminal defense in the jurisdiction in which they reside. Which of the following statements is inadmissible in the divorce trial?

A. The husband bragged to his good friend, a Lutheran minister, that he had made love with an attractive waitress at their golf club.

B. The husband admitted to his wife a year before she filed for divorce that he had an affair with the waitress from the golf club.

C. During one of their sessions, the husband told a psychiatrist he was consulting for depression that he no longer got any pleasure out of his marriage, but he was excited about an affair he was having with someone at his golf club.

D. At the husband's deposition in the divorce case, the wife's lawyer asked him whether he had ever had sexual relations with anyone other than his wife while married and the husband refused to answer, asserting his Fifth Amendment privilege against self-incrimination.

ANALYSIS. If the husband objects to testimony from the minister on the ground of the spiritual advisor privilege, his objection will be overruled. The husband did not make the statement to the minister for the purpose of receiving spiritual or religious advice. He was simply bragging about his sex life. The statement in **A** is admissible. The husband may not object to the statement to his wife on the ground of the marital communications privilege, because this is an action for divorce between the marital partners. The privilege does not apply in the divorce case. Thus the statement in **B** is admissible. The husband was entitled to claim the Fifth Amendment privilege and to decline to admit to adultery in his deposition. In this civil case, however, the fact that the husband took the Fifth Amendment in his deposition is admissible. The wife's lawyer may argue that the finder of fact can infer from the fact that he took the Fifth that his answer would not have been helpful to his case. Thus the exercise of the Fifth Amendment in **D** is admissible. The statement by the husband to his psychiatrist is privileged. It was a confidential communication made for the purpose of receiving counseling for a mental or emotional condition. The statement in **C** is inadmissible.

 # Avery's Picks

1. Question 1   **C**
2. Question 2   **B**
3. Question 3   **A**
4. Question 4   **C**

6

Witnesses and Impeachment

The most common way of introducing evidence at trial is through the testimony of witnesses. The rules (and to a limited extent the common law) provide the requirements a person must meet to be a witness, the methods with which the parties may examine and cross-examine witnesses, and the means that parties may use to test the credibility of witnesses. Handling witnesses effectively at trial is a matter of art, but the place to start is with a thorough mastery of the rules.

A.   Witness Competency and Requirements

Under Rule 601, every person is competent to be a witness, except as otherwise provided in the Rules. Rules 605 and 606 specify that the trial judge is not permitted to testify in the case pending before her, and that a member of the jury is not permitted to testify before the jury in the trial in which the juror is sitting. Other than that, there are no limitations on who is competent to be a witness.

Rule 603 provides that every witness must take an oath or affirm that she will testify truthfully. There are no technical requirements with respect to the wording of the oath or affirmation. The rule simply provides that it must be "in a form designed to impress that duty on the witness's conscience." If a witness is unwilling to promise to tell the truth, the witness may not testify. Unlike at common law, a young child is deemed competent to be a witness. The child must, however, be able to satisfy the requirement of Rule 603. A judge may refuse to allow a child to testify if the child is unable to appreciate the difference between truth and falsity, or the necessity of testifying truthfully.

Rule 602 requires that witnesses, other than experts, "may testify to a matter only if evidence is introduced sufficient to support a finding that the witness has personal knowledge of the matter." Experts are allowed to testify based on vicarious knowledge, as we discuss in Chapter 7. All other witnesses must satisfy the personal knowledge requirement. That means that a witness may testify only about something observed with one of the five senses: the witness has seen it, heard it, smelled it, tasted it, or physically felt it. Foundation evidence that a witness has personal knowledge may be provided by the witness's own testimony.

QUESTION 1. Defendant is on trial for the rape of a child under the age of fourteen. The prosecutor called an eight-year-old girl who testified that she, the defendant, the alleged victim, and several other people had spent the night at a vacation house on the evening of the alleged offense. The prosecutor then asked what the witness observed when the victim came to their bedroom late at night. The witness would say that she "had an instinct that something had happened" to the victim, and that the defendant "had done something sexual with the victim." The defendant's objection to this testimony should be:

A. Sustained, the witness has no personal knowledge.
B. Sustained, the witness cannot testify about something that happened to someone else.
C. Sustained, the eight-year-old girl is not competent to testify.
D. Overruled.

ANALYSIS. At common law, young children were often held incompetent to testify. But under the Federal Rules, every witness is deemed competent. To the extent that a young witness may lack some understanding of matters requiring greater life experience, the opponent may explore that on cross-examination, but it does not render the witness incompetent. Thus **C** is incorrect. **B** is incorrect because the objection is phrased too broadly. A witness may testify about things that happened to other people, but only if the witness observed what happened. This witness, however, did not observe what happened to the alleged victim, and did not observe any contact between the defendant and the victim. The witness lacked personal knowledge regarding those matters. The witness was merely speculating about what might have happened. Thus **A** is the correct answer and **D** is incorrect.

QUESTION 2. The defendant is on trial for assault and battery against his wife. Testimony established that the wife left their home after the alleged assault and went to her daughter's house, but then returned home after only three days. The defendant would argue that returning home was inconsistent with her claim that her husband had assaulted her. The prosecutor called the daughter as a witness and asked her why her mother returned home so quickly. The daughter would testify that her mother was concerned that her husband and son were abusing drugs and alcohol and that there were firearms in the house. The defendant's objection to this testimony should be:

A. Sustained, the evidence is not relevant.
B. Sustained, marital privilege.
C. Sustained, the witness lacks personal knowledge.
D. Overruled, the witness probably has observed and knows what is going on in her parents' home.

ANALYSIS. Evidence that the alleged victim returned home because she was concerned about drugs, alcohol, and firearms is relevant to rebut the argument that her early return home suggested she had never been assaulted. Thus **A** is incorrect. As an aside, a better argument with respect to the substance of the evidence would have been that the testimony constituted evidence of other acts that could be used as improper character evidence, and that the risk of unfair prejudice substantially outweighed probative value. That would have presented the court with a more difficult decision. How the judge would rule on that issue could depend on what other evidence there was about what was going on in the home, and we needn't try to resolve that here.

Let's move on to the remaining answer choices provided for this question. There is a common law privilege that protects confidential communications between spouses, but the daughter was not testifying about any communications between her parents. Thus **B** is incorrect.

What about **D**? Can the judge assume that the daughter has been in her parents' home and has personal knowledge of the alcohol, drugs, and weapons? It is important to remember that the proponent of evidence has the burden of establishing facts that provide the necessary foundation for admissibility, including on the issue of personal knowledge. Here there is nothing in the question demonstrating that the prosecutor met that burden with respect to the daughter's personal knowledge and the court could not just assume that such knowledge existed. There are two problems here. The prosecutor did not show that the daughter had personal knowledge that the father and son were abusing drugs and alcohol and that there were firearms in the home; nor did the prosecutor show that the daughter had personal knowledge that this was the reason her mother returned home. She did not testify, for example, that her mother told her that was why she was going home. In the ordinary course, one person cannot testify about what is in another person's mind. Thus **D** is incorrect and **C** is the correct answer.

The requirement of personal knowledge is important, but students often overlook it. Not only students—the last question is based on a Massachusetts case where the trial judge improperly admitted the daughter's testimony and as a result the defendant's conviction was reversed on appeal when the court held the witness lacked personal knowledge.

B. Mode and Order of the Examination of Witnesses

Rule 611 governs the examination of witnesses. It gives the trial judge discretion to control the mode and order of examining witnesses in order to get at the truth, avoid wasting time, and to protect witnesses from harassment or undue embarrassment. In the ordinary course the prosecution in criminal cases and the plaintiff in civil cases present all their witnesses first and the defense calls witnesses only after the prosecution or plaintiff has rested. The court may allow witnesses to testify out of order, however, for the above mentioned purposes.

The party who calls a witness begins with direct examination and then the opposing party may cross-examine the witness. The scope of cross-examination should be limited to the matters testified to on direct examination. After the opponent does a cross-examination, the proponent of the witness may conduct a re-direct examination limited to matters raised on cross-examination. Re-cross-examination is rare and is usually allowed only with respect to any new matters raised on re-direct examination.

On direct examination counsel may not use leading questions, with some exceptions as discussed below. Leading questions are questions that suggest to the witness the answer counsel desires the witness to give. Leading questions are permitted on cross-examination.

As noted above, ordinarily the scope of cross-examination is limited to matters discussed on direct examination. In other words, if the direct examination did not touch on a given topic, it is improper for the cross-examiner to ask about it. The cross-examiner has the option to recall the witness when presenting her case, and then conduct a direct examination of the witness on the topic in question. That may prove impractical or inefficient, however, and in such cases the court may permit the cross-examiner to ask about matters outside the scope of direct examination. When the court allows cross-examination to go beyond the scope of direct, counsel is limited to non-leading questions as to those matters, as though she were conducting a direct examination.

C.   Direct Examination

1. Form of the Question

As just mentioned, on direct examination counsel should not ask the witness leading questions, that is, questions that suggest the desired answer. "You first met the plaintiff on December 1, isn't that right?" is a leading question. Any question that begins with a phrase like "isn't it true that," or ends with a phrase like, "isn't that correct?" is a leading question. The absence of such phrases, however, does not guarantee that a question is non-leading. The idea is that the witness is supposed to be providing the evidence, not the lawyer conducting the examination. The issue is whether in the context of the examination the question unnecessarily suggests the answer to the witness. For example, if an important issue at trial is the time at which the witness arrived at the scene, the question, "Did you arrive at the scene at eleven o'clock?" would be a leading question. On the other hand, "What time did you arrive at the scene?" would not be leading. A good way to avoid leading is to ask questions that begin with the following words: "who, what, where, why, when, how."

Rule 611(c) states that on direct examination leading questions may be used "as necessary to develop the witness's testimony." The rule states that ordinarily the court should allow leading questions during the direct examination of a hostile witness, an adverse party, or a witness identified with an adverse party. In addition, judges will usually allow leading questions where a witness has a limited understanding of the proceedings due to age, mental disability, or difficulty with the English language. Ordinarily leading questions are permitted to establish preliminary matters that are not really contested (e.g., age, occupation, place of residence, and the like). The court may sometimes permit leading questions if the witness's memory has failed, or the witness is confused.

2. When the Witness Cannot Remember: Refreshing Recollection and Prior Recollection Recorded

Witnesses sometimes cannot remember the facts the examiner expects them to relate. A judge may permit counsel to ask some leading questions to trigger the witness's memory, but on important matters judges usually do not allow lawyers to use leading questions to put answers in the witness's mouth.

The rules for refreshing recollection and prior recollection recorded provide the acceptable techniques that the lawyer can use when a witness has a failure of memory. Rule 612 describes refreshing recollection, a method of awakening a witness's memory so that she is able to testify to what she recalls. When a witness cannot access sufficient memories to testify accurately and completely, Rule 803(5) permits the lawyer to read from a report or memorandum the witness made previously.

> **Rule 612. Writing Used to Refresh a Witness's Memory**
>
> **(a) Scope.** This rule gives an adverse party certain options when a witness uses a writing to refresh memory:
>
>   **(1)** while testifying; or
>
>   **(2)** before testifying, if the court decides that justice requires the party to have those options.
>
> **(b) Adverse Party's Options; Deleting Unrelated Matter.** Unless 18 U.S.C. §3500 provides otherwise in a criminal case, an adverse party is entitled to have the writing produced at the hearing, to inspect it, to cross-examine the witness about it, and to introduce in evidence any portion that relates to the witness's testimony. If the producing party claims that the writing includes unrelated matter, the court must examine the writing in camera, delete any unrelated portion, and order that the rest be delivered to the adverse party. Any portion deleted over objection must be preserved for the record.
>
> **(c) Failure to Produce or Deliver the Writing.** If a writing is not produced or is not delivered as ordered, the court may issue any appropriate order. But if the prosecution does not comply in a criminal case, the court must strike the witness's testimony or—if justice so requires—declare a mistrial.

Counsel may use a writing to refresh a witness's memory either while she is on the stand or before she takes the stand. Let's first discuss refreshing recollection that occurs while the witness is on the stand. For example, suppose the witness is a police officer who has investigated an automobile accident. He testifies to what he did at the scene, including measuring the length of skid marks behind the defendant's vehicle, but in court he cannot remember how long the skid marks were. Rule 612 then permits the following:

Counsel: Officer, if I showed you your report, would that refresh your recollection?
Officer: It might.
Counsel: Officer, I want you to read this report silently and let me know when you have finished.
Officer: I'm done.
Counsel: Did reading that report refresh your recollection as to the length of the skid marks?
Officer: Yes.
Counsel: Please hand the report back to me. (Pauses.) How long were the skid marks?
Officer: Sixty feet.

The lawyer shows the officer the report in order to see if it will restore the officer's memory as to the length of the skid marks. Counsel is not asking the officer to read the skid mark measurement to the jury. If reading the report silently does not awaken the officer's memory, he should say so, for example, "Well, I see what it says in this report, but honestly, it does not bring back my memory." On the other hand, we all know that sometimes looking at a report, a letter, a memo, or the like, may trigger one's memory with respect to details that one has been unable to recall. In that case, the witness is truly testifying from memory. That is what Rule 612 is designed to facilitate.

The rule provides that if counsel uses a writing to refresh a witness's memory on the stand, the adverse party is entitled to inspect it, to cross-examine the witness about it, and to introduce in evidence any portion that relates to the witness's testimony. The rule also provides that the court may impose sanctions for the failure to disclose the writing. If the witness uses a writing to refresh her memory before taking the stand, the court has discretion with respect to whether the writing has to be disclosed to the adverse party. The reference to 18 U.S.C. §3500 relates to the Jencks Act, which provides the procedure for disclosing witness statements to the defense in criminal cases.

Sometimes a witness has a failure of memory, and it cannot be refreshed. A report that the witness has written in the past constitutes hearsay if it is introduced to prove the truth of matters in the report. We will discuss hearsay in detail in Chapter 8. For now, it is enough to say that the report would be inadmissible in evidence, except for the fact that the Rule 803 (5) provides an exception for such reports if certain conditions are met.

(5) Recorded Recollection.
A record that:

> (A) is on a matter the witness once knew about but now cannot recall well enough to testify fully and accurately;
> (B) was made or adopted by the witness when the matter was fresh in the witness's memory; and
> (C) accurately reflects the witness's knowledge.

If admitted, the record may be read into evidence but may be received as an exhibit only if offered by an adverse party.

Under this rule it is permissible to read the pertinent parts of a witness's report to the jury when the witness testifies that she made the writing when the matter was fresh in her memory, that the writing accurately reflected her knowledge at the time, and that she now has insufficient recall to testify fully and accurately about the matter. The proponent of the evidence may not introduce the report as an exhibit, but the adverse party may.

The difference between refreshing recollection and recorded recollection is that for the former the source of the evidence is the witness's present memory, after it has been refreshed, and for the latter the source of the evidence is the writing itself.

QUESTION 3. Defendant is being prosecuted on a charge of armed bank robbery. The prosecution calls the bank teller as a witness. When asked how the male bank robber was dressed, the teller says that she can't remember. The prosecutor then hands the teller a photocopy of a police report and asks the teller whether it refreshes her memory. The report summarizes the descriptions of the perpetrator that the teller and other witnesses gave to the officer.

The Defendant's objection to this procedure should be:

A. Sustained, because the report contains hearsay statements of witnesses other than the bank teller.
B. Sustained, the teller has not testified that she reviewed the report at the time it was prepared or that the report accurately summarized her statement to the police officer.
C. Overruled.

ANALYSIS. A lawyer examining a witness may show the witness anything to refresh her recollection. It does not matter whether it contains hearsay, or whether it is a statement by someone other than the witness. The issue is only whether it evokes a present recollection by the witness. If it does, she may testify to her refreshed recollection. Thus the correct answer is **C**. Opposing counsel is entitled to examine what was shown to the witness and cross-examine her about what precisely it was that she claims refreshed her recollection.

QUESTION 4. In a wrongful death case following an automobile accident, the plaintiff's lawyer called the investigating detective to testify about the accident scene. When the lawyer asked the detective whether there was any broken glass or other debris in the roadway and, if so, where any such debris was located, the detective could not recall. The prosecutor then handed the detective his report and asked, "What does your report say about glass and debris?" (The report described the location of glass and debris in considerable detail.) The defendant's objection to the last question should be:

A. Overruled. Refreshing recollection.
B. Overruled. Prior recollection recorded.
C. Sustained. Leading.
D. Sustained.

ANALYSIS. The witness has a failure of recollection. The rules provide two methods for dealing with this, but the plaintiff's lawyer has not properly used either of them. He has not asked the detective to look at his report to see if it refreshes his recollection. He has simply asked him to tell the jury what the report says. Choice **A** is incorrect because the lawyer did not attempt to refresh the recollection of the witness. Choice **B** is incorrect because the lawyer has not laid the foundation for recollection recorded. He did not establish that the report was written when the matter was fresh in the witness's memory, nor did he establish that the report was accurate when made.

The defendant's objection must be sustained. The question was not leading, however. It did not suggest the answer to the witness; the question took no position on whether there was glass or debris in the road or where any such debris was. Thus **C** is incorrect. Choice **D** is the correct answer. The proper ground for the objection would be hearsay, but we will wait under Chapter 8 to discuss that topic in detail.

D.   Cross-Examination and Impeachment

Cross-examination is the principal vehicle for testing the credibility and reliability of live testimony. Extended discussion of the art of cross-examination is beyond the scope of the present volume. We discuss here the substantive issues that the cross-examiner may raise and the other methods the rules provide for impeaching witnesses.

The cross-examiner is allowed to use leading questions and is well advised to do so. Leading questions permit counsel to control the witness. Essentially the examiner provides the substance of the testimony and permits the witness merely to agree or disagree with the assertions contained in the questions.

At the outset we must note that Rule 607 provides, "The credibility of a witness may be attacked by any party, including the party calling the witness." Thus where a party is surprised by the testimony of its own witness, the party may impeach that witness. In the ordinary case, however, it is the opposing party who has an interest in doing something to cause the jury to discount the testimony of a witness.

1. General and Specific Impeachment

A cross-examiner has several ways to impeach the direct testimony of an adverse witness. Some of them fall into the category of general impeachment—something showing that in general the jury should discount the testimony of the witness. Others constitute specific impeachment—something suggesting that a particular assertion by the witness may not be true or accurate.

The techniques that are available for general impeachment include: (1) showing that the witness is biased, prejudiced, or subject to some influence that could affect the reliability or truthfulness of his or her testimony; (2) showing that the witness suffers from a defect in sensory or memory capacity, or that something interfered with his or her ability to perceive the event in question; and (3) evidence that the witness has poor character for truthfulness. The methods of specific impeachment are: (1) evidence of a prior inconsistent statement; and (2) contradicting the witness's testimony through other witnesses or exhibits. Under Rule 610, it is not proper to impeach a witness with evidence of beliefs or opinions on matters of religion. We discuss all the permissible methods of impeachment in this chapter.

2. Cross-Examination Compared with Extrinsic Evidence

The cross-examiner can impeach a witness either by asking the witness questions, or by introducing evidence from another source. Anything other than testimony from the witness's own mouth is referred to as "extrinsic evidence." Extrinsic evidence includes testimony from another witness, physical exhibits, and writings, recordings or photographs. Impeaching a witness through extrinsic evidence takes more time than simply asking the witness a question on cross-examination, and so the rules put some limits on the use of extrinsic evidence to impeach.

The general rule is that one cannot use extrinsic evidence to impeach a witness on "collateral matters." Collateral matters are facts that are not closely related to the elements of a claim or defense. They include background facts, details that are not dispositive, and other facts that are introduced to create interest or color for a story. The cross-examiner may not employ extrinsic evidence to contradict a witness's trial testimony on such matters. Nor may the cross-examiner contradict a witness on collateral matters with her own prior inconsistent statements, although in practice judges often allow it. Courts may make an exception and allow extrinsic evidence to contradict where a fact, although collateral, is one that the witness could not possibly have been mistaken about if she actually made the observations she claims to have made.

QUESTION 5. At trial the cross-examiner asks a witness to an automobile collision at an intersection how many cars were parked on the east side of the street where the accident occurred. She answers "three." The cross-examiner has photographs taken immediately after the accident that show four parked cars. The cross-examiner may impeach the witness by:

A. Introducing the photographs into evidence.
B. Calling a different witness to testify there were four cars.
C. Introducing a police report from an officer who responded immediately to the scene that states there were four cars.
D. All of the above.
E. None of the above.

ANALYSIS.   How many cars were parked on the side of the street is not significant with respect to any of the claims or defenses in the case, and is a collateral matter. The three suggested methods of proving there were four cars are all competent ways of proving that, but the court will not take the time to permit any of them. The correct answer is **E.**

QUESTION 6. A witness testifies that he witnessed the defendant commit an assault and battery in a department store in New Orleans on August 29, 2005 (the date of Hurricane Katrina). The cross-examiner asks what the weather was like on that day, and the witness replies, "Sunny and mild all day." The cross-examiner may impeach the witness by:

A. Introducing a certified report of the National Weather Service documenting the hurricane conditions on August 29, 2005.
B. Calling a witness who was present in New Orleans on that day.
C. Introducing an authenticated videotape of the hurricane conditions in New Orleans on that day.
D. All of the above.
E. None of the above.

ANALYSIS.   The weather conditions are not significant with respect to the elements of assault and battery, nor would they have affected the ability of the witness to observe the event inside a store. No one who was actually in New

Orleans that day, however, could have been unaware of the hurricane, and the witness's incorrect answer suggests he was not present at the incident he claimed to have witnessed. Under these circumstances the court should allow contradiction although the weather would otherwise be a collateral matter. The correct answer is **D.** Each of the methods described in **A, B,** and **C** would be a permissible way to prove the conditions of the hurricane.

3. *Bias, Prejudice, Corrupting Influences*

Witnesses who are biased in favor of or against one of the parties in a case, or biased or prejudiced with respect to an important issue in a case, may consciously or unconsciously shade their testimony as a result. Although the Federal Rules of Evidence do not mention impeachment on the basis of bias or prejudice, the Supreme Court has held that this is an integral part of the common law that was not abrogated by the Rules. Moreover, the Court has held that bias is not a collateral matter and it may be demonstrated either through cross-examination or extrinsic evidence.

4. *Defect in Testimonial Capacity or Ability to Observe*

Disqualifications of witnesses that were recognized at common law, for example, for children, insane people, and convicted felons, have been eliminated by the rules. Weaknesses in a witness's testimonial capacity, however, may be used to impeach a witness. The adverse party may introduce evidence showing that the witness's ability to perceive, remember, and relate the facts was compromised in some manner.

QUESTION 7. The defendant is charged with stabbing his girlfriend to death outside a bar late at night. Which of the following potential witnesses will not be allowed to testify?

A. A four-year-old girl who was walking home with her mother at the time of the incident and who will say she recognizes the defendant as the attacker.

B. The victim's mother who was not present but who will say that if someone harmed her daughter it must have been the defendant.

C. A man who left the bar falling down drunk who will say that the victim was unarmed.

D. The defendant's mother who will say that the defendant was home at the time watching television with her.

ANALYSIS.   The age and ability of the child to understand what she was seeing are factors the jury can take into account in deciding how much weight to give her testimony, but she is a competent witness and will be allowed to testify.

Similarly, the impairment of the drunken man does not disqualify him as a witness. The fact that the defendant's mother is probably biased in his favor may be brought out on cross-examination, but she will be allowed to testify. In other words, the weaknesses of the witnesses in **A**, **C**, and **D** are appropriate matters to use in impeaching them, but they do not render them incompetent as witnesses. The victim's mother, who was not present, however, has no personal knowledge of the event and will not be allowed to testify that the defendant stabbed her daughter. The correct answer is **B**.

QUESTION 8. In a libel action, a witness testifies that before the alleged defamation was published, the plaintiff enjoyed a good reputation. Which of the following types of evidence might the adverse party use to impeach the witness?

A. Asking the witness on cross-examination, "Isn't it true that your business makes $200,000 worth of sales to the plaintiff each year?"
B. If the witness denies the business relationship, introducing into evidence documentary proof of the sales contracts for $200,000 between the witness and the plaintiff.
C. Asking the witness on cross-examination, "Isn't it true that you are an atheist?"
D. All of the above.
E. **A** and **B**, but not **C**.

ANALYSIS. Rule 610 specifically prohibits impeachment on the basis of religious beliefs or opinions, so **C** and **D** are not correct. Choice **A** is a straightforward cross-examination question to show the witness has a reason to be biased in favor of the plaintiff and it would be allowed. Moreover, if the witness denies the relationship, the cross-examiner may introduce extrinsic evidence of it, since bias is not a collateral matter. Thus **B** is correct as well, and **E** is the correct answer.

5. Demonstrating that a Witness Is by Nature Not Truthful

The adverse party is allowed in various ways to demonstrate that a witness is by nature not truthful. This is an exception to the general bar against character evidence in Rule 404. The adverse party may: (1) call a character witness to give reputation or opinion testimony that another witness is not truthful, under Rule 608(a); (2) cross-examine the witness in question about specific instances of his or her conduct in the past that suggest poor character with respect to telling the truth, under Rule 608(b); (3) introduce evidence that the witness has been convicted of certain crimes, under Rule 609. One must pay careful attention to the technical requirements of the Rules when using these methods of impeachment.

a. Character Witnesses In the first method, the opponent calls other witnesses to provide information regarding the witness's character for truthfulness.

> Rule 608. A Witness's Character for Truthfulness or Untruthfulness
>
> **(a) Reputation or Opinion Evidence.** A witness's credibility may be attacked or supported by testimony about the witness's reputation for having a character for truthfulness or untruthfulness, or by testimony in the form of an opinion about that character. But evidence of truthful character is admissible only after the witness's character for truthfulness has been attacked.

After a witness has testified, the adverse party may call a different witness to testify about the first witness's character for truthfulness. Let's call the first witness a "fact witness," and the other witness a "character witness." The character witness's testimony must be either an opinion about the fact witness's character for truthfulness, or testimony about the fact witness's reputation for truthfulness. The party must establish that the character witness knows the fact witness well enough to have a foundation for forming an opinion of his or her character for truthfulness, or that the character witness has discussed the fact witness with others and is familiar with his or her reputation with respect to character for truthfulness. The character witness may not refer to specific instances of conduct by the fact witness on direct examination. On cross-examination, however, the court has discretion to allow the other party to question the character witness about relevant specific instances of the fact witness's conduct. We discussed this use of questions about specific acts in Chapter Four, in the section Cross-Examination of the Character Witness.

Here is an example of character evidence with respect to truthfulness:

Prosecutor:	Sir, do you know Mr. Smith, who testified that at the time of the crime he was at the movies with the defendant?
Character W:	Yes, I know him.
Prosecutor:	How do you know him and under what circumstances do you see him?
Character W:	We have worked in the same shop for fifteen years. I see him at work every day and at various work-related functions during the year. Also, we have lived on the same block for the past five years.
Prosecutor:	Do you have an opinion about his character with respect to truthfulness?
Character W:	I do.
Prosecutor:	What is your opinion?
Character W:	He is untruthful. I wouldn't believe a thing he said.

b. Cross-Examination about Specific Conduct Suggesting Poor Character for Truthfulness In this method, the opponent tries to get the witness to provide the information that impeaches his character for truthfulness.

Rule 608. A Witness's Character for Truthfulness or Untruthfulness

(b) **Specific Instances of Conduct.** Except for a criminal conviction under Rule 609, extrinsic evidence is not admissible to prove specific instances of a witness's conduct in order to attack or support the witness's character for truthfulness. But the court may, on cross-examination, allow them to be inquired into if they are probative of the character for truthfulness or untruthfulness of:

(1) the witness; or

(2) another witness whose character the witness being cross-examined has testified about.

By testifying on another matter, a witness does not waive any privilege against self-incrimination for testimony that relates only to the witness's character for truthfulness.

Under Rule 608(b) the court may permit a cross-examiner to ask a witness about specific instances of conduct by that witness that reflect poorly on his or her character for truthfulness. The conduct must have probative value with respect to the character of the witness for truthfulness or untruthfulness. For example, the cross-examiner might ask a witness about making untruthful statements on an application for a job, making misrepresentations about his income in order to obtain a mortgage, or maliciously filing a false complaint against another person. Asking the witness about a violent act that he committed, however, does not reflect on truthfulness and would be improper.

The party seeking to impeach the witness is limited to bringing out the facts through cross-examination, and is not permitted to prove the conduct through extrinsic evidence such as documents or other witnesses. Some authors say that the cross-examiner is obliged to "take the answer" of the witness if the witness denies the misconduct in question. This is not exactly true. The cross-examiner may not introduce extrinsic evidence to contradict the witness, but he may press the witness with further questions, making the inquiries more and more specific and pointed with the intent to force the witness to acknowledge the misconduct.

In order to question the witness about specific misconduct, the cross-examiner must have a good faith basis for believing in the existence of the facts. If the opposing party objects, the cross-examiner must be prepared to advise the court of the basis for asking the question.

The last sentence of Rule 608(b) means that a witness may decline to answer questions about prior misconduct if the answer could subject him to criminal prosecution. In other words, merely by testifying as a witness in a case a person does not sacrifice his Fifth Amendment rights. Rule 608(b) does not override the Fifth Amendment.

QUESTION 9. In a prosecution of the defendant for murder, the prosecution called defendant's former cellmate from the county jail as a witness. The cellmate testified that the defendant was placed in his cell after he was arrested, and that defendant admitted to him that he committed the murder. In the defense case, defendant's lawyer called a character witness who testified that he has lived in the same neighborhood with the cellmate for twenty years and has discussed his reputation for truthfulness with others numerous times. Which of the following would be permitted by the rules?

A. Defense lawyer asks the character witness what the cellmate's reputation for truthfulness is in the neighborhood, and the character witness says, "People say you can't believe a word he says."
B. Defense lawyer asks the witness whether he believes the cellmate's testimony about what the defendant said to him.
C. Defense lawyer asks the character witness to give examples of lies that people say the cellmate has told.
D. The character witness testifies, "My neighbor downstairs says that in her opinion the cellmate is the worst liar she has ever known."

ANALYSIS. The adverse party is allowed to call a character witness to impeach a fact witness's *character for truthfulness*, but not to give an opinion about whether his specific testimony in the case is truthful. Choice **B** is incorrect because the question calls for an opinion about the credibility of the cellmate's specific testimony, not his general character. The question in **C** asks for specific instances of lying. Choice **C** is incorrect, because the testimony of a character witness has to be in the form of opinion or reputation about character, not specific instances of conduct. Reputation testimony is the sum total of what people in the community say about someone, not the words of a single person, and for that reason **D** is incorrect. To the extent the neighbor's words are opinion testimony, they are hearsay, in that the witness is reporting the neighbor's assertion about the cellmate to prove the truth of the assertion. If the neighbor in question came to court and demonstrated that she knew the cellmate well enough to form an opinion of his character for truthfulness, she would be able to give her opinion (in which case she could be cross-examined), but one character witness cannot testify to what another character witness might say. Choice **A** is the correct answer because the question properly asks for the cellmate's reputation in the community with respect to his character for truthfulness.

QUESTION 10. During discovery, a party obtains documentary evidence that an adverse witness fabricated items on his resume when he applied for his current job, falsely claiming to have a degree from a prestigious school. Which of the following methods of impeachment is not permissible?

A. Asking the witness on cross-examination whether he listed the school in question on his resume and whether he actually attended that school.

> **B.** If the witness denies any falsity and claims he did attend the school, asking detailed follow-up questions about the school in question, such as what dorm he was in, who his advisor was, etc., to try to expose the falsehood.
>
> **C.** If the witness denies any falsity and claims he did attend the school, calling the Registrar from the school to testify that the witness never attended.

ANALYSIS.   Asking the witness whether he falsely claimed to have attended a school he did not attend falls squarely within what is permitted by Rule 608(b). Lying on one's resume certainly is evidence of poor character for truthfulness, and **A** is therefore permissible. The rule, however, prohibits proving that the conduct occurred through extrinsic evidence, and therefore one may not call the Registrar to testify, as in **C**. Nor could one introduce records from the school, or any other exhibits. The resume with the false statement on it is not admissible. Rule 608(b) authorizes "inquiring into" the conduct in question on cross-examination, and that permits the cross-examiner to ask follow-up questions as suggested in **B**. It would be good practice to use cross-examination to paint the witness into a corner so that he felt obligated to admit his misconduct. The correct answer as to which method of impeachment is impermissible is **C**.

> **QUESTION 11.** The Defendant in a criminal case calls a Witness to testify that the police officer who testified against Defendant is a member of Witness's golf club and he has known her for 10 years and discussed her many times with other members of the club. Which of the following may the Witness *not* testify to?
>
> **A.** His opinion of the officer's character for veracity.
> **B.** His knowledge of the officer's reputation with respect to veracity.
> **C.** That the officer lied about her job on her application to join the golf club.
> **D.** That the officer told him on the sixth green at the club one day that she hated the Defendant and would say anything to send him to prison.

ANALYSIS.   Defendant is allowed to call a character witness to testify to a fact witness's character for truth and veracity. The character witness may do so either by expressing her own opinion of the fact witness's character, or by reporting the fact witness's reputation for truth and veracity. Thus **A** and **B** are incorrect answers. Bias is also a permissible issue for impeachment and the Witness may testify that the officer admitted her bias against the Defendant to him. **D** is also an incorrect answer. The correct answer is **C**. Whether the fact witness committed a specific act in the past that demonstrates poor character for veracity may only be raised on cross-examination of the fact witness. It may not be shown by extrinsic evidence, such as the testimony of another witness.

c. Proof of Conviction of Crime to Suggest Poor Character for Truthfulness   The third method for proving poor character for truthfulness is to show that the witness has been convicted of a crime. The practice is based on the notion that someone who has violated the criminal law has demonstrated a sufficient willingness to flout social norms that he might be more willing to commit perjury than another witness. Rule 609 limits the sorts of crimes that can be used for this purpose and the circumstances under which such impeachment is permissible.

> **Rule 609. Impeachment by Evidence of a Criminal Conviction**
>
> **(a) In General.** The following rules apply to attacking a witness's character for truthfulness by evidence of a criminal conviction:
>
> (1) for a crime that, in the convicting jurisdiction, was punishable by death or by imprisonment for more than one year, the evidence:
>
> (A) must be admitted, subject to Rule 403, in a civil case or in a criminal case in which the witness is not a defendant; and
>
> (B) must be admitted in a criminal case in which the witness is a defendant, if the probative value of the evidence outweighs its prejudicial effect to that defendant; and
>
> (2) for any crime regardless of the punishment, the evidence must be admitted if the court can readily determine that establishing the elements of the crime required proving—or the witness's admitting—a dishonest act or false statement.
>
> **(b) Limit on Using the Evidence After 10 Years.** This subdivision (b) applies if more than 10 years have passed since the witness's conviction or release from confinement for it, whichever is later. Evidence of the conviction is admissible only if:
>
> (1) its probative value, supported by specific facts and circumstances, substantially outweighs its prejudicial effect; and
>
> (2) the proponent gives an adverse party reasonable written notice of the intent to use it so that the party has a fair opportunity to contest its use.

Two categories of criminal convictions are admissible under the rule: (1) felonies, that is, crimes where the possible sentence exceeds one year, or is death; and (2) crimes which require proof of an untruthful act or a false statement. With respect to felony convictions, the witness does not have to have received a sentence exceeding one year for the conviction to be admissible. The rule merely requires that the crime carried a potential penalty of more than one year.

(1) Felony Convictions   When impeaching a witness with a felony conviction, the rule requires the court to use a balancing test to determine the admissibility of the conviction. With respect to the balancing test, the rule distinguishes between impeachment of a criminal defendant and impeachment of all other witnesses. Felony convictions may be used to impeach a witness other than a criminal defendant as long as Rule 403 does not bar them. The conviction is

admissible as long as the probative value of the conviction is not substantially outweighed by the risk of unfair prejudice, or considerations of wasting time, delay, cumulative evidence, confusion, or misleading the jury. Ordinarily the principal concern is the risk of unfair prejudice.

You must pay careful attention to what constitutes probative value and risk of prejudice in this context. The probative value of any criminal conviction used for impeachment depends upon how much it tells us about the likelihood the witness is lying, and how important credibility issues are in the case. Some crimes are more probative of character for untruthfulness than others, although there is no chart that lists the probative value of all crimes in this respect. But a judge might find, for example, that a conviction for grand theft is more probative of untruthfulness than a conviction for an assault and battery that arose out of a sudden confrontation. A recent conviction is generally considered to be more probative of a witness's current character than an older conviction. Whether the witness has lived a blameless life since the conviction or has continued to be in conflict with the law will affect the probative value of the conviction.

The risk of prejudice for a felony conviction used for impeachment is the risk that the jury will use the felony conviction as evidence about what happened in the underlying event. For example, if the prosecutor uses a conviction to impeach a criminal defendant's alibi witness there is a risk the jury will be more inclined to convict the defendant because he associates with a felon, reasoning that "birds of a feather, flock together." Criminal convictions used to impeach witnesses may tar the party who called the witness for a variety of reasons.

The trial judge must assess the likelihood that the jury's verdict might be unfairly affected by the use of a felony conviction to impeach a witness, and weigh that against the significance of the impeachment value of the conviction. For witnesses other than a criminal defendant, the balancing test is weighted in favor of admissibility—the conviction is inadmissible only where the risk of unfair prejudice substantially outweighs the probative value.

When the witness is the criminal defendant the test is weighted in favor of exclusion. Felony convictions are admissible to impeach a criminal defendant only where the prosecution can show that the probative value of the evidence outweighs the risk of unfair prejudice to the defendant. The probative value of the conviction for impeachment depends upon how much it tells us about the likelihood the defendant is lying, how important it is for the defendant to be able to testify on his own behalf, and how important credibility issues are in the case. The reality is that if a defendant knows he will be impeached with a previous conviction he is much less likely to testify. Where the facts are such that the defendant's testimony is crucial to presenting his side of the story, allowing impeachment based on a prior conviction will likely result in depriving the jury of important probative evidence.

It is essential to remember that the probative value of the defendant's previous conviction does *not* depend upon how much it tells us about how likely it is that the defendant committed the crime. The only legitimate value of evidence admitted under Rule 609 is its impeachment value—what it says about the defendant's character for truthfulness as a witness.

The risk of unfair prejudice is usually high for convictions used to impeach a criminal defendant. The jury may conclude the defendant is a bad person and vote to convict although the evidence does not establish guilt beyond a reasonable doubt. This risk of unfair prejudice is particularly high where the previous conviction is for the same or a similar offense to the crime charged in the case on trial. The jury may use the previous conviction for propensity purposes, concluding the defendant's character is such that he is inclined to commit this sort of crime and therefore is probably guilty. Remember that similarity between the previous conviction and the crime charged increases the risk of unfair prejudice, but does not increase the probative value of the evidence for impeachment purposes.

(2) Convictions Involving a Dishonest Act or False Statement   Some crimes require proof of an element establishing that the defendant committed a dishonest act or false statement. In this context the word "dishonest" does not refer to criminal behavior generally, it specifically means an act that was untruthful or deceitful. Perjury is the paradigmatic offense of this type. Other crimes that would qualify include misrepresentation, fraud, embezzlement, bigamy, and similar offenses. Larceny is a crime that may or may not involve dishonesty or false statement. Simply putting something in one's pocket and walking out of a store without paying for it would not involve a false statement. Larceny by trick, however, would fall within this category of crimes. A trial judge will not conduct a "mini-trial" to determine whether a false statement was involved in the commission of the offense. The rule specifies that a conviction is admissible only "if the court can readily determine" that the necessary element was present. That can be done where the element is set forth in the statutory definition of the offense, the language of the indictment, a bill of particulars, or the like.

If an offense falls within this category there is no balancing test to determine admissibility. The court must permit impeachment with convictions for crimes involving dishonesty or false statement. A trial judge has no discretion to exclude such evidence.

(3) Ten-Year Limitation   For the most part, convictions that are more than ten years old are inadmissible. The ten years is measured from the date of conviction or release from confinement, whichever is later. For example, if a witness was convicted fifteen years before trial and served ten years in prison, release from confinement would be five years before trial and the conviction would not be barred by the ten-year limitation.

Convictions more than ten years old are admissible only where their probative value, supported by specific facts and circumstances, substantially outweighs their prejudicial effect. This is a high burden. In addition, the party seeking to use such a conviction must give pretrial notice to the opponent.

(4) Other Issues   Rule 609(c) provides that where a witness has received a pardon, annulment, or certificate of rehabilitation and the person has no subsequent felony convictions, the conviction is inadmissible for impeachment. If the pardon, annulment, or equivalent was based on a finding of innocence, the conviction is inadmissible whether or not there have been subsequent convictions.

Rule 609(d) provides that juvenile adjudications are admissible for impeachment only in criminal cases and with respect to witnesses other than the defendant. They are admissible only if an adult's conviction for the same offense would be admissible for impeachment, and only where such evidence is "necessary to fairly determine guilt or innocence."

A conviction may be used for impeachment, even if the case is on appeal, pursuant to Rule 609(e). The opponent, however, may bring out that there is an appeal pending.

QUESTION 12. Plaintiff sued defendant in tort for injuries suffered in an automobile collision. Plaintiff called an eyewitness who testified on direct examination that the defendant ran a red light and crashed into the side of plaintiff's car. Plaintiff testified that plaintiff had the green light when he entered the intersection, and defendant testified that defendant had the green light. Which of the following items of evidence would definitely be inadmissible under Rule 609?

A. Evidence that the plaintiff was convicted of perjury twelve years before trial.

B. Evidence that the plaintiff's witness was adjudicated as a juvenile delinquent nine years before trial, based on murdering his brother.

C. Evidence that the plaintiff's witness was convicted of armed robbery and sentenced to pay a fine of five hundred dollars three years before trial.

D. Evidence that the defendant was convicted of larceny under one hundred dollars, a misdemeanor, where the bill of particulars indicated the offense was committed by lying about the number of bottles of water in his shopping cart when checking out at Costco.

ANALYSIS.   The plaintiff's conviction for perjury might be admissible if the plaintiff served a prison sentence from which he was released within the past ten years, because the age of the conviction is measured either from the date of conviction or the date of release from confinement, whichever was later. Even if the plaintiff served no time, the court could admit the conviction if it found that its probative value for impeachment substantially outweighed the risk of unfair prejudice. Thus **A** is incorrect, because the conviction is not definitely inadmissible. The armed robbery conviction would be admissible to impeach the plaintiff's witness as long as its probative value was not substantially outweighed by the risk of unfair prejudice. Although the witness was only sentenced to a fine, the potential penalty for armed robbery exceeds one year. Thus **C** is incorrect. Given the information in the bill of particulars, the defendant's larceny conviction was for a crime involving dishonest or false statement. It is thus admissible for impeachment, although the offense was only a misdemeanor, and therefore **D** is incorrect. Only **B** is an example of something that would definitely be inadmissible, because juvenile adjudications cannot be used to impeach witnesses in civil cases. **B** is the correct answer.

6. Impeachment with Prior Inconsistent Statements

The opponent may impeach specific testimony of a witness by showing that he has made prior inconsistent statements. For example, suppose that a witness testifies at trial that the plaintiff had the green light when she entered the intersection where a collision occurred. If the witness had said at an earlier time that the plaintiff entered the intersection on the red light, the opponent could bring that out to impeach the witness. The idea is that the witness is not reliable on this point because she has given inconsistent accounts at different times. The opponent may bring out the inconsistent statement either on cross-examination or by introducing extrinsic evidence of it.

Ordinarily proof of a prior inconsistent statement is only admissible to impeach the witness's trial testimony, not to prove that the prior inconsistent statement was true. Where the witness made the prior inconsistent statement under oath in a formal proceeding, however, the prior statement is admissible for its truth and is not considered hearsay. We discuss such prior inconsistent statements in Chapter Eight, in the section on Rule 801(d). If the witness did not make the prior inconsistent statement under oath in a formal proceeding, its evidentiary value is limited to showing that the witness has contradicted himself, which undermines the reliability of his trial testimony. Rule 613 governs prior inconsistent statements used for purposes of impeachment.

> Rule 613. Witness's Prior Statement
>
> (a) **Showing or Disclosing the Statement During Examination.** When examining a witness about the witness's prior statement, a party need not show it or disclose its contents to the witness. But the party must, on request, show it or disclose its contents to an adverse party's attorney.
>
> (b) **Extrinsic Evidence of a Prior Inconsistent Statement.** Extrinsic evidence of a witness's prior inconsistent statement is admissible only if the witness is given an opportunity to explain or deny the statement and an adverse party is given an opportunity to examine the witness about it, or if justice so requires. This subdivision (b) does not apply to an opposing party's statement under Rule 801(d)(2).

As the rule provides, where the opponent brings out a prior inconsistent statement during cross-examination it is not necessary to show it to the witness before asking him about it. If opposing counsel requests it, however, it must be shown to him or her. Where a party introduces a prior inconsistent statement through extrinsic evidence, the rule requires that at some point the witness must be given an opportunity to explain or deny it, and the opposing party must have an opportunity to examine the witness about it, unless the prior inconsistent statement is one made by the opposing party.

QUESTION 13. The defendant is on trial for murder. An eyewitness told the investigating detective that she saw the defendant shoot the victim. At the trial, however, the witness testifies it was too dark at the time of the event and she has no idea who shot the victim. The prosecution calls the detective and asks him to state what the witness told him. The defendant objects. The court should:

A. Sustain the objection and exclude the testimony because the prosecution is impeaching its own witness.
B. Overrule the objection and allow the detective to testify.
C. Overrule the objection and allow the testimony subject to a limiting instruction that it is admissible only for the purpose of impeaching the witness and not for the purpose of proving that the defendant shot the victim.

ANALYSIS. The prosecution is impeaching its own witness, but that is allowed under Rule 607. Thus **A** is incorrect. The prosecution is attempting to introduce extrinsic evidence of a prior inconsistent statement by the witness. That is permissible as long as the witness is given an opportunity at some point to explain or deny the prior statement and the defense counsel is given an opportunity to question the witness about it. The court must give a limiting instruction, however, because the prior statement was not made under oath in a formal proceeding and is admissible only for purposes of impeachment, not to prove the truth of the prior statement. Thus **B** is incorrect and **C** is the correct answer.

QUESTION 14. Assume the court allows the detective to testify and the government calls him as a witness. He testifies that the witness told him she had a good view of the shooting and was certain that it was the defendant who shot the victim. The judge gives an appropriate limiting instruction. The government rests without offering any other evidence. The defendant moves for a directed verdict of not guilty. How should the court rule?

A. Deny the motion for a directed verdict.
B. Grant the motion for a directed verdict.

ANALYSIS. Choice **B** is the correct answer. The court must grant the motion for a directed verdict because the prosecution never introduced any evidence that the defendant shot the victim. This example allows you to see the real effect of the limiting instruction the court gave. The detective's testimony about what the witness said was admitted only to show that the witness told conflicting stories, which impeached her trial testimony that it was too dark for her to see the shooter. The detective's account of what she said was not admitted to prove the truth of what she said, and thus provided no evidence that the defendant shot the victim. In the absence of any other evidence, the prosecution failed to prove that the defendant shot the victim.

E. Rehabilitation of Witnesses

Where the opponent has attacked the character of a fact witness for truthfulness, the proponent may call a rebuttal character witness to give opinion or reputation testimony that the fact witness has good character with respect to truthfulness. Good character evidence with respect to truthfulness is admissible, however, only after a fact witness's character for truthfulness has been attacked. Testimony by a character witness that the fact witness has poor character for truthfulness, cross-examination under Rule 608(b) about specific conduct, and proof of a criminal conviction constitute an attack on a witness's character for truthfulness. Impeachment through evidence of bias or prejudice does not amount to an attack on character for truthfulness. Most people have biases and prejudices, and it is only natural for witnesses to be biased in favor of parties with whom they have enjoyed a good relationship in the past. That does not demonstrate poor character for truthfulness in general. Demonstrating that a witness has defects in testimonial capacity also does not constitute poor character for truthfulness, nor does proof that a witness has made prior inconsistent statements. Contradicting a fact witness's testimony through other witnesses or exhibits is usually not an attack on character for truthfulness, although in some situations it may be.

F. Miscellaneous Matters

Rule 610 provides that evidence of a witness's religious beliefs or opinions is not admissible to attack or support the witness's credibility.

Rule 614 permits the court to call witnesses on its own motion, and provides that such the parties are entitled to cross-examine such witnesses. The rule also provides that the court may ask questions of witnesses called by the parties.

Rule 615 provides that at a party's request, the court must order witnesses sequestered so that they cannot hear other witnesses' testimony. The court may also issue such an order on its own. But this rule does not authorize excluding: (a) a party who is a natural person; (b) the representative of a party that is not a natural person; (c) a person whose presence is essential to presenting the party's claim or defense (the party's attorney, for example, or an expert witness who needs to hear the testimony of other witnesses); or (d) a person authorized by statute to be present.

QUESTION 15. The Closer. The defendant is on trial for the murder of a bank teller. The prosecution alleges that he shot and killed the teller during a bank robbery. The prosecution called a security guard from the bank, who testified that he was present during the robbery and saw the defendant shoot the teller. Defense counsel has a copy of the grand jury testimony of the security guard, where he testified that he was too frightened to look at the robbers and could not identify the person who shot the teller. The defense lawyer's investigator has found a witness, Mr. Smith, who says that he has known the security guard very well for years and in this witness's opinion, the security guard is a liar. The investigator has also interviewed another teller from the bank, who says that he got a very good look at all of the robbers and the defendant was not one of them. Defense counsel also has a copy of the security guard's employment application. In response to a question that asked him to list all of his previous employment, he failed to disclose a job from which he had been fired two years before he applied to work at the bank. Which of the following is not a permissible method for defense counsel to use to impeach the security guard:

A. Calling the other teller to contradict the security guard's testimony.
B. Introducing the grand jury testimony as an exhibit.
C. Calling Mr. Smith to testify that in his opinion the security guard has poor character for truthfulness.
D. Introducing the security guard's employment application as an exhibit.

ANALYSIS.   Contradiction is a permissible method of specific impeachment and there is nothing that would bar the defendant from calling a witness to say that the defendant was not in the bank. Thus **A** is a permissible method of impeachment. The security guard made a statement in the grand jury that is inconsistent with his trial testimony. The defense may ask him about it on cross-examination, but it is also permissible to prove the prior inconsistent statement with extrinsic evidence, as long as the security guard has an opportunity to explain or deny the inconsistent grand jury testimony and the prosecutor has an opportunity to examine him about it. Thus **B** is a permissible method of impeachment. It is permissible to impeach a fact witness by calling a character to witness to give his opinion of the fact witness's character for untruthfulness. Thus **C** is a permissible method of impeachment. The correct answer to the question is **D**. Under Rule 608(b) it would have been permissible for defense counsel to ask the security guard about lying on his employment application during cross-examination. It is not permissible, however, to introduce extrinsic evidence of prior acts by the witness to show that he has poor character for truthfulness. Thus **D** would be an impermissible method of impeachment.

 # Avery's Picks

1. Question 1   **A**
2. Question 2   **C**
3. Question 3   **C**
4. Question 4   **D**
5. Question 5   **E**
6. Question 6   **D**
7. Question 7   **B**
8. Question 8   **E**
9. Question 9   **A**
10. Question 10   **C**
11. Question 11   **C**
12. Question 12   **B**
13. Question 13   **C**
14. Question 14   **B**
15. Question 15   **D**

7

Opinions and Expert Testimony

CHAPTER OVERVIEW

A. Lay Opinions
B. Expert Testimony
   1. Subject Matter of Expert Testimony
   2. Qualifications of Experts
   3. Reliability of Scientific Principles and Methods
   4. Factual Basis for Opinions by Experts
   5. Opinions on Ultimate Issues
   6. Court Appointed Experts

 Avery's Picks

Common law courts generally did not allow lay witnesses to testify in the form of opinions or inferences drawn from observations. The theory was that lay witnesses should simply testify to the facts. Drawing inferences from the facts was thought to be the purview of the jury. A more modern approach takes into account that there is no clear line between fact and opinion.[1] Statements of "fact" invariably involve some drawing of inferences on the part of the speaker. The Federal Rules of Evidence recognize this by eliminating the general bar against opinion testimony by lay witnesses.

The Federal Rules of Evidence also liberalized the rules with respect to opinion testimony by experts. Another significant change occurred several years after the adoption of the Rules, when the Supreme Court decided *Daubert v. Merrell Dow Pharmaceuticals, Inc.*, 509 U.S. 579 (1993). The *Daubert* case ushered in a new era of how courts determine the reliability of scientific

---

1. For an interesting discussion of this issue, see *Beech Aircraft Corp. v. Rainey*, 488 U.S. 153 (1988), which we discuss in Chapter 8 in connection with the public records exception to the hearsay rule.

and expert evidence. As a result the Federal Rules were amended to reflect the holding in that case. Expert evidence is extremely important in an increasing number of cases. A competent lawyer needs to master the art of examining and cross-examining experts. Trial advocacy skills are beyond the scope of this book, but one must start with a working knowledge of the rules that govern expert testimony, which we discuss below.

A.   Lay Opinions

Rule 701 governs the admissibility of lay opinion evidence.

> **Rule 701. Opinion Testimony by Lay Witnesses**
> If a witness is not testifying as an expert, testimony in the form of an opinion is limited to one that is:
>   (a) rationally based on the witness's perception;
>   (b) helpful to clearly understanding the witness's testimony or to determining a fact in issue; and
>   (c) not based on scientific, technical, or other specialized knowledge within the scope of Rule 702.

The rule explicitly permits a lay witness to draw inferences based on observations and to express them in the form of an opinion. As mentioned above, the rule reflects the understanding that there is no clear line between "facts" and "inferences" or "opinions." In addition, the rule is based on the practical reality that it may be difficult or impossible for a witness to disaggregate her conclusion about an event into a set of discrete "factual" observations. For example, a witness's testimony that another person appeared to be "frightened" may be based on numerous observations about the person's speech, breathing, facial expressions, eye movements, and many other things. The witness may not have taken conscious note of these individual observations. If we make the witness testify about these specific manifestations of fear rather than permitting her to express her conclusion that the subject was frightened, it is possible she will simply make things up, consciously or unconsciously. Rather than forcing the witness to struggle with listing each feature she observed, the rule permits her to use a "shorthand" description that has meaning to the average juror. To the extent it is desirable to elicit further specifics, they can be fleshed out during further direct examination or on cross-examination.

The requirement that a lay opinion be rationally based on the perceptions of the witness imposes the personal knowledge requirement on such testimony. A lay witness cannot base her opinions on facts observed by others. Nor may a lay witness base an opinion on speculation or assumptions about the facts.

The requirement that a lay opinion be helpful to the trier of fact means that a witness may not testify to opinions that the trier of fact could just as easily reach. For example, we would not permit a lay witness to give an opinion about the age of another person present in the courtroom because the jurors would be equally able to form their own opinions.

Lay witnesses are able to testify to opinions about a wide variety of things. Examples include: the speed of a vehicle, the age of a person, whether a person was intoxicated, taste sensations, and the value of one's own land. Witnesses may give an opinion about the emotional, mental, or physical state of another person: for example, whether someone was nervous, angry, depressed, tired, and the like. A lay witness, however, may not testify to a mental condition that requires expert diagnosis—for example, that someone was a paranoid schizophrenic.

QUESTION 1. Plaintiff sued prison officials and guards for injuries he sustained when guards allegedly used unreasonable and excessive force against him. The defendants did not designate any expert witnesses during discovery, as required by the Federal Rules of Civil Procedure. At trial defendants called the deputy superintendent of security at the prison as a lay witness to testify about the interpretation of policy and procedures relating to security in the state's Department of Corrections. Plaintiff objected to testimony on that issue from the deputy superintendent. The court should:

A. Exclude the testimony because the defendants failed to comply with discovery requirements concerning expert testimony.
B. Exclude the testimony because the witness's opinions are not relationally based on his perceptions.
C. Admit the testimony as proper lay opinion testimony.

ANALYSIS. The issue here is whether the deputy superintendent is giving lay opinion testimony or expert testimony. Rule 701 permits lay opinions only where the opinion is not based on specialized knowledge within the scope of Rule 702. Does the question of how to handle security issues in an institution that contains men convicted of violent crimes require specialized knowledge? Of course it does. Policymakers draft policies and procedures based on the accumulated experience of people in the corrections field and prison guards receive training on the use of force and other measures in handling security problems. In the case on which this question is based, the court concluded that the deputy superintendent would be giving "paradigmatic expert testimony."[2]

One reason for section (c) of Rule 701 is to deter parties from avoiding their discovery responsibilities with respect to expert testimony by describing testimony as a lay opinion when it is really coming from an expert. Since

---

2. *Giles v. Rhodes*, 2000 WL 1425046 (S.D.N.Y. 2000).

the testimony of the deputy superintendent here is expert testimony, the testimony is not admissible as lay opinion. Thus **C** is incorrect. Because it is not lay opinion, the requirement of Rule 701 that opinions be rationally based on the perceptions of the witness does not apply. Thus **B** is incorrect. The correct answer is **A**; the testimony should be excluded because the defendants failed to comply with the discovery rules with respect to expert testimony.

QUESTION 2. Plaintiff sued defendant for injuries sustained in a collision between their cars at an intersection. Plaintiff alleged that the defendant was speeding and entered the intersection by running the red light. Defendant claimed that he had the green light and was driving at a normal rate of speed, and that it was the plaintiff who ran a red light. At the trial the plaintiff called a witness who testified he was standing on the sidewalk at the intersection, that he saw both cars approach the intersection, and that he could see the traffic signal from his location. When plaintiff's counsel asked the witness what happened next, the witness stated, "The defendant's car came barreling into the intersection against the red light really fast. The guy must have been drunk." The defendant moved to strike this testimony. The court should:

A. Overrule the objection because the witness gave proper lay opinion testimony.

B. Sustain the objection and exclude the witness's statements.

C. Admit the first sentence of the testimony, but strike the statement, "The guy must have been drunk."

ANALYSIS.   The witness would be allowed to testify in the form of opinions if they were rationally based on his perceptions. He has testified that he saw the cars approaching and that he could see the traffic signal. His opinions that the defendant was driving "really fast" and that he ran the red light appear to be rationally based on his observations. The first sentence of his testimony is admissible. Choice **B** is incorrect because it would be error to exclude everything the witness said. The witness's opinion that the defendant was drunk, however, does not appear to be based on anything other than his manner of driving. There could be many other explanations for the defendant's driving behavior, and it is not rational to conclude that he must have been drunk. That is merely speculation on the part of the witness. Choice **A** is incorrect because it would be error to admit everything the witness has said. The correct answer is **C**. The court should allow the first sentence, but grant the motion to strike as to the second statement and instruct the jury to ignore it.

B.   Expert Testimony

Rule 702 sets forth the basic requirements for expert witnesses.

Rule 702. Testimony by Expert Witnesses

A witness who is qualified as an expert by knowledge, skill, experience, training, or education may testify in the form of an opinion or otherwise if:

(a) the expert's scientific, technical, or other specialized knowledge will help the trier of fact to understand the evidence or to determine a fact in issue;

(b) the testimony is based on sufficient facts or data;

(c) the testimony is the product of reliable principles and methods; and

(d) the expert has reliably applied the principles and methods to the facts of the case.

We'll take up each of the requirements for expert testimony in the following sections.

1.   Subject Matter of Expert Testimony

The rule establishes two requirements for expert testimony. First, the subject matter must be scientific, technical, or other specialized knowledge. Second, such knowledge must assist the trier of fact in understanding the evidence or determining the facts. Where the subject matter is beyond the knowledge of the average juror, expert testimony is plainly appropriate. Suppose plaintiff has filed a medical malpractice case alleging that the defendant doctor was negligent in failing to properly diagnose her illness. Expert testimony on the question of whether the defendant doctor's performance met the appropriate standard of care is clearly appropriate, because the average juror does not have the medical training necessary to perform a medical diagnosis.

A field does not have to be as esoteric as medicine for expert testimony to be helpful to the jury in understanding or determining the facts. For example, some research suggests that untrained jurors are as accurate at handwriting comparison as expert document examiners. Nonetheless, it might be helpful to the jury to have testimony from a document examiner who explains what to look for in comparing handwriting samples—such as locations where pressure was applied to the pen, places where the writer lifted the pen off the page, and the like.

To be helpful to the trier of fact, an expert's testimony must "fit" the facts of the case. This imposes a standard on expert testimony that is more demanding than the low threshold for relevance under Rule 401. The trial judge must determine whether scientific or technical principles described by an expert have "a valid scientific connection to the pertinent inquiry as a precondition to admissibility."[3] Expert testimony may be misleading because of the difficulty

---

3.   *Daubert v. Merrell Dow Pharmaceuticals, Inc.*, 509 U.S. 579, 591 (1993).

that lay jurors have in evaluating it. On the remand of the *Daubert* case from the Supreme Court, the Ninth Circuit concluded that the fit requirement compels federal judges to exclude scientific evidence "unless they are convinced that it speaks clearly and directly to an issue in dispute in the case, and that it will not mislead the jury."[4]

On certain issues, expert testimony is not only permitted, but required. Findings of fact as to technical matters beyond the scope of ordinary experience may not be warranted in the absence of expert testimony supporting such findings. Expert testimony is usually required on issues of medical causation, the standard of care in professional malpractice actions, questions of causation involving engineering propositions, and many other matters.

The conclusions of experts are not binding on the trier of fact. Where expert testimony has been admitted, trial judges routinely instruct jurors that they should evaluate it like any other testimony and may reject any expert testimony in whole or in part.

QUESTION 3. Plaintiff sued Defendant for negligence that caused an auto accident. Plaintiff claimed to have suffered a herniated disc as a result of the collision. He testified he had never had back pain before the accident, but experienced excruciating pain beginning the day after the incident. He introduced medical records to prove that he received treatment for a herniated disc and sought to recover his medical costs and an additional amount for pain and suffering. After the conclusion of the evidence, the Defendant sought a partial directed verdict barring the Plaintiff from recovering any damages for a herniated disc. How should the court rule?

A. Grant the defendant's motion for a partial directed verdict.
B. Deny the defendant's motion.

ANALYSIS. Expert testimony is required to prove that a given cause is responsible for a medical condition. The mere fact that the Plaintiff's herniated disc developed *after* the accident is not sufficient to prove that it was *caused* by the accident. *Post hoc ergo propter hoc* is a logical fallacy. Therefore the Plaintiff had a failure of proof with respect to the cause of the herniated disc and the Defendant's motion should be granted. **A** is the correct answer.

---

4. *Daubert v. Merrell Dow Pharmaceuticals, Inc.*, 43 F.3d 1311, 1321, n.17 (9th Cir. 1995).

2. Qualifications of Experts

Rule 702 requires that experts be qualified by "knowledge, skill, experience, training, or education" to address the scientific, technical, or other specialized knowledge issues in their testimony. The proponent has the burden of establishing the expert's qualifications and should begin the examination of the witness by asking about her education, training, experience, publications, previous experience as an expert witness, and similar matters. The opponent is not permitted to short circuit the proponent's demonstration of the witness's qualifications by forcing the proponent to agree to a stipulation that she is qualified. The opponent will be given an opportunity to question the witness about qualifications if he desires to do so before the witness begins testifying about substantive matters.

The trial judge decides under Rule 104(a) whether an expert is qualified. Once the judge has determined that a proposed expert is qualified, further questions the opponent may raise about her education, training, knowledge, and professional experience go to the weight the jury may give her testimony and not its admissibility.

The language of Rule 702 makes explicit that advanced education is not the only method of acquiring specialized knowledge. Experts may acquire the necessary qualifications on the job, in the field, or through other training or study. An expert does not necessarily have to be a specialist within her profession to be qualified to testify. Whether a person qualified as an expert on one subject is qualified to give an opinion on a somewhat related subject depends on the circumstances.

QUESTION 4. The defendant is on trial for conspiracy to import marijuana and arson on the high seas. The prosecution has alleged that the defendant set fire to the shrimp boat on which he was transporting marijuana when he saw a Coast Guard vessel approaching. The boat was in flames and the defendant was nearby in a rowboat when the Coast Guard reached the shrimper. The prosecution has called an arson investigator from Miami who was trained at the FBI academy in arson investigation. He has investigated fires of suspicious origin, including on boats in the harbor, for twenty years. The prosecution intends to ask the investigator about his conclusion that the fire was started intentionally, which he based on burn patterns that demonstrated that it was a fire with two points of origination. While questioning the witness about his qualifications, defense counsel established that the witness had never before investigated a fire on the high seas and could not opine about whether the motion of a ship at sea could simulate the appearance of a two-origin fire. The defendant objects to any further testimony from this witness. The court should:

A. Sustain the defendant's objection because the issue of how the fire started is an issue of fact and not an appropriate subject for expert testimony.
B. Sustain the defendant's objection because the witness is not qualified to testify about whether this fire on the high seas was arson.
C. Overrule the defendant's objection and allow the witness to testify as a lay witness.
D. Overrule the defendant's objection and allow the witness to testify as an expert.

ANALYSIS. The first issue here is whether the question of whether the fire was intentionally set is an appropriate subject matter for expert testimony. It is true that it will be up to the jury in the case to determine, as a question of fact, whether the fire was intentionally set. The scientific and technical information the arson investigator possesses, however, will be of assistance to the jury in making that determination. There can be little question that arson investigation involves scientific and technical issues beyond the knowledge of a layperson. Thus **A** is incorrect. For the same reason, if the court were to determine that the proposed witness was not qualified to testify as an expert, it would be error for the court to permit the witness to testify as a lay witness. As we discussed above, Rule 701(c) specifically limits lay opinion testimony to matters that do not require scientific or technical expertise. Thus **C** is incorrect.

The issue here comes down to whether the fact that the witness has no experience investigating fires on the high seas renders him unqualified to give an opinion in this case. It does not. The witness's general training and experience as an arson investigator qualify him to testify about the factors that should be taken into account in determining whether a fire was intentionally set, and about the significance of a two-origin fire. The weaknesses in his experience with or knowledge regarding boats on the high seas go to the weight the jury might give his conclusions. It is possible to poke some holes in the training or knowledge of most expert witnesses. A good cross-examiner will use that to raise doubts in the minds of the jurors about the conclusions the expert has expressed. Judges, however, will usually qualify experts whose general education, training, and experience permit them to provide assistance to the jury on scientific and technical matters. Choice **D** is the correct answer and **B** is incorrect.

3. *Reliability of Scientific Principles and Methods*

Rule 702 requires that expert testimony be based on "reliable principles and methods" and that the principles and methods be reliably applied to the facts of the case. This language was added to the rule after the decision of the Supreme Court in *Daubert v. Merrell Dow Pharmaceuticals, Inc.*, 509 U.S. 579

(1993). *Daubert* established that the trial judge must act as a gatekeeper with respect to scientific and expert evidence. The judge must make a preliminary determination under Rule 104(a) that such evidence is reliable before submitting it to the jury.

The Court in *Daubert* set forth several factors that trial judges might take into account in determining whether scientific evidence is reliable: (1) whether the technique or theory has been tested; (2) whether the technique or theory has been subjected to peer review or publication in peer reviewed journals; (3) the potential rate of error of the principles or methods; (4) whether there are established standards or controls for using the principles or methods; and (5) whether the principles and methods have been generally accepted in the relevant scientific community. These factors do not constitute a checklist for the admissibility of expert or scientific evidence. Some of the factors do not apply to certain types of evidence or scientific fields. A trial judge has discretion with respect to which of the factors to take into account in a particular case. A judge may also take into account other factors that bear on the reliability of scientific or technical evidence. For example, one factor not mentioned in *Daubert* that is commonly used is whether a witness has developed a theory or method specifically for use in the litigation at hand, or whether the expert uses the principle or method in question in her other work.

Before *Daubert* federal courts determined the reliability of scientific and expert evidence simply by asking whether the principles and methods were generally accepted in the relevant scientific community. The *Daubert* approach permits courts to take into account the other factors described above. This may result in a conclusion that evidence is reliable, even though it has not yet achieved general acceptance. Conversely, it may result in a conclusion that evidence is unreliable, even though it had previously been generally accepted for a substantial length of time.

In making a decision about reliability under Rule 104(a) trial judges are not constrained by the rules of evidence. Judges may consider affidavits from other experts, articles in scientific and technical journals, government reports, decisions by other courts, and similar materials. The testifying expert's own assurance that her methods are reliable, however, is not sufficient to warrant a finding of reliability.

In Question 4 above we considered proposed testimony by an arson investigator who had concluded that a fire was intentionally set. In addition to the subject matter and qualifications issues we explored there, the government would have to show that the principles and methods employed by the witness were reliable in order for his testimony to be admissible. For example, the prosecution might have to show that the following were reliable: analysis of burn patterns; analysis based on the presence of certain chemicals in residue; the use of gas chromatography and mass spectrometry to isolate those chemicals; the theory that a two-origin fire suggests arson; and analysis based on the presence of "accelerants."

4. *Factual Basis for Opinions by Experts*

Rule 703 governs what constitutes an appropriate factual basis for an expert's opinion.

> **Rule 703. Bases of an Expert's Opinion Testimony**
> An expert may base an opinion on facts or data in the case that the expert has been made aware of or personally observed. If experts in the particular field would reasonably rely on those kinds of facts or data in forming an opinion on the subject, they need not be admissible for the opinion to be admitted. But if the facts or data would otherwise be inadmissible, the proponent of the opinion may disclose them to the jury only if their probative value in helping the jury evaluate the opinion substantially outweighs their prejudicial effect.

An expert may base her opinion on facts of which she has personal knowledge, facts made known to her at trial, or facts made known to her outside of the courtroom. An example of an expert opinion based on personal knowledge is the testimony of a surgeon who has operated on the plaintiff and now testifies about the plaintiff's injuries. Facts may be made known to the expert at trial either by allowing her to listen to the testimony of other witnesses, or by posing a hypothetical question to the expert based on the facts in evidence. The rules do not require the proponent to present the opinions of an expert by using hypothetical questions, but they do not prohibit it. The decision about whether to use hypothetical questions with an expert is up to the proponent. Facts may be presented to the expert outside the courtroom by giving the expert reports, records, deposition transcripts, photographs, or other materials to read or review.

The Federal Rules substantially broadened the type of facts that an expert can take into account in forming opinions. Rule 703 permits an expert to base an opinion on facts or data that are not admissible in evidence, "[i]f experts in the particular field would reasonably rely on those kinds of facts or data in forming an opinion on the subject." Among other things, an expert may rely on hearsay statements from sources who do not testify at trial, as long as experts in her field would consider reliance on that sort of information to be reasonable.

That an expert is allowed to base an opinion on inadmissible evidence creates a dilemma. In the ordinary course, both the proponent and the opponent of the expert's testimony would like the jury to know what facts the expert's opinion is based on. The proponent would like to be able to show the jury that the expert has a solid basis in fact for her opinion, and that her opinion is logically based on the facts considered. The opponent would like to argue just the opposite, namely that the expert's conclusions do not follow logically from the facts she reviewed. Where the expert has relied on material that would be inadmissible in evidence, there is a risk of unfair prejudice that comes from disclosing the material. The jury may not limit its use of the material to assessing the reasonableness of the expert's conclusions, but may assume that the underlying facts or data are true. Where those facts or data are inadmissible in evidence, this would be improper.

The Federal Rules respond to this dilemma in Rule 705.

Rule 705. Disclosing the Facts or Data Underlying an Expert's Opinion
Unless the court orders otherwise, an expert may state an opinion—and give the reasons for it—without first testifying to the underlying facts or data. But the expert may be required to disclose those facts or data on cross-examination.

As you can see, Rule 705 allows the proponent to ask an expert to state her opinions and the reasons for them, without first asking the witness to state the facts or data on which her opinions are based. It is not necessary for the proponent to refer to the inadmissible underlying facts or data the witness relied upon. The proponent may go directly to the witness's conclusions and opinions.

The rules permit the opponent, on cross-examination, to ask the witness what facts or data she relied upon. Whether the cross-examiner chooses to do that is a tactical matter. If cross-examination brings out the inadmissible evidence, the opponent may ask the court to give a limiting instruction, so that the jury is advised that it may not consider the underlying facts and data as substantive evidence.

What about the proponent? The proponent is probably not satisfied with jumping directly to the opinions by the expert without first introducing the material the expert considered in forming those opinions. The opinions are not as persuasive when they are divorced from their factual basis. The proponent can have the expert give a general description of the nature of the materials she considered in forming her opinion. For example, where a criminal defendant is making an insanity defense, a psychiatric expert could testify she interviewed members of the defendant's family, talked to his friends, and read the defendant's diary. But she could not testify about what the family members and friends said, or what she read in the diary, all of which would be hearsay if considered for its truth, without seeking a ruling by the court.

If we look back at the last sentence of Rule 703, we see that the proponent can disclose facts or data that constitute the basis for an opinion where they consist of inadmissible evidence, "only if their probative value in helping the jury evaluate the opinion substantially outweighs their prejudicial effect." In order to disclose the inadmissible evidence that the expert based her opinion on, the proponent must convince the judge that this balancing test has been met. The probative value of the disclosure is how much assistance knowing the basis for the opinion will assist the jury in evaluating the expert's conclusions (limited to that purpose the evidence in our example is not hearsay). The risk of unfair prejudice is the risk that the jury will not be able to follow the court's limiting instruction and will consider the underlying facts or data for their truth (for that purpose the evidence in the example would be hearsay).

QUESTION 5. The defendant is on trial for murder and has pleaded not guilty by reason of insanity. The defense calls two psychiatrists to testify that at the time of the incident the defendant was suffering from a crack cocaine-induced psychosis, with hallucinations and delusions. Psychiatrist No. 1 would testify that she could tell that the defendant's behavior was driven by cocaine-induced hallucinations simply by looking into his eyes. She has filed an affidavit stating that she has had great success with this method in the past and that it never fails. Psychiatrist No. 2 interviewed the defendant, gave him a battery of standard psychological tests, read his diary, and interviewed his family and friends. Based on all the information she gathered she reached her conclusions. Which of the following statements is not true?

A. The prosecution's objection to testimony from Psychiatrist No. 1 should be sustained.

B. The prosecution's objection to testimony from Psychiatrist No. 2 should be overruled.

C. On cross-examination by the prosecution Psychiatrist No. 2 can be required to relate what she read in the defendant's diary, what the defendant said to her, and what his family and friends told her.

D. Defense counsel must establish the factual basis for the conclusions reached by Psychiatrist No. 2 before asking her to state her diagnosis of the defendant.

ANALYSIS. Choice **A** is a true statement. Psychiatrist No. 1 employs an unusual methodology and the defense has provided no support for the reliability of her approach other than her own testimony. The judge will exclude her testimony. On the other hand, Psychiatrist No. 2 has employed an ordinary methodology that is generally accepted in her field. It is unlikely that the prosecution would object to her testimony on reliability grounds. If it did, it would be easy enough to support the reliability of her approach through application of the *Daubert* factors. Choice **B** is a true statement.

Psychiatrist No. 2 has relied on several statements that would constitute hearsay—the defendant's out of court statements, the diary, and statements from family and friends. We take up hearsay in the next chapter and so we will not analyze here why these statements are hearsay, or whether they could fall within any exceptions to the hearsay rule. Assuming they are hearsay and inadmissible, it is nonetheless permissible for the expert to rely on this material because it is the type of material psychiatrists generally and reasonably rely upon. Despite the fact that these statements are inadmissible in evidence, however, the opposing counsel has a right under Rule 705 to elicit this information on cross-examination. The prosecutor is entitled to show what Psychiatrist No. 2 relied upon in order to challenge the legitimacy of the conclusions she reached. Thus **C** is true. The statement in **D** is not true. Under Rule 705 the defense counsel does not have to bring out the basis for the expert's opinion before asking her to state her conclusions. In this case defense counsel could ask Psychiatrist No. 2 to give her diagnosis of the defendant without first disclosing the specific facts or data on which she based her opinion.

5. *Opinions on Ultimate Issues*

At common law neither lay witnesses nor experts were allowed to give an opinion on the ultimate issues in a case. Rule 704 has abandoned that absolute restriction.

> **Rule 704. Opinion on an Ultimate Issue**
>
> (a) **In General—Not Automatically Objectionable.** An opinion is not objectionable just because it embraces an ultimate issue.
>
> (b) **Exception.** In a criminal case, an expert witness must not state an opinion about whether the defendant did or did not have a mental state or condition that constitutes an element of the crime charged or of a defense. Those matters are for the trier of fact alone.

Under the Federal Rules an expert may give opinions that reach the ultimate issues in the case. For example, an expert may testify that a product was unreasonably dangerous, that poison caused the death of a victim, or that pilot error was the cause of an airline crash.

Despite Rule 704, however, there are still limits on what opinions an expert may give. We do not permit experts to express opinions that embrace legal conclusions. An expert may not testify that the plaintiff was "negligent," or that a criminal defendant was "guilty." Statements that come too close to legal conclusions are also inadmissible. A police officer may not testify, for example, that while conducting surveillance from a van with tinted windows he witnessed a "drug sale," because that in effect is a conclusion with respect to the defendant's guilt. It is the judge's role to instruct the jury on the law. If an expert expresses a legal conclusion, that conclusion inevitably includes a definition of what the law is. Such testimony by an expert invades the province of the court to determine the law.

Experts are also not permitted to express an opinion about whether a given witness has testified truthfully in the trial. For example, a doctor who examined a child who complained of sexual abuse may not testify that the child was telling the truth.

Section (b) creates an additional exception to Rule 704. In a criminal case an expert may not express an opinion about "whether the defendant did or did not have a mental state or condition that constitutes an element of the crime charged or of a defense."[5] The limitation in section (b) means that an expert may not testify that a defendant was legally insane at the time of his actions,

---

[5]   Congress added this exception to the rule after John Hinckley shot President Ronald Reagan and was found not guilty by reason of insanity.

or that as a result of a mental disease or defect he was unable to appreciate the wrongfulness of his conduct or to conform his conduct to the law. Nor could an expert testify that a defendant was mentally incapable of premeditation.

An expert may testify to a diagnosis of the defendant, for example, that he was suffering from paranoid schizophrenia at the time of the incident. The expert may describe the symptoms of paranoia and may explain the effect of hallucinations and delusions on the thought processes of someone who is mentally ill. The expert must leave it to the jury, however, to draw the ultimate conclusion that the defendant was legally insane.

6. *Court Appointed Experts*

Rule 706 authorizes the trial judge to appoint experts, either on its own or at the suggestion of one or more parties. Appointed experts must advise the parties of their findings, sit for a deposition by any party, appear to testify if called by a party, and may be cross-examined by any party, including the party who called the expert.

QUESTION 6. The Closer. The defendant is on trial for murder, charged with killing his wife. The prosecution contends that the defendant hit her over the head with a hammer near a large pond, about a mile from their home outside Boston. The defendant told the police that he went to look for his wife who had gone out for a walk. He said that he found her draped over a log, bleeding profusely from her head. At trial the potential witnesses include the pathologist who performed the autopsy, a psychiatrist who examined the defendant at the request of defense counsel, a police detective, and an oncologist who had been treating the wife for cancer. Which of the following is inadmissible?

A. Testimony from the pathologist based on his observations, training, and experience, that the cause of death was blunt trauma to the head.
B. Testimony from the psychiatrist that the defendant loved his wife.
C. Testimony from the detective based on his training at the FBI fingerprint school and his twenty years of experience that he lifted latent fingerprints from the handle of the hammer, but they did not match those of the defendant.
D. Testimony from the oncologist based on her observations of the deceased, medical records, and X-rays, that, despite the wound to the head, it was cancer that was the cause of death.

ANALYSIS. May the pathologist testify based on vicarious knowledge that he obtained during his training? Yes, because expert witnesses are not confined to testifying on the basis of personal knowledge, as otherwise required by Rule 602. Expertise in any subject builds upon the collected wisdom of that field. Choice **A** is admissible evidence. May the detective testify to his negative results—the absence of a match with respect to the fingerprints? Yes, negative results are as probative as positive results. The detective is a qualified fingerprint expert and his opinion is helpful to the jury in determining whether there is a reasonable doubt as to the defendant's guilt. Choice **C** is admissible in evidence. Is the oncologist's testimony barred because she is expressing an opinion on the ultimate issue of whether it was the blunt trauma or the cancer that caused the death of the victim? No, under Rule 704 the fact that her opinion embraces an ultimate issue in the case does not render it inadmissible. Choice **D** is admissible evidence. The subject matter of the proposed testimony by the psychiatrist is not scientific, technical, or other specialized knowledge. The psychiatrist cannot tell us, as an expert, whether the defendant truly loved his wife. Nor could the psychiatrist testify that the defendant would be telling the truth if defendant stated he loves his wife. Choice **B** is inadmissible.

 ## Avery's Picks

1. Question 1   **A**
2. Question 2   **C**
3. Question 3   **A**
4. Question 4   **D**
5. Question 5   **D**
6. Question 6   **B**

8

Hearsay

CHAPTER OVERVIEW

A. Definition of Hearsay
   1. Assertions
   2. The Purpose for Which a Party Offers a Statement
   3. Statements That Can Be Offered Both to Prove the Truth of an Assertion and for a Different Purpose
   4. When the Witness Is Testifying About Something She Said Out of Court

B. Exceptions to the Hearsay Rule
   1. Multiple Hearsay
   2. Statements Defined as Non-Hearsay by the Rules
      a. Former Statements
         (1) Inconsistent Statements
         (2) Consistent Statements
         (3) Statements of Identification of a Person
      b. Statement by Party Opponent
   3. Exceptions Under Rule 803
      a. Present Sense Impression and Excited Utterance
      b. State of Mind, Emotions, or Physical Condition
      c. Statements Made to Obtain Medical Diagnosis or Treatment
      d. Recorded Recollection
      e. Business Records
      f. Public Records
      g. Vital Statistics
      h. Absence of Records
      i. Ancient Documents
      j. Market Reports and Commercial Publications
      k. Learned Treatises
      l. Reputation Concerning Character

Most people, whether lawyers or not, know that witnesses are not supposed to testify to "hearsay." Most non-lawyers would not, however, be able to define the term. The average person probably believes that hearsay is equivalent to rumors, as suggested by the popular expression, "That's just hearsay," often used to reject facts when there is no source provided for the information. Knowledge of the legal definitions of hearsay and the hearsay exceptions is limited to lawyers and law students who have studied Evidence. There is no need, however, to mystify the concept. Anyone who learns a few simple definitions and takes a logical approach to the analysis can master the subject. We show you how in this chapter.

Throughout this chapter, remember that under Rule 104(a) the judge determines whether an out of court statement is hearsay and whether the proponent has established the foundation for any exemption from or exception to the hearsay rule.

A. Definition of Hearsay

Hearsay is defined as an out of court statement offered to prove the truth of an assertion made in the statement. By "out of court" we mean a statement not made on the witness stand in the current trial or hearing. The statement might have been made in a courtroom some other time, for example, in a previous trial, but we consider it an "out of court" statement if it was not made on the witness stand in the current proceeding. "Out of court" statements include those the witness herself has made on other occasions.

Here are a couple of simple examples of hearsay statements. Suppose the prosecutor in a murder case calls a witness to testify about a conversation with her sister concerning a shooting the sister saw. The prosecutor asks the witness, "What did your sister tell you about the shooter?" The witness's answer, "My sister said the defendant shot the victim," is hearsay. The sister's statement was not made on the witness stand in this case, it contains an assertion, and the prosecutor is offering it to prove the truth of the assertion, namely, that the defendant shot the victim.

For a second example, suppose that an eyewitness testified at a murder trial five years ago that she saw the defendant shoot the victim. The defendant was convicted, but appealed and won a new trial. In the meantime, the eyewitness has died. At the new trial, the prosecutor offers the transcript of the eyewitness's testimony at the first trial. The testimony was not given on the witness stand in this proceeding, it contains an assertion, and the prosecution is offering it to prove that assertion, namely, that the defendant shot the victim. The transcript is hearsay. (You will learn that there is an exception to the hearsay rule for previous testimony such as this, but we will talk about that when we get to exceptions. For now it is important to recognize that the transcript of previous testimony falls within the definition of hearsay.)

To get deeper into this, let's look at Rule 801, which provides the applicable definitions that separate hearsay from other "out of court" statements.

> **Rule 801. Definitions That Apply to This Article; Exclusions from Hearsay**
>
> (a) **Statement**. "Statement" means a person's oral assertion, written assertion, or nonverbal conduct, if the person intended it as an assertion.
>
> (b) **Declarant**. "Declarant" means the person who made the statement.
>
> (c) **Hearsay**. "Hearsay" means a statement that:
>
> (1) the declarant does not make while testifying at the current trial or hearing; and
>
> (2) a party offers in evidence to prove the truth of the matter asserted in the statement.

We use the term "witness" to refer to the person on the witness stand at the trial, and the term "declarant" to refer to the person who made the out of court statement. When the witness testifies about something the declarant said or did, it will be hearsay if: (1) the declarant intended to make an assertion, and (2) the party offering the evidence is doing so in order to prove the truth of the assertion.

It is important to have a reliable method you can use to apply the rules to an out of court statement to determine whether something is hearsay. If you try to jump immediately to the bottom line of whether hearsay is present, you will often get the wrong answer. Instead, follow these simple steps in this order:

(1) Identify the words or conduct in question.
(2) Identify the declarant.
(3) Determine whether the declarant intended to make an assertion.
(4) If there is an assertion, determine whether the party is offering the evidence to establish the truth of the assertion, or for a different reason.

Let's go back to the first example we mentioned above—the witness who would testify to what her sister told her about a shooting. In that example, the words in question are, "The defendant shot the victim." The declarant is the witness's sister. She intended to make an assertion, and the prosecutor is offering it for the purpose of proving that assertion, namely, that the defendant shot the victim.

At the beginning, students often confuse the issues in steps 3 and 4. It is important to recognize that they are separate questions. Step 3 asks whether the declarant intended to make an assertion. Step 4 asks for what purpose the party is offering the evidence. To keep these things straight, remember that it is the declarant's intent that determines whether there was an assertion (step 3), but it is the intent of the lawyer offering the evidence that determines for what purpose it is offered (step 4).

1. Assertions

An oral or written assertion is simply a declaration or allegation of a fact or opinion. The assertion need not be expressed in a declarative sentence; it may be made or implied in a question or an exclamation as well. All of the following are assertions: "There is a pothole in front of you." "Do you see the pothole in front of you?" "Look out for the pothole in front of you!" Both the question and the exclamation imply the existence of the pothole and thus are assertive.

You don't need words to make a statement. Nonverbal conduct is a "statement" if the declarant intends for his conduct to be assertive. A nod of the head, a wink, a gesture, or any other physical conduct may be intended to convey an assertion. If someone flies a flag at half-mast to honor a person who recently died, the conduct of flying a flag at half-mast is an assertion that the flag owner respects the person who died.

The issue with respect to nonverbal conduct is whether the declarant has taken an action for its own sake, that is, to accomplish some purpose inherent in the act, or whether he has taken the action to communicate an assertion. Do not be confused by the fact that conduct may have meaning whether or not the person who engaged in the conduct intended to make an assertion. We may infer something an actor thought from his conduct, but that does not mean that he intended to make an assertion.

For example, if the captain of a ship assigns a particular sailor to be a lookout, we may infer that the captain believed that sailor had good eyesight. The captain, however, did not assign the sailor to be the lookout in order to communicate his opinion of the sailor's eyesight; he assigned him to the post to get the job done. In this example the nonverbal conduct was not for the purpose of making an assertion.

QUESTION 1. A murder victim was hacked to death with a machete. The defendant is on trial for the murder. Which, if any, of the following pieces of evidence contains an assertion that defendant owns a machete?

A. A witness will testify that defendant's mother said, "My son has a machete."

B. A police officer will testify that she went to the defendant's home and asked his mother, "Does your son have a machete?" The officer will testify that without saying a word, the mother went to another room in the house and came back and handed the officer a machete.

C. The defendant's neighbor will testify that the defendant's mother came to her house and asked, "Did you borrow my son's machete? I can't find it anywhere."

D. None of the above.

E. All of the above.

ANALYSIS.   The defendant's mother is the declarant in **A, B,** and **C.** In **A,** she makes a simple declaration that her son has a machete; this is an assertion. In **B,** she uses no words, but her nonverbal behavior is intended to answer the officer's question affirmatively and constitutes an assertion that the machete she hands over belongs to her son. In **C,** although framed as a question, her words constitute an assertion that her son has a machete. The correct answer is **E.**

QUESTION 2. Plaintiff was injured while riding in the defendant's car when the defendant lost control of the vehicle and was unable to stop before he ran into a tree. Defendant claims that the plaintiff assumed the risk of riding in the car, because plaintiff was with him an hour before the accident when he picked his car up at the garage and the mechanic said to the defendant, "Those brakes are nearly shot." If the defendant testifies to what the mechanic said, is there an out of court assertion?

A. No, because the statement was made to the defendant, not the plaintiff.

B. Yes.

ANALYSIS.   Here there is a simple declaration by the mechanic that the defendant's brakes were "nearly shot." It does not matter to whom the statement was made. The question we must focus on is whether, under the circumstances, the mechanic, who is the declarant, intended to make an assertion. Clearly he did, and it is not significant that the plaintiff was merely a bystander. **B** is the correct answer.

QUESTION 3. Defendant is on trial for possession of marijuana with intent to sell. He admits that he was the owner of the marijuana that the police found in his dormitory room, but claims it was for his personal use. The prosecutor called a witness to testify that the defendant told him the day before his arrest that if he had any marijuana to sell, he would hang a necktie on the handle of the door to his room. A neighbor in the dorm is prepared to testify that the night before the arrest he saw the defendant hang a necktie on the door handle. Was there an assertion?

A. No, the defendant did not make any statement.
B. Yes.

ANALYSIS. In this case the defendant has not made any verbal statements, oral or written. If he had simply left a necktie or other clothing on the door handle or lying around in his room because he was messy, there would be no statement. But here the evidence from another witness established that leaving a necktie on the handle to the door was a signal that the defendant had marijuana to sell. Under these circumstances it is apparent that the defendant engaged in the conduct in question intending to make an assertion. It is as though he put a sign on his door that said, "I have marijuana to sell." The correct answer is **B**; there was an assertion.

QUESTION 4. The defendant is on trial for the murder of the victim. The defendant had been having an affair with the victim. The defendant's theory of the case is that the victim's wife killed him. To prove that the wife was home at the time of the murder, defendant offers the testimony of a neighbor that the victim never shoveled snow due to a back injury, and that his wife invariably did all the snow shoveling. The neighbor would testify that it snowed heavily on the night that victim was killed and that she observed that the walk in front of the victim's home was freshly shoveled at least twice during the evening hours, although she did not see who did it. Is the neighbor testifying about an assertion?

A. Yes, shoveling the sidewalk was an assertion that the victim's wife was home.
B. No.

ANALYSIS. In cases of nonverbal conduct, it is particularly important to identify the conduct in question and the declarant. Here the conduct is shoveling the snow, and the person who did it would have been the victim's wife, so she would be the declarant. Did she do so in order to make an assertion that she was home? No. She shoveled the walk to clear away the snow and make the sidewalk safe. In other words, she engaged in the conduct in question for its own sake, not to communicate anything. Shoveling snow was not intended to be a signal, unlike hanging the necktie on the doorknob in the previous question. Therefore **A** is incorrect, and the correct answer is **B**, there was no assertion.

2. The Purpose for Which a Party Offers a Statement

There are several purposes for which parties may offer out of court statements, other than to prove the truth of assertions in the statements. Whether another purpose is relevant will depend upon substantive law. Such evidence questions cannot be resolved in the abstract. It is essential to consider the elements of the cause of action or crime that is being tried.

For example, in the last question in the preceding section, we said that the mechanic's statement, "Those brakes are nearly shot," contained an assertion. For what purpose other than the truth of the assertion could the defendant owner of the car offer this evidence? If tort law in his jurisdiction recognizes the doctrine, his defense to the plaintiff's case could be assumption of the risk. Then he would offer the mechanic's statement to show that the plaintiff heard it and chose to ride in the car despite his awareness of the risk of doing so. The plaintiff had *notice* of the possible defective condition of the brakes, and thus assumed the risk of riding in the car. If offered for that purpose, the statement is not hearsay. Notice is a frequent purpose for offering statements that takes them outside the hearsay rule.

Another common purpose for offering out of court statements is that making the statements has independent legal significance that does not depend on their truth. The words have operative significance that renders them legal acts. For example, the words that constitute an offer and an acceptance result in the formation of a contract. Words that are false and defamatory constitute the tort of defamation, for example, the false statement, "Jones is a thief." Uttering certain words, for example a threat, may constitute a crime. If words constitute the formation of a contract, or are tortious, or amount to a criminal act, then we consider them to be a *verbal act* and offering them to prove the existence of a contract, tort, or crime is not hearsay.

We also might offer words as circumstantial evidence of the state of mind of the person who speaks them. For example, imagine that a teacher walks into class the first day and says to the students, "Good morning, I am Napoleon Bonaparte." If someone later starts proceedings to have the teacher committed to a mental hospital and a student testifies to what the teacher said, that would not be hearsay. The words are not offered to prove that the teacher is Napoleon. On the contrary, they are offered to prove that the teacher is delusional.

When the proponent offers an out of court statement that contains an assertion, the opponent can be expected to object on hearsay grounds. In order to rule on the objection, the judge must determine the purpose for which the proponent is offering the evidence. Typically the judge will do this by asking counsel what the purpose of the offer is.

Here is a typical colloquy that demonstrates the process. Plaintiff has a police officer on the witness stand in an automobile accident case.

> Plaintiff's counsel: Officer, what did the eyewitness say to you when you
> were investigating the accident?

Defense counsel:	Objection, your Honor, hearsay.
The court:	Counsel, approach the side bar.
The court:	Plaintiff's counsel, what do you expect the answer will be?
Plaintiff's counsel:	Your Honor, I expect him to say that the eyewitness told him the BMW (which was the defendant's car) ran the red light.
The court:	For what purpose are you offering this evidence?
Plaintiff's counsel:	To prove the light was red for the defendant.
The court:	Objection sustained.

If plaintiff's counsel were offering the evidence for a different purpose, he would have to advise the judge of that. Consider this example from a "slip and fall" case, where plaintiff alleges that she fell on some salad oil on the floor of the defendant's supermarket. A witness who was in the store at the time is on the stand.

Plaintiff's counsel:	Did you happen to hear any conversation between any other customer and the store manager before the plaintiff's accident?
Witness:	Yes.
Plaintiff's counsel:	What did the customer say to the store manager?
Defense counsel:	Objection, your Honor, hearsay.
The court:	Counsel, approach the side bar.
The court:	Plaintiff's counsel, what do you expect the answer will be?
Plaintiff's counsel:	Your Honor, I expect she will say that she overheard another customer tell the store manager that there was salad oil on the floor of aisle three.
The court:	What is the purpose for which you are offering this testimony?
Plaintiff's counsel:	We are not offering it to prove that the salad oil was on the floor, your Honor. We have other evidence that will show that. We are offering this testimony only to show that the manager was on notice that there might be salad oil on the floor. Other evidence will show that he took no action, and that is what we say constituted the negligence in this case.
The court:	Objection overruled. I'll give an appropriate limiting instruction.

In this example, the words in question are "There is salad oil on the floor of aisle three." The declarant is the customer who made that statement to the manager, and she intended to make an assertion. But here the proponent provides the court with a relevant purpose for the evidence other than to prove that assertion, namely, to show that the manager had notice of a potential problem. Thus, the evidence is not hearsay.

Let's look at some other situations to explore the purposes for which out of court statements containing assertions might be offered.

QUESTION 5. A murder victim was hacked to death with a machete. Defendant is on trial for the murder. The prosecution calls a witness who would testify that she heard the defendant's mother say that her son owns a machete. Is the witness's testimony hearsay?

A. No, because she is not testifying to any assertions.
B. No, because the prosecution is trying to prove that Defendant killed the victim, not that he owned a machete, so the testimony is not offered to prove the truth of any assertions.
C. Yes, the prosecution is offering the evidence to prove the truth of the mother's assertion.

ANALYSIS.   First we identify the words in question, "My son owns a machete." The declarant is the defendant's mother. Did she intend to make an assertion? Yes, that her son owned a machete; therefore **A** is incorrect. For what purpose did the prosecutor offer this evidence? Choice **B** represents a mistake that students frequently make when they are first learning about hearsay—it confuses the prosecution's ultimate goal (proving that the defendant killed the victim) with the specific purpose of offering this piece of evidence. The issue in analyzing hearsay is what the specific purpose of this item of evidence is, which is usually just a step toward the party's final goal. Here the purpose is to show that the defendant owned a machete and thus had the means to commit the crime. The evidence is offered to prove the truth of the mother's assertion and therefore is hearsay. Choice **C** is correct.

QUESTION 6. The defendant, Mr. Driscoll, lives in Minneapolis. The plaintiff, a ten-year-old boy, delivers the afternoon paper. Plaintiff claims that he fell and broke his leg when he slipped on ice on the front walk of defendant's home while delivering his paper. Defendant denies there was any ice on his sidewalk and says that Plaintiff fell while running during a snowball fight with his friends. At the trial, plaintiff calls defendant's neighbor to testify that from her living room she heard someone outside yell on the afternoon of plaintiff's injury, "Hey, Mr. Driscoll. You better get that ice off your front walk." The neighbor could not see defendant's front walk herself from inside her house. Is the testimony hearsay?

A. Yes.
B. No, because the declarant's words are not a "statement."

> **C.** No, because plaintiff is not offering the testimony to prove the truth of an assertion.
>
> **D.** The correct answer depends upon the purpose for which plaintiff is offering the evidence.

ANALYSIS.   "Hey, Mr. Driscoll. You better get that ice off your front walk," are the words in question and the person who said them is the declarant. Choice **B** may be a tempting answer, because declarant's words are in the form of an imperative, rather than a simple declaratory statement. But whether words contain an assertion does not depend upon the form of a sentence. Here declarant's words certainly convey the assertion that there is ice on defendant's walk, and thus **B** is not correct.

If plaintiff were offering the testimony to prove that there was ice, it would be hearsay. There is a different purpose for which the evidence might be offered, however—to show that defendant had notice that there was ice on his sidewalk at the time in question. If the evidence were offered for that purpose, it would not be hearsay. As is often the case, the judge needs to be told for which purpose the plaintiff is offering the evidence before she can rule on whether it is hearsay, and thus the correct answer is **D**.

QUESTION 7. In a drug case against a single defendant, the government seeks to prove that he was the supplier of cocaine to a group of men who sold it on the street. It offers as an exhibit a page from the address book of one of the men containing defendant's address and cell number. How should the court rule on defendant's objection?

A. Exclude the evidence because it is hearsay.

B. Exclude the evidence because it is not relevant.

C. Admit the exhibit because it does not contain any assertions.

D. Admit the exhibit because it is not hearsay.

ANALYSIS.   The words in question are defendant's address and cell number and the owner of the address book is the declarant. Did he intend to make any assertions? Yes, namely that defendant lives at a certain address and has a certain cell phone number. Therefore **C** is incorrect.

In thinking about whether there is a purpose for this evidence other than proving those assertions, you must determine whether the exhibit has any other relevance and, if so, what it is. The entries show that defendant's address and number were of interest to the owner of the address book. That makes it more likely that defendant was the cocaine supplier than it would be if the seller did not have his contact information. The address book page, therefore, is relevant (which means we can rule out **B** as the answer), and for a purpose other than proving the truth of the assertions in the entry. The government is not trying to prove where defendant lives or what his number is, but merely that there was an entry in the defendant's address book for defendant. Therefore the evidence is not hearsay and the court should admit the exhibit. **D** is the correct answer.

QUESTION 8. The defendant is charged with soliciting an act of prostitution. The prosecutor calls a police officer who testifies that while working undercover he drove into a neighborhood where prostitutes were suspected of working. He slowed down and a provocatively clad woman, the defendant, approached his car. He rolled down the window and said, "Hey there." The officer would testify that she said, "I'll have sex with you for two hundred dollars." Is the officer's testimony about what she said hearsay?

A. Yes, the defendant's statements are offered for the truth of an assertion.
B. No, there was no assertion.
C. No, there was a verbal act.

ANALYSIS. The declarant is the defendant and the words in question are, "I'll have sex with you for two hundred dollars." The words amount to an assertion, and so **B** is incorrect. But the mere uttering of these words constitutes a crime, whether or not the assertion is true. The prosecution has charged the defendant with soliciting prostitution, not committing an act of prostitution. Inviting the witness to have sex for money is a completed crime. This is a verbal act and not hearsay. Thus **C** is the correct answer.

Choice **A** is incorrect because the defendant's words would constitute the commission of a crime even if the defendant did not intend to have sex with the witness, but merely to rob him once she got him in a private space. The prosecution is not offering the words to prove that they were true, merely that they were spoken, and hence the crime of solicitation was committed.

3. Statements That Can Be Offered Both to Prove the Truth of an Assertion and for a Different Purpose

Often out of court statements are capable of being used both to prove the truth of an assertion, and for another purpose. In such cases, there is a risk that the jury might use the statement for its truth, even though the proponent is not offering it for that purpose. Ordinarily the judge controls that risk by giving the jury a limiting instruction under FRE 105, explicitly advising them that the statement does not constitute evidence of the truth of the assertion. If the opponent does not believe a limiting instruction will be effective, he should object on the ground that the risk of unfair prejudice (the risk the jury will use the statement to prove the assertion) would substantially outweigh the probative value of the evidence (the significance of the other purpose for which the evidence is offered).

For example, imagine that the colloquy in the salad oil case we discussed previously had continued as follows after the Judge said he would admit the evidence and give a limiting instruction:

Defense counsel: Your Honor, we object under Rule 403 on the ground that the risk of unfair prejudice substantially outweighs the probative value of this evidence. We think, with all respect, that the jury will not be able to follow your limiting instruction and will use the customer's statement to conclude there actually was salad oil on the floor.

The court: Overruled. From the pretrial memorandum, I know that the plaintiff has substantial other evidence that there was salad oil on the floor, so the risk that the jury will use this evidence for that purpose is not significant. The real issue in this case is what the manager knew, and the probative value of this evidence on that score is high.

QUESTION 9. In an employment discrimination case, the female plaintiff has sued the company that employed her for sexual harassment committed by a male co-worker. Plaintiff plans to testify that she told the supervisor of her division that the male co-worker repeatedly touched her inappropriately, made offensive sexual remarks and constantly interfered with her ability to do her work. Is her testimony hearsay?

A. No, if offered to prove that the supervisor had notice of her allegations.

B. No, if offered to prove that the male co-worker sexually harassed her.

C. No, and it may be offered to prove both that the supervisor had notice and that the male co-worker harassed her.

D. Yes, and it is inadmissible regardless of the purpose for which it is offered.

ANALYSIS.   The words in question are what the plaintiff said to the supervisor about the male co-worker's actions. Plaintiff is the declarant. She intended to assert that the male co-worker engaged in the behavior described. If offered to prove that he engaged in that behavior, it would be hearsay, thus **B** and **C** are incorrect. However, if plaintiff offered this evidence merely to show that the supervisor had notice of her claims, it would not be for the purpose of proving the truth of the assertions and therefore not hearsay. Thus **A** is correct and **D** is incorrect.

The court could give a limiting instruction that this evidence can only be used to prove notice to the supervisor and not to prove that the male co-worker committed the harassment. What if the defendant objects that the limiting instruction is not likely to be effective and the risk of unfair prejudice substantially outweighs probative value? The risk of unfair prejudice is the likelihood that the jury will use this testimony to find that the male co-worker sexually harassed the plaintiff. In this case, that is not very likely. Plaintiff is on the stand. She can testify about what her co-worker did to her directly, without putting it in the context of what she told the supervisor. The jury is going to hear her allegations against the male co-worker in any event, so there is virtually no risk of unfair prejudice in allowing her to testify that she told the supervisor about them. On the other hand, that the supervisor had notice is highly probative in plaintiff's case against the company. The judge should overrule the defendant's objection.

4. When the Witness Is Testifying About Something She Said Out of Court

Sometimes a witness is testifying about something that she said on an earlier occasion. In other words, the witness and the declarant are the same person. Where the witness is quoting his or her own words, is the earlier statement hearsay? With some exceptions, the answer is yes, if the statement contains an assertion and the party is offering it to prove the truth of the assertion. The exceptions are for certain prior inconsistent statements, certain prior consistent statements, and statements of identification of another person. The exceptions are set forth in FRE Rule 801(d)(1), and are discussed in the next section.

QUESTION 10. The witness is a fourteen-year-old boy who saw a drive-by shooting in which one of his neighbors was killed. The witness got a good look as the car slowed down, the shooter leaned out of his window, gun in hand, and fired three shots into the unarmed neighbor from a distance of about ten feet. He told the police what he saw and is willing to describe the incident in court. At trial, the witness begins by testifying that there was a shooting incident while he was walking home from school and the police came. The prosecutor asks him what he said to the police officer about the shooting. How should the court rule on the defendant's objection to that question?

A. Sustain the objection, hearsay.
B. Overrule the objection—he is not expected to make assertions.
C. Overrule the objection—the prosecution is not offering his testimony to prove the truth of any assertions he made to the police officer.
D. Overruled—not hearsay because the witness is on the stand and can be cross-examined.

ANALYSIS.   The words in question are what the witness said to the officer. The witness was the declarant. Choice **D** may be a tempting answer. The witness could be cross-examined about what he said to the police officer. But the Federal Rules do not define hearsay in terms of the absence, in the ordinary case, of an opportunity to cross-examine the declarant. They define hearsay by asking whether the declarant made an assertion and whether the proponent is offering the evidence to prove the assertion. **D** is incorrect. Here the witness's statement to the officer of how the shooter killed the victim contains several assertions (the shooter acted deliberately, fired from a close distance, and the victim was unarmed), and the prosecution is offering the evidence in order to prove them. Thus **B** and **C** are incorrect, and the correct answer is **A**. To get the witness's story admitted, the prosecutor should simply ask him what happened, rather than asking what he told the police officer.

B.   Exceptions to the Hearsay Rule

There are three sources for exceptions to or exemptions from the hearsay rule. Rule 801(d) defines certain statements as not hearsay, and exempts them from the bar against hearsay. Rule 803 lists hearsay exceptions that can be used whether or not the declarant is available to testify. Rule 804 contains hearsay exceptions that can only be invoked when the declarant's testimony is not available.

Remember, whenever you are confronted with an out of court statement, you should always first determine whether it is hearsay. Once you have determined that the statement is hearsay, analyze whether the statement falls within an exception to the hearsay rule.

1. Multiple Hearsay

Some statements contain multiple declarants and multiple potential assertions. In other words, one out of court statement contains one or more other out of court statements. Rule 805 governs this situation.

> **Rule 805. Hearsay Within Hearsay**
> Hearsay within hearsay is not excluded by the rule against hearsay if each part of the combined statements conforms with an exception to the rule.

Suppose the witness on the stand in a murder case testifies, "David told me that Dana told him that she saw the defendant shoot the victim." That is multiple hearsay. In any multiple hearsay problem, it is essential to carefully identify each of the declarants and what that person said or did. Here the two declarants are David and Dana. Dana said, "I saw the defendant shoot the victim." David said, "Dana told me she saw the defendant shoot the victim." Each declarant made an assertion, and we may assume that the prosecutor is offering each statement for the truth of its assertion. For the witness's testimony to be admissible there would have to be an exception for each declarant.

Some instructional materials tell students to look for an exception for each level of hearsay. Analyzing "levels" of hearsay is not really helpful. It is much easier and more reliable to analyze these problems by identifying all the declarants, and determining whether there is an exception for each declarant.

A potential case of multiple hearsay may actually have only one hearsay statement, because only one of the assertions may be offered for its truth. For example, in a defamation case, a witness testifies, "My neighbor told me that the defendant said that the plaintiff cheated on an exam, and I lost a lot of respect for the plaintiff." The declarants are the neighbor and the defendant. The declarant neighbor said to the witness, "The defendant said the plaintiff cheated on an exam." That statement contains an assertion, and if plaintiff were offering it to prove that is what the defendant said, then it would be hearsay. The declarant defendant said, "The plaintiff cheated on an exam." That statement contains an assertion, but in this defamation case the plaintiff is not offering to prove that the assertion was true. Indeed, the plaintiff claims the assertion was false and defamatory. The statement by the defendant is a verbal act and not hearsay. For the witness's testimony to be admissible, it would only be necessary to find an exception for the declarant neighbor.

We will examine some multiple hearsay statements below as we work through the various exceptions and exemptions to the hearsay rule.

2. Statements Defined as Non-Hearsay by the Rules

a. Former Statements   Rule 801(d) provides:

> **(d) Statements That Are Not Hearsay**. A statement that meets the following conditions is not hearsay:
>> **(1) A Declarant-Witness's Prior Statement**. The declarant testifies and is subject to cross-examination about a prior statement, and the statement:
>>> **(A)** is inconsistent with the declarant's testimony and was given under penalty of perjury at a trial, hearing, or other proceeding or in a deposition;
>>> **(B)** is consistent with the declarant's testimony and is offered:
>>>> **(i)** to rebut an express or implied charge that the declarant recently fabricated it or acted from a recent improper influence or motive in so testifying; or
>>>> **(ii)** to rehabilitate the declarant's credibility as a witness when attacked on another ground; or
>>> **(C)** identifies a person as someone the declarant perceived earlier.

For Rule 801(d) to apply the declarant must testify at the proceeding and the opponent must have an opportunity to cross-examine the declarant about the statement. The fact that the declarant made the previous statement may be proved through the testimony of the declarant or other evidence.

Statements described in Rule 801(d) would ordinarily be considered hearsay, in that they contain assertions and are offered in evidence to prove the truth of those assertions. The drafters of the Federal Rules, however, decided to define them as "not hearsay." The Rules treat them as exemptions from the bar against hearsay.[1]

(1) Inconsistent Statements   Rule 801(d)(1)(A) treats prior inconsistent statements of the declarant under oath at a formal proceeding differently from other prior inconsistent statements. Under Rule 613, in the ordinary course the cross-examiner may use an inconsistent statement to show that a witness has made a contradictory statement at a different time only to demonstrate unreliability and to impeach the witness's credibility. The cross-examiner may not use the previous statement to prove the truth of what it asserted. Under Rule 801(d)(1)(A), if the declarant made the prior inconsistent statement subject to the penalty of perjury at a formal proceeding, he or she testifies at the current proceeding, and is now subject to cross-examination, the previous inconsistent statement may be introduced to prove its truth.

QUESTION 11. A witness testifies at a drive-by shooting murder trial that she saw the defendant at the wheel of the car and saw him shoot the victim with a handgun through the open window. The prosecutor does not ask her how many people were in the car. Before beginning cross-examination, the defense lawyer offers to introduce the witness's grand jury testimony that there were three people in the car. The defense theory is that one of the others was actually the shooter. The prosecutor's objection should be:

A. Overruled, but the court should give a limiting instruction that the statement may only be used to show the existence of an inconsistent story under Rule 613.
B. Overruled, the statement is admissible under Rule 801(d)(1)(A).
C. Sustained, hearsay.

ANALYSIS.   The witness was the declarant and the defense lawyer is seeking to use her grand jury testimony to prove the truth of her assertion that there were three people in the car. She has testified at the trial and is available for cross-examination, even though the cross-examination has not begun. She gave her previous statement under oath at a formal proceeding. Thus, if the defense lawyer were offering an inconsistent statement it would be admissible to prove its truth. **B** would be the correct answer, and there would be no need for a limiting instruction as provided in **A**. However, the previous statement is

---

1. Not all states that have adopted the Federal Rules have adopted these exemptions from the hearsay rule.

not inconsistent with her trial testimony; it merely includes additional details that do not contradict what she said on direct examination. Because there is no inconsistency, the statement does not fall within Rule 801(d)(1)(A). Because the defense lawyer is offering the previous statement for the truth of its assertion, the statement is hearsay. Choice **C** is correct.

If the defense lawyer had begun by asking the witness how many people were in the car and she testified there was only one, then her grand jury testimony would be inconsistent with her trial testimony. Under those circumstances, the defense could offer the grand jury testimony for its truth under Rule 801(d)(1)(A).

QUESTION 12. Plaintiff sues defendant for damages in tort, alleging that defendant ran a red light and ran her over as she was crossing the street in the crosswalk. At trial defendant calls a witness who testifies that defendant had the green light when he entered the intersection. On cross-examination, plaintiff offers to introduce the witness's deposition, in which he testified under oath that defendant had the red light. The court's ruling should be:

A. Sustained, hearsay.
B. Overruled, the statement is admissible under Rule 801(d)(1)(A).
C. Overruled, but the court should give a limiting instruction that the statement may only be used to show the existence of an inconsistent story under Rule 613.

ANALYSIS.   The witness was the declarant and the plaintiff is offering the assertion in his deposition testimony to prove that it was true that the defendant had a red light. The statement is not hearsay, however, because the witness was under oath at a formal proceeding when he made a prior statement inconsistent with his trial testimony, he has testified at the trial, and he is subject to cross-examination concerning the deposition testimony. **A** is incorrect and **B** is the correct answer. Because the requirements of Rule 801(d)(1)(A) are met, the evidence is not subject to the limiting instruction described in **C**.

QUESTION 13. After a shooting in a bar, the police interview an eyewitness at the police station. They take a sworn statement from him, which is videotaped and taken down by a stenographer. The witness states that he saw defendant shoot the victim. At trial the prosecutor calls the witness and he testifies that he saw the defendant in the bar, but a stranger that he had never seen before or since was the shooter. The prosecutor then offers the videotaped sworn statement in evidence and defense counsel objects. The objection should be:

A. Sustained, hearsay.

> **B.** Overruled, the statement is admissible under Rule 801(d)(1)(A).
> **C.** Overruled, but the court should give a limiting instruction that the statement may only be used to show the existence of an inconsistent story under Rule 613.

ANALYSIS.   The witness was the declarant and the prosecutor might be offering his videotaped statement to prove the truth of his assertion that defendant shot the victim. If so, it would be hearsay, and **A** would be correct. The witness's previous statement is inconsistent with his trial testimony. It does not come within Rule 801(d)(1)(A), however, because courts would not consider an interview in the police station to be the sort of formal proceeding contemplated by the rule, even though the witness was sworn and a stenographer was present. Choice **B** is therefore incorrect. The prosecutor could offer the statement merely to impeach the witness under Rule 613. Choice **C** is the correct answer. If the statement is admitted with a limiting instruction that it cannot be used to prove that defendant shot the victim, it is not hearsay and therefore **A** is incorrect. Remember, under Rule 607 a party may impeach its own witness.

(2) Consistent Statements   Ordinarily a witness is not allowed to testify that she has made previous statements consistent with her trial testimony. If a party offers previous consistent statements on direct examination in order to vouch for the credibility of the witness, they are considered hearsay and are inadmissible.

If the opponent, however, has attacked the credibility of the witness, part (B) of the rule provides that consistent statements may be admissible in two circumstances. Under section (1), if the opponent suggested that the witness has recently made the story up, or is testifying for an improper motive or under an improper influence, the proponent may offer a prior consistent statement to be admitted to prove the truth of the statement. The previous statement need not have been under oath, or made at a formal proceeding. The Supreme Court has ruled, however, that the prior consistent statement is only admissible if it was made before the motive to fabricate arose or the improper influence was brought to bear on the witness.[2] Under section (2), the proponent may offer a prior consistent statement to rehabilitate the declarant's credibility if attacked on another ground, such as an inconsistency in the witness's testimony, or a charge of a faulty memory.[3] Prior consistent statements offered under either section (1) or (2) are admissible as substantive evidence of the assertions in the statements, not merely for rehabilitation.

---

2. *Tome v. United States*, 513 U.S. 150 (1995).
3. Section (2) was added by amendment in 2014.

QUESTION 14. Roger Rat robbed a bank with another man. When they were arrested, Rat made a deal with the prosecutor to become a cooperating witness and testify against his accomplice. At the accomplice's trial, Rat testified that he was only the getaway driver, and the accomplice entered the bank and shot the bank guard. On cross-examination, accomplice's defense counsel brought out that the prosecution had promised to drop the charges against Rat, put him in the witness protection program, and set him up with a new identity and employment. The defense lawyer suggested that Rat had made up the story against her client in order to please the government and get a good deal for himself. The prosecutor then called Rat's brother to testify that before he knew he was suspected of involvement in the robbery, Rat had confessed his participation in the robbery to him, supplying the same details about his participation and that of the accomplice he had testified to in court. The defendant's objection should be:

A. Sustained, hearsay.
B. Overruled, the statement is admissible under Rule 801(d)(1)(B).
C. Overruled, but the court should give a limiting instruction that the statement may only be used to bolster the credibility of the witness.

ANALYSIS.   Rat is the declarant and the statement to his brother contains an assertion the prosecutor could use for its truth. If the prosecutor had attempted to introduce the account Rat gave to his brother before the defense lawyer charged that Rat's trial testimony was fabricated, the prior consistent statement would have been hearsay and **A** would be the correct answer. The rule, however, allows the testimony to be admitted after there has been a suggestion of fabrication. Moreover, it is admissible not only to bolster Rat's trial testimony, but also to prove the truth of Rat's statement to his brother. Therefore, **B** is correct and **C** is incorrect because no limiting instruction is required.

If Rat had not spoken to his brother until after he made his deal with the prosecution, the statement to him would be inadmissible. The fact that a witness tells a consistent story after the motive to fabricate arose is not very significant.

(3) Statements of Identification of a Person   Eyewitness testimony plays a significant role in many trials. Scientific research has demonstrated that there are many reasons why eyewitness testimony may be unreliable. Identification by a witness on the stand of a defendant in the courtroom is particularly questionable. The witness has probably received a great deal of feedback confirming the identification as a result of various proceedings before trial. Moreover, it is hardly surprising that a witness would identify the defendant sitting at the defense table. Rule 801(d)(1)(C) therefore allows testimony about an earlier identification, which was probably made under less suggestive conditions, as long as the witness testifies at trial and is subject to cross-examination.

QUESTION 15. The witness is a bank teller who was forced to empty her cash drawer into a bag by an armed robber. At the police station she identified the defendant as the robber by his photograph in a series of eight photos the investigating officer showed her. The witness died before trial. The prosecutor calls the investigating officer to testify that the witness had picked the defendant's photo out of those shown to her by the police as that of the robber. Defense counsel's objection should be:

A. Sustained, hearsay.
B. Sustained, the prior identification was not made under oath.
C. Sustained, the defendant's lawyer had no opportunity to cross-examine the witness at the time of the original identification.
D. Overruled.

ANALYSIS.   The witness was the declarant and her statement picking out the defendant's photo contains an assertion that could be offered to prove its truth. It is hearsay, and **A** is correct, unless the evidence falls within Rule 801(d)(1)(C). This evidence does not fall within the rule, because the witness did not testify and was not subject to cross-examination concerning the statement at trial. Remember that the witness must testify at trial and be subject to cross-examination for all three categories of statements under Rule 801(d)(1). The rule does not require that a prior identification be made under oath or at a formal proceeding to be admissible, or that there was an opportunity to cross-examine the witness at the time of the original identification. Choices **B** and **C** are incorrect for that reason.

QUESTION 16. The victim identified the defendant in a lineup at the police station as the man who assaulted her and snatched her purse. The prosecutor calls the victim as a witness at the trial, and asks her, "When you viewed the eight subjects at the lineup, what did you do or say?" Defendant objects on hearsay grounds. The prosecutor tells the judge that she expects the victim to answer, "I pointed to the defendant as my attacker." What is the correct ruling for the court to make on the defense objection?

A. Sustained, hearsay.
B. Sustained, the testimony is not inconsistent with anything the witness said at the trial.
C. Overruled, admissible under Rule 801(d)(1)(B) as a prior consistent statement.
D. Overruled, admissible under Rule 801(d)(1)(C) as a statement of identification.

ANALYSIS.   The victim was the declarant and her assertion at the lineup that the defendant attacked her is offered to prove the truth of that assertion. It is not hearsay, however, because it falls within Rule 801(d)(1)(C) as a prior identification of a person after perceiving him. Choice **D** is the correct answer, and **A** is wrong. The statement would not be admissible as a prior consistent statement, because there has been no suggestion that the trial testimony was fabricated. Thus **C** is incorrect. The fact that it is not admissible as a prior consistent statement, however, does not mean that it cannot be admitted as a prior identification. To be admissible as prior identification the statement does not have to be inconsistent with any trial testimony, therefore **B** is incorrect.

Notice that it does not matter that the statement is inadmissible as either a prior inconsistent statement or a prior consistent statement. The proponent only needs to find one exemption or exception to the hearsay rule to justify admitting the statement.

b. Statement by Party Opponent   The final exemption from the rule against hearsay is for a statement by the opposing party. A party to a lawsuit may introduce any statement made by the opposing party and it is not barred by the hearsay rule. The opponent may object to the evidence on such other grounds as may exist, but Rule 801(d)(2) provides that such statements are simply not considered hearsay.

> **801(d)(2) An Opposing Party's Statement.**
> The statement is offered against an opposing party and:
>   (A) was made by the party in an individual or representative capacity;
>   (B) is one the party manifested that it adopted or believed to be true;
>   (C) was made by a person whom the party authorized to make a statement on the subject;
>   (D) was made by the party's agent or employee on a matter within the scope of that relationship and while it existed; or
>   (E) was made by the party's coconspirator during and in furtherance of the conspiracy.
>   The statement must be considered but does not by itself establish the declarant's authority under (C); the existence or scope of the relationship under (D); or the existence of the conspiracy or participation in it under (E).

The simplest example is when the opposing party is an individual person and he personally makes a statement (section (2)(A) of the rule). Suppose the plaintiff, Paul, sues the defendant for assault and battery. Plaintiff offers evidence that defendant stated to one of his friends a couple of days after the incident, "I really clobbered Paul the other night." The statement is not considered hearsay and is admissible. If it were a criminal case and the prosecution had the same evidence available, it could also offer the friend's testimony, because the prosecution and the defendant are opposing parties in a criminal case.

Lawyers and judges frequently call statements by a party opponent "admissions." The term is misleading and you will be able to analyze things more clearly if you avoid using it. A statement by a party does not have to admit anything, or be incriminating, or be against the declarant's interest, to be admissible. It can be something that was entirely self-serving at the time the party made the statement and it still falls within this rule.

In addition, the declarant (the opposing party) does not have to have personal knowledge of the subject matter of his statement. This rule is really breathtakingly simple. Any statement a party makes is not hearsay if the opposing party offers it in evidence. There are no other requirements that have to be met. Remember, a party cannot introduce his own statement under this rule, only statements by the *opposing party*.

The rule gets a little more complicated when we move beyond direct statements by an individual person who is an opposing party. Let's work through the rest of the rule to discuss these cases.

Section (2)(B) provides that an opposing party may offer a statement that the other party "manifested that it adopted or believed to be true." A party can adopt the statement of another person either explicitly or implicitly. Suppose plaintiff has sued defendant, a young adult, for causing a traffic accident. Plaintiff has evidence that after the accident a witness said to the defendant, "You ran that red light." If the defendant nods affirmatively, or says, "I know," he has explicitly adopted the statement. The plaintiff may then introduce the statement of the witness and the defendant's response as a statement by a party opponent.

In the same scenario, suppose the eyewitness made the statement in the presence of the defendant and the defendant's mother and the defendant made no response and said nothing. Plaintiff can argue that the defendant adopted the statement of the witness implicitly through silence, because if his mother was present, one would expect him to deny the statement if it were not true. There are three requirements for an adoption by silence: (1) the party heard the statement; (2) the party understood the statement; and (3) a reasonable person in the party's position, under all the circumstances, would have denied the statement if it were not true. If those requirements are met, the judge may admit the statement of the witness and the defendant's silence as a statement by a party opponent.

Whether there is an adoption by silence and whether it is admissible against a criminal defendant involves two separate questions when a police officer is present. The first question is whether introducing evidence of an adoption by silence would violate the defendant's constitutional rights. If the police have given a suspect in custody the *Miranda* warnings and advised him of his right to remain silent, the prosecution cannot introduce an adoption by silence in the presence of a police officer against a criminal defendant. It would violate the suspect's constitutional rights to advise him that he has a right to remain silent, but then introduce his silence against him in evidence. If a person has not been arrested, however, or if he has been arrested but not yet advised of his rights, it does not violate his constitutional rights to introduce an adoption by silence against him, even if a police officer is present.

The second question is whether under the circumstances a reasonable person would have denied the statement if it were not true. The presence of a police officer is a factor to take into account in this inquiry. A reasonable person might decide to remain silent in the presence of a police officer even in the face of a false statement, reasoning that it is better to say nothing than to run the risk of being misunderstood or misquoted, or of encouraging further conversation that might go in an unanticipated direction.

A party can also adopt the statement of another by taking some action that manifests a belief that the statement is true. Suppose the prosecution is trying the defendant on the charge of extortion, and claims he sent threatening emails to the victim. The prosecutor has a witness who would testify that he was at the defendant's apartment and he said to the defendant, "You've got a lot of incriminating evidence on that computer." The defendant said nothing, but immediately turned on his computer and reformatted his hard drive, erasing everything that was on it. The prosecution could introduce the witness's remark and the defendant's action as a statement by a party opponent, arguing that erasing the hard drive was an adoption of the witness's remark.

Section (2)(C) of the rule provides that a statement by an agent of a party who is authorized to make statements upon the subject matter of the statement is a statement by the party. This is pretty straightforward. Where a party has authorized his lawyer, accountant, press representative, spokesperson, or similar agent to make statements on a given subject matter, the opposing party may offer them under this rule. This was the rule at common law and the Federal Rules broke no new ground in adopting it.

The Federal Rules went further than the common law, however, in section (2)(D). This section says statements will be deemed to be the statements of a party if an agent or employee of the party makes statements concerning something within the scope of his agency or employment during the agency or employment relationship. This means that the agent or employee does not have to be specifically authorized to make statements for the statements to be considered the statements of the employer. They simply must relate to the scope of the agent or employee's duties and be made while the agency or employment is ongoing. For example, suppose a machine manufactured and sold by the defendant corporation injured the plaintiff. Plaintiff has evidence that an engineer employed by defendant who worked on the design of the machine said to a government inspector, "This machine is dangerous and really needs to be redesigned." The statement related to something within the scope of the engineer's employment, and as long as he made it while the defendant employed him, the plaintiff could offer it against the defendant corporation as a statement by a party opponent.

Under both (2)(C) and (2)(D) to lay a foundation for admissibility it is necessary to establish that the declarant was an agent or an employee of the opposing party at the time of the statement. The judge makes that decision and the standard is preponderance of the evidence. In determining whether the proponent has established agency or employment, the judge must take into account the contents of the statement in question, but the statement by itself is not sufficient to make the necessary showing. Some additional evidence of agency or employment is required.

Let's look at some questions before we take up the final section of the rule concerning co-conspirator statements.

QUESTION 17. The defendant is on trial for the murder of his wife. The victim died from arsenic poisoning. The defendant claims to have no knowledge of how she ingested the poison. The prosecutor called a neighbor of the couple to the stand. She testified that she knew the defendant and his wife well. The prosecutor asks, "In the month before she died, did you talk to the defendant about his relationship with his wife?" The neighbor answers, "Yes." The prosecutor then asks, "What did the defendant say?"

At this point, defense counsel objects. At side bar the prosecutor tells the judge that the neighbor will recount how the defendant complained about his wife's obsession with money and said he "despises her and cannot fathom how he ever married her." The objection should be:

A. Sustained, hearsay.
B. Sustained, not relevant.
C. Sustained, improper character evidence respecting the victim.
D. Overruled.

ANALYSIS. First, let's dispose of the objections that do not relate to the hearsay issue. Is the fact that the defendant told his neighbor that he "despised" his wife relevant to whether or not he murdered her? Of course. The fact that he despised her does not conclusively prove that he killed her. It does, however, make it more likely that he was the killer than it would be without that evidence. **B** is incorrect. **C** is also incorrect. It is not clear that the defendant's attitude toward his wife was based on her character. More importantly, this evidence is not being offered to prove that she acted in accord with her character or a character trait.

The evidence is not inadmissible hearsay. The words in question are an out of court statement offered to prove the truth of the assertion that the defendant despised his wife. The defendant, however, is a party opponent of the prosecution, which is offering the evidence. This is as straightforward an example of Rule 801(d)(2)(A) as one could find. Hence, **A** is incorrect, and **D** is the correct answer.

> **QUESTION 18.** The defendant is on trial for a robbery that took place in Boston on New Year's Eve in 2012. His defense is that he was not in Boston at that time, but was home in New York at a party. He has alibi witnesses who will testify they were with him at the party in New York. The prosecution has a witness who would testify that she was discussing ice sculptures with the defendant in January 2013 and he said to her, "You should have seen the amazing ice sculptures I saw at the First Night celebration in Boston on New Year's Eve a couple of weeks ago." The defense objection to this testimony should be:
>
> **A.** Sustained, hearsay.
> **B.** Overruled.

ANALYSIS. The prosecution is offering a statement by the defendant, the opposing party, and therefore it is exempt from the hearsay rule and **B** is the correct answer and **A** is incorrect. Notice that at the time the defendant made the statement there was nothing incriminating about it and it did not amount to an admission or confession that he committed the robbery. A statement does not have to be against the interest of the party at the time it is made for it to be admissible as a statement by a party opponent; it merely has to be offered in evidence by the opposing party.

> **QUESTION 19.** The defendant is on trial for the murder of her husband. The prosecutor calls a neighbor who would testify that two weeks before the husband's death, the defendant told him that her husband had said that he wanted a divorce and she was furious about it. The prosecutor offers the neighbor's testimony at trial. How should the court rule on the defendant's objection?
>
> **A.** Sustained, the husband's statement is offered for its truth and there is no hearsay exception for it.
> **B.** Sustained, the defendant's statement is offered for its truth and there is no hearsay exception for it.
> **C.** Overruled, there are two hearsay statements and there is an exception for each one.
> **D.** Overruled, statement by a party opponent.

ANALYSIS. The first thing one must note is that this is a potential multiple hearsay problem. There are two declarants, the defendant and the husband. The husband's statement was, "I want a divorce." The defendant's statement was, "My husband said he wants a divorce and I'm furious about it." Let's take the declarant husband's statement first. It contains an assertion, but the prosecutor is not offering it for the truth of the assertion, but rather for the effect the statement had on the defendant when she heard it. It does not matter whether the husband really wanted a divorce; what is important is that he told the defendant he did and she got furious (providing her with a motive to kill him). The husband's statement is not hearsay because the prosecutor did not offer it to prove the truth of the assertion in it, thus **A** and **C** are both incorrect.

The defendant's statement contains an assertion and the prosecutor is offering it to prove the truth of the assertion, that her husband told her he wanted a divorce and she got furious. But the prosecution is offering a statement by the defendant, the opposing party. The statement is exempt from the hearsay rule and is admissible, thus **D** is the correct answer and **B** is incorrect.

QUESTION 20. The plaintiff is suing the defendant Cola Corporation for injuries she suffered when her car was hit by a U-Haul truck. At the accident scene, the driver said he was driving the truck for the Cola Corporation and he ran a red light and the accident was his fault. At trial the plaintiff offers the driver's statement against the defendant Cola Corporation. The defense objection should be:

A. Sustained, hearsay.
B. Overruled, statement by a party opponent.

ANALYSIS. The declarant was the driver and he made assertions that he was working for the Cola Corporation and that the accident was his fault. The plaintiff is offering both assertions for their truth. If there were a sufficient foundation that the driver was in fact an employee of the defendant Cola Corporation, the statement would be admissible against the corporation as a statement by a party opponent under Rule 801(d)(2)(C). The statement involved something within the scope of the driver's employment and was made during the period of his employment. The only evidence that the corporation employed him, however, was the statement itself, which is insufficient. Thus **B** is incorrect and the correct answer is **A**. The statement must be excluded as inadmissible hearsay.

QUESTION 21. The plaintiff is suing the defendant Cola Corporation for injuries she suffered when her car was hit by a truck. The plaintiff has testified that at the accident scene she observed that the truck said "Cola Corporation" on the side, that the driver was wearing coveralls that said "Cola Corporation" on the back, and that the truck was filled with bottles of Cola. She would also testify that she saw the driver at a bar later that night and he said that he was employed by the Cola Corporation, and that he ran a red light and the accident was his fault. At trial the plaintiff offers the driver's statement against the defendant Cola Corporation. The defense objection should be:

A. Sustained, hearsay.
B. Overruled, statement by a party opponent.

ANALYSIS. In this question there is ample evidence in addition to the statement by the driver that the defendant Cola Corporation employed him. The issue here is whether it matters that he made the statement when he was off duty at the bar. It does not. The rule does not require that agents or employees make statements while they are on duty for them to be admissible against the employer. All that is required is that the declarant makes the statement during the existence of the employment relationship. There is no evidence that the company fired the driver before he spoke, so the statement is admissible as a statement by a party opponent. **B** is correct and **A** is incorrect.

Under section (2)(E) of the rule, the opposing party may introduce certain statements of a co-conspirator of a party and such statements are not considered hearsay. Joint venturers are treated the same as co-conspirators under the rule, but we will refer simply to co-conspirators for the sake of simplicity.

The following requirements must be established by a preponderance of the evidence to lay the foundation for the admissibility of co-conspirator statements:

1. There was a conspiracy and the declarant was a member of the conspiracy at the time he made the statement.
2. The party against whom the statement is offered was a member of the conspiracy at the time of the statement.
3. The statement was made during the conspiracy.
4. The statement was made in furtherance of the conspiracy.

A conspiracy does not have to be formally charged or pled for co-conspirator statements to be admissible, but the existence of the conspiracy must be established by a preponderance of the evidence. The judge makes the decision as to whether the elements of the foundation have been established. The judge must take into account the contents of the statement in making this decision, but the statement itself is not sufficient to establish the existence of the conspiracy or the participation of the declarant and the party against whom it is offered in it. Some additional evidence is necessary.

Suppose that the prosecution has charged the defendant with conspiracy to import and sell marijuana. There is evidence that the defendant and the declarant had telephone calls in which they discussed their plans to import and sell marijuana, that the declarant traveled to Mexico to buy marijuana, and that the defendant organized others to sell the product in the United States. The prosecution has evidence that during the time the scheme was ongoing an undercover agent posing as a potential customer asked the declarant whether the product was any good, and he said, "This is the best weed you can get in Mexico." The declarant's statement is admissible against the defendant as a statement by a party opponent. They were both members of the conspiracy at the time, the statement was made during the conspiracy, and the statement was in furtherance of the conspiracy because it was made to market the product. The statement would be admissible even if the declarant were not a defendant in the case on trial. If the conspiracy had ended or if either the declarant or the defendant had withdrawn from the conspiracy before the statement was made, the statement would not be admissible.

In complicated trials a party may offer co-conspirator statements against the opposing party before all the evidence has been introduced that would establish the foundation for admissibility. In such cases the proponent of the evidence advises the court what additional evidence he expects to offer and the court may admit the co-conspirator statement provisionally, pending later receipt of the necessary foundation evidence. If such evidence is not forthcoming, the opponent would be entitled to have the co-conspirator statement struck from the record and the court would advise the jury to disregard it.

QUESTION 22. The defendant is on trial for bank robbery. The prosecution has introduced evidence that there was a conspiracy of several men to rob the bank, that the defendant met several times with the other conspirators, that three of the other conspirators entered the bank with guns and took money, and that police found some of the money from the robbery at the defendant's apartment. The prosecution has evidence that the police arrested one of the men who entered the bank and questioned him at the jail. He stated that the defendant was the getaway driver for the robbery. The prosecution calls the officer who questioned that individual to testify about what he said. The defendant's objection should be:

A. Sustained because the defendant is not charged with conspiracy.
B. Sustained because the other evidence that the defendant was a member of the conspiracy is circumstantial.
C. Sustained, the statement was not made while the declarant was a member of the conspiracy and was not in furtherance of the conspiracy.
D. Overruled.

ANALYSIS. It is not necessary for conspiracy to be formally charged in the indictment for co-conspirator statements to be admissible, so **A** is incorrect. There does have to be proof that the defendant was a member of the conspiracy. Here there is the declarant's statement that the defendant was the getaway driver, evidence that he met with other conspirators, and evidence that proceeds of the robbery were in his apartment. The fact that the other evidence of his involvement is circumstantial is not fatal. Circumstantial evidence is as legitimate as direct evidence, so **B** is incorrect. The arrest of the declarant, however, terminated his participation in the conspiracy. Moreover, telling the police that the defendant was the getaway driver did not further the aims of the conspiracy. Thus **C** is the correct answer and **D** is incorrect.

QUESTION 23. Defendant and Co-Defendant have been indicted for conspiracy to sell cocaine. The government has offered sufficient evidence that each was a member of the conspiracy. A Police Officer testifies that he participated in a search with a warrant of Defendant's apartment and found a handwritten note on stationery with Co-Defendant's name at the top, signed with her name, and dated during the period of the alleged conspiracy, which he identifies. The note reads, "I have found an excellent source for cocaine that I will tell you about the next time I see you." A previous expert witness has identified a fingerprint on the note as belonging to Co-Defendant. Defendant's objection to the prosecution's offer in evidence of the note should be:

A. Sustained, hearsay.
B. Sustained, with leave to the prosecution to offer the note only if Co-Defendant testifies and there is a limiting instruction to admit it only against her.
C. Sustained, insufficient authentication in the absence of expert testimony to identify the handwriting.
D. Overruled, co-conspirator statement.

ANALYSIS. We will deal with authentication in Chapter 9. The general rule is that an item may be authenticated by evidence that is sufficient to convince the trier of fact by a preponderance of the evidence that the item is what the proponent of the evidence claims it to be. Here, if the jury credits the testimony of the fingerprint expert, there is sufficient evidence to conclude that the note came from Co-Defendant. **C** is incorrect. The note is hearsay because it contains an assertion and is offered to prove the truth of the assertion, namely that Co-Defendant planned to tell Defendant about a source she found for cocaine. It falls within the exception for co-conspirator statements because it was made during the pendency of the conspiracy by a member of the conspiracy and is being offered against a Defendant, who also was a member of the conspiracy. Thus A is incorrect. Statements within the co-conspirator hearsay exception are admissible in evidence against both Defendant and Co-Defendant. **B** is incorrect and the correct answer is **D**.

3. *Exceptions Under Rule 803*

The largest category of hearsay exceptions is found in Rule 803. These exceptions may be used whether or not the declarant is available as a witness at the proceeding at which the hearsay is admitted. There are 23 exceptions under this rule, but we will discuss here only those most commonly used.

In order to introduce a statement under a hearsay exception, the proponent must first elicit sufficient facts from the witness to establish that the exception applies to the statement. The burden of establishing the foundation for the exception is on the proponent. The court, under Rule 104(a), decides whether the facts elicited are sufficient to establish the foundation. In addition to the requirements of the individual exceptions, the proponent also must show that the declarant had personal knowledge of the matter asserted in the statement.

A party may introduce statements by any declarant that fall within one of the hearsay exceptions. A party may not introduce his own words as a statement by a party opponent, because under Rule 801(d)(2), one can only offer statements by the opposing party. However, a party could introduce his own out of court statement if it fell within a hearsay exception, for example, as a present sense impression or an excited utterance.

a. Present Sense Impression and Excited Utterance Rule 803 provides the following exceptions:

> **(1)** *Present Sense Impression.* A statement describing or explaining an event or condition, made while or immediately after the declarant perceived it.
> **(2)** *Excited Utterance.* A statement relating to a startling event or condition, made while the declarant was under the stress of excitement that it caused.

These two exceptions are somewhat similar, but there are differences between them. A declarant voices a present sense impression when she describes or explains an event or condition at the very moment she observes it, or *immediately* thereafter. The content of the statement itself may be considered in determining whether it was made contemporaneously with the observation. The event does not have to be exciting or dramatic. For example, if we wanted to prove that the defendant was wearing a purple dress on the evening of the crime, the statement by someone who saw her at that time, "My, what a lovely purple dress you are wearing," would be admissible under exception (1).

A statement is an excited utterance when the declarant has experienced or observed a startling event or condition and says something that relates to that event while she is still under the stress of excitement it caused. The justification for the exception is that the declarant speaks before she has collected herself enough to be able to dissemble. For example, if someone witnessed a high speed auto collision and, still trembling from shock, said, "That red car must have been going a hundred miles an hour," the remark would be admissible to prove the speed of the car under exception (2).

The requirement of contemporaneity is strictly enforced with respect to present sense impressions. The statement must be made at the time of the observation or immediately thereafter, not several minutes later. With respect to excited utterances, the issue is not how much time has passed since the event took place, but whether or not the declarant is still under the stress of the event. This may be demonstrated by the content of the statement, the apparent physical and/or emotional condition of the declarant, the circumstances of the startling event, what transpired between the event and the statement, and what prompted the making of the statement. Sufficient stress to suspend the ability of the declarant to fabricate lasts for a short period of time for most startling events. Some courts, however, have admitted as an excited utterance a statement made several hours after the event where circumstances suggested that the declarant would still be under great stress. This might be the case, for example, for a child who had been sexually abused and then remained in the presence of the abuser.

QUESTION 24. The defendant planned a road trip in his car. Before the trip, he took the car to a garage to have it examined by a mechanic. While he was inspecting the brakes, the mechanic said, "Wow. The brakes are nearly shot. You should have them replaced before the trip." Defendant went on the trip without making any repairs, and was unable to stop the car while going down a mountain road. He crashed into plaintiff's car. Plaintiff sued the defendant. The mechanic has passed away, but plaintiff called a witness from the garage to testify to the mechanic's statement about the brakes, to prove both that the brakes were defective and that the defendant was on notice of it. The defendant's hearsay objection should be:

A. Sustained, hearsay.
B. Overruled, the statement is offered for the effect on the listener.
C. Overruled, present sense impression.
D. Overruled, excited utterance.

ANALYSIS. The declarant is the mechanic and his assertion that the brakes were "nearly shot" is offered for its truth, to prove they were defective. It is hearsay, but **A** is not correct because it falls within an exception. The real question is which one. It cannot be an excited utterance because there was no startling event. Observing faulty brakes is a routine event for an auto mechanic, thus **D** is incorrect. The mechanic makes his statement about the brakes at the very moment he is observing their condition, and thus his remark is a present sense impression. Choice **C** is the correct answer. Although plaintiff also offered the statement to prove that the defendant had notice of the defect, that was not the statement's only purpose. Because plaintiff offered the statement to prove that the brakes were defective as well, **B** is incorrect.

QUESTION 25. A police officer responded to a call to investigate a domestic disturbance. When he arrived, the victim was on her front porch, sobbing and trembling. There were several cuts on her arms and she was holding a towel against herself to try to stop the bleeding. The officer asked, "What happened?" The victim moaned and said, "My boyfriend cut me." The state prosecuted the boyfriend, but the victim refused to testify against him. The prosecutor calls the officer to testify to what the victim said. The boyfriend's defense lawyer's objection should be:

A. Sustained, hearsay.
B. Sustained, no personal knowledge.
C. Overruled, present sense impression.
D. Overruled, excited utterance.

ANALYSIS. The declarant is the victim and the prosecution is offering her assertion that her boyfriend cut her for its truth. It would be hearsay and inadmissible unless it falls within an exception. The victim has personal knowledge of how she was stabbed, so **B** is incorrect. Because we do not know how much time elapsed between the assault and the statement, we cannot establish that the statement followed immediately after the event. **C**, present sense impression, is therefore incorrect. A knife attack is certainly a startling event, and the facts demonstrate that the victim was still under the stress of the event—she was still bleeding, sobbing, and trembling. Choice **D** is correct.

We noted above that whether a declarant was still under the stress of the startling event might be shown, in part, by what prompted the statement. When the declarant responds to a question, her statement is not as spontaneous as when she makes it in the absence of a question. She has a tendency to think about how to frame her answer. The mere fact that a statement is in response to a question, however, does not always preclude admissibility as an excited utterance. Each case must be viewed on the basis of all the circumstances that existed at the time.

QUESTION 26. The police arrested a young woman and then got a search warrant to search her home, where she lived with her mother. The mother asked the police why they were there and they said they had arrested her daughter for terrorism, as a suspect in a conspiracy to blow up some government buildings. The mother burst into tears upon hearing this news and began tearing her hair. Sobbing, she said, "I bet her new boyfriend got her into this." At the trial of the daughter and her boyfriend the prosecutor calls one of the police officers as a witness and offers to have him testify as to what the mother said. The defendants' objection should be:

A. Sustained, hearsay.
B. Sustained, no personal knowledge.
C. Overruled, excited utterance.
D. Overruled, present sense impression.

ANALYSIS. The declarant is the mother and her assertion that the boyfriend got her daughter into the conspiracy is offered for its truth. She is not describing anything that she is observing at the moment, so her statement does not fall under the present sense impression exception and **D** is incorrect. Learning that her daughter had been arrested was a startling event, and she was still under the stress of it when she made her statement. Her statement related to the arrest. Thus it would seem to qualify for the excited utterance exception. She has no personal knowledge of the substance of her statement, however. Because of that, **C** is incorrect. Choice **B** is the correct answer. In this example the statement is excluded by the personal knowledge requirement and not the rule against hearsay, so **A** is incorrect.

Remember, personal knowledge is required for all witnesses (except experts) and all hearsay declarants. The only exception to this general requirement is that personal knowledge is not required for statements by party opponents.

b. State of Mind, Emotions, or Physical Condition   Rule 803 creates a hearsay exception for the following type of statement:

> **(3) Then-Existing Mental, Emotional, or Physical Condition.** A statement of the declarant's then-existing state of mind (such as motive, intent, or plan) or emotional, sensory, or physical condition (such as mental feeling, pain, or bodily health), but not including a statement of memory or belief to prove the fact remembered or believed unless it relates to the validity or terms of the declarant's will.

A statement which described the declarant's mental, emotional, sensory, or physical condition at the time the statement was made is admissible under this exception. Obvious examples include statements such as: "I'm depressed," "My back is killing me this morning," and "I love you." The state of mind exception also includes statements of intent, such as, "I am planning to go to New York tomorrow," or "If you don't pay the money you owe me, I will break your arm."

In order for a statement to be admissible under the state of mind exception, the declarant's state of mind must be relevant to a claim or defense. Evidence of an intent or plan to take an action is relevant, for example, where the question is whether the declarant later took the action in question. Evidence that the declarant intended to do something makes it more likely that he performed the act in question than it would be in the absence of evidence of his intent.

The Rule 803(3) exception makes statements about what the declarant intends to do in the future admissible, but not statements about what he did or observed in the past. The rule excludes evidence of a memory or belief to prove that an event happened or condition existed in the past. For example, suppose the declarant stated, "I saw an auto accident yesterday and I remember that the taxi ran the red light." One could argue that his memory of what he saw reflects his state of mind. That interpretation of the rule, however, would swallow the rule against hearsay. Any time a speaker put "I believe," or "I remember" in front of an assertion, it would fall within the state of mind exception. Rule 803(3) explicitly provides that such statements may not be admitted under this exception, unless the statements relate to the terms or validity of the declarant's will, for example, statements by the declarant that he has made or revoked a will.

In homicide cases there is often evidence that the victim had expressed a fear that the defendant would harm her. Suppose a witness would testify that the victim said, "I'm afraid that my husband is going to kill me." The victim is the declarant, she has made an assertion, and the prosecutor would be offering it to prove the truth of the assertion. A prosecutor may attempt to introduce the statement under the state of mind exception, but it would be error for the court to admit it. The state of mind of the victim is not relevant to the charge of homicide. The only relevance the declarant's fear of her husband has is that it reflects her memory or belief that her husband did something in the past that made her fear him. To make "I'm afraid my husband is going to kill me" relevant, we have to read it as though she said, "My husband threatened to kill me," or "My husband beat me up." Those statements are clearly assertions about what the husband did, not about the victim's state of mind. Appellate courts have reversed numerous murder convictions because trial judges mistakenly admitted hearsay statements of fear by victims.[4]

Statements of fear by a homicide victim are only relevant where the nature of the defense makes the victim's state of mind a relevant factor. Suppose a husband and wife separated and the wife was murdered. The husband was seen in the vicinity of her home near the time of the murder. To explain his presence, he told a police officer that his wife had invited him to her house so they could jointly write a letter to their son at camp. The prosecutor has evidence that the wife told several people that she was deathly afraid of her husband and did not want to be alone with him. Under these circumstances the

---

4.   See, e.g., *Com. v. Qualls*, 425 Mass. 163 (1997).

victim's state of mind is relevant because it undercuts the defendant's claim that he was invited to her house.[5] Absent a defense that creates a similar issue, the state of mind of a homicide victim would not be relevant.

QUESTION 27. The plaintiff was badly injured in an automobile accident and spent several weeks recovering after he was released from the hospital. He has sued the driver of the other car for damages, including pain and suffering. At trial, the plaintiff's wife would testify that for six weeks after he came home from the hospital he complained of pain in his back and right hip every morning. The defendant's objection to the testimony should be:

A. Sustained, hearsay.
B. Sustained, the wife has no personal knowledge of the plaintiff's pain.
C. Overruled, statement by a party opponent.
D. Overruled, statement of then-existing physical condition.

ANALYSIS. The plaintiff is the declarant and his assertions that he was suffering from pain each day are offered for their truth. The testimony would be inadmissible hearsay unless it falls within an exception. Choice **B** is incorrect because the wife is not required to have personal knowledge of the pain. A witness who testifies about a hearsay statement need only have personal knowledge that the statement was made, not of the underlying facts asserted in the statement. Plaintiff is offering his own statements through the testimony of his wife, and not statements of an opposing party, thus **C** is incorrect. Plaintiff's complaints of pain to his wife are precisely the sort of statements contemplated under the exception for statements concerning his then-existing physical condition. Choice **D** is the correct answer.

QUESTION 28. The defendant is on trial for the murder of his wife. The prosecution calls a neighbor who would testify that two weeks before her death, the victim told her that she was planning to leave the defendant and take her children with her and that she intended to tell her husband that evening that she was leaving and wanted a divorce. The defense objection to this evidence should be:

A. Sustained, hearsay.
B. Overruled, present sense impression.
C. Overruled, excited utterance.
D. Overruled, state of mind.

---

5. Under these facts the Supreme Judicial Court of Massachusetts held the victim wife's statements of her fear of the defendant were admissible in *Com. v. Magraw*, 426 Mass. 589 (1998).

ANALYSIS. The declarant is the victim and she made an assertion that she was planning to leave her husband and to tell him about it. The prosecution is offering the evidence to prove the truth of the assertion. It is hearsay unless it falls within an exception. It does not qualify as a present sense impression because the declarant was not describing something she was observing, but rather something she was thinking. Thus **B** is incorrect. Nor is the statement an excited utterance because there no evidence of a startling event or that the declarant was under the spell of a startling event. Thus **C** is incorrect. The declarant has made a statement of her intent to do something, which qualifies as a comment on her state of mind. Her state of mind in this case is relevant, because if she told her husband of her plans it would provide a possible motive for him to murder her. Choice **D** is the correct answer and **A** is incorrect.

QUESTION 29. The Defendant is on trial for the murder of her elderly aunt. The perpetrator beat the victim to death. The Defendant has denied any knowledge of the assault. The prosecutor calls a neighbor to the stand, who testifies that she was at her kitchen window on the morning of the aunt's death. She says that she saw the Defendant enter the house and shortly thereafter heard screaming. She recognized the aunt's voice. The prosecutor asks, "What did she scream?" Defense counsel objects and at side bar, the prosecutor tells the judge that the neighbor heard the victim shout, "Let go of my wrist. You're hurting me." The defense objection should be:

A. Sustained, hearsay.
B. Sustained, because FRE 803(3) does not apply to the victim of a homicide.
C. Overruled, because Virginia's statement falls within one or more hearsay exceptions.
D. Overruled, because the contents of the scream constitute a statement by a party opponent.

ANALYSIS. The words in question were spoken by the victim of the murder. The victim is not a party to the case, and thus not the party opponent of the prosecution. **D** is incorrect. The words in question contained two assertions: that someone had ahold of her wrist, and that the person was hurting her. The evidence is offered to prove the truth of those assertions, and would be hearsay unless it falls within an exception.

The Rule 803(3) exception includes statements regarding then-existing physical pain, and statements relating to the declarant's state of mind. However, we've said that statements by a homicide victim that she feared the defendant are generally not admissible under this rule. Her fear cannot be used to show that the defendant did something to her in the past, because that would constitute a statement of memory of a past event, which the rule forbids. It is too broad, however, to say that Rule 803(3) never applies to the victim of a homicide. Thus, **B** is incorrect.

The words in question here are admissible as a present sense impression, possibly as an excited utterance, and as a statement of then-existing pain. **C** is the correct answer, and **A** is incorrect.

c. Statements Made to Obtain Medical Diagnosis or Treatment   Rule 803(4) recognizes a hearsay exception for statements made for the purpose of obtaining a medical diagnosis or treatment:

> (4) **Statement Made for Medical Diagnosis or Treatment.**
> A statement that:
>> (A) is made for—and is reasonably pertinent to—medical diagnosis or treatment; and
>> (B) describes medical history; past or present symptoms or sensations; their inception; or their general cause.

In practice the most common use of this exception is for statements made to obtain medical treatment. Reliability is the justification for admitting hearsay statements made to get treatment. A patient usually tells his doctor the truth about his medical condition because he wants the doctor to prescribe a course of treatment that will be effective. We can imagine reasons why someone might make untrue or inaccurate statements to a medical provider, but most of the time the information is probably reliable. The common law recognized the hearsay exception for statements made to obtain medical treatment.

The Federal Rules go further than the common law and also recognize an exception for statements made to obtain a diagnosis, even where no treatment is contemplated. For example, a plaintiff in a personal injury case may see a doctor recommended by his attorney so that the doctor can testify as an expert witness at trial. Under these circumstances, there is less reason to assume the statements the plaintiff makes to the doctor are reliable. In fact, a person seeking damages may be motivated to exaggerate his symptoms or injuries. The rule admits hearsay statements in these cases because when the doctor testifies about his diagnosis, it is likely that one party or the other will ask the doctor what the plaintiff told the doctor, in order to explore the basis for the doctor's expert opinions about the patient's condition. If offered to prove the truth of what the plaintiff said, such statements are hearsay. One way of dealing with this hearsay would be to require a limiting instruction that the plaintiff's statements are admissible only to assist the jury in weighing the doctor's opinion and not for their truth. Rule 803(4) does not take that option, but instead brings the statements within this exception and relies on cross-examination and argument by the opposing party to make the point that the jury is free to question the credibility of the plaintiff.

The exception applies not only when the declarant made statements directly to a medical provider, but also when the declarant made statements to a third party to pass on to a medical provider. For example, if the declarant was so ill he could not comfortably make a telephone call, he might tell a family member what he was experiencing and ask that person to call the doctor. The statements to the family member would fall within the exception.

In addition the declarant does not have to be the person who is ill for the exception to apply. A third person with knowledge of what happened to the patient, or what the patient is experiencing, might call for medical assistance. In that event the third person is the declarant and his statements fall within the exception. So in the previous example, the statements of the family member who calls the doctor's office are admissible. For statements from a third party, however, it is essential to show that the declarant has personal knowledge of the patient's history or condition.

In order for hearsay statements to be admissible under this exception, the content of the statement must be pertinent to diagnosis or treatment. Statements concerning the patient's history that are relevant only with respect to liability issues, such as who was at fault in causing injuries, are not admissible. Suppose a patient went to the emergency room after an automobile accident and told the nurse or doctor, "I was driving my car and was struck from behind by a blue Toyota driven by a white male. The impact threw me forward and I cracked my head on the windshield." That the patient's car was struck by another car from behind, and that the patient struck his head on his windshield, would be pertinent to diagnosis and treatment. The fact that it was a blue Toyota and the description of the driver would not be. Those parts of the statement would be hearsay if offered for their truth, and would not be admissible under this exception. Whether a given piece of information is pertinent to medical diagnosis or treatment may not be obvious to a layperson. In such cases a medical witness can lay the foundation for admissibility by testifying why the information is medically significant.

QUESTION 30. The plaintiff sued the defendant for running into him with his car while plaintiff was crossing the street. Plaintiff claims that he suffered a herniated disc as a result of the accident. At trial, plaintiff called the treating physician as a witness and she would testify that plaintiff told her that he had pain in his lower back, that the pain sometimes shot down into his legs, and that the pain began several hours after the accident. How should the court rule on the defense objection?

A. Overruled, statements made to obtain medical treatment.
B. Overruled as to the description of the pain, but sustained with respect to the statement that the pain began several hours after the accident.
C. Overruled, statement by a party opponent.
D. Sustained, hearsay.

ANALYSIS. The declarant is the plaintiff and the words in question are what the plaintiff told the doctor. They contain assertions, and plaintiff is offering them to prove the truth of those assertions, so they are hearsay. The plaintiff is offering his own statements, so they are not statements by an opposing party and **C** is incorrect. The declarant made the statements to obtain medical treatment and so they appear to fall within the exception. That the pain began shortly after the accident suggests that the accident caused the pain. Should the objection be sustained to this part of the statement, as **B** suggests? No. The rule permits statements about history, inception of symptoms, and causation, as long as the information is pertinent to diagnosis and treatment. The identity of the other driver in the accident would not be pertinent to treatment, but the fact that the pain was caused by a traumatic incident would be. Thus **A** is the correct answer and **B** and **D** are incorrect.

QUESTION 31. The plaintiff sued the defendant for civil assault and battery, seeking damages for a traumatic brain injury. Plaintiff called a nurse from the emergency room as a witness. She described the head injuries she observed and now is prepared to testify that the police officer who brought the plaintiff to the ER for treatment said that the plaintiff suffered injuries when someone struck him in the head with a blunt object. How should the court rule on the defendant's objection to the testimony about what the police officer said?

A. Admissible, statement for purposes of medical treatment.
B. Inadmissible, the patient did not make statement to a medical provider.
C. Inadmissible, the statement is not pertinent to treatment.
D. Inadmissible, declarant lacked personal knowledge.

ANALYSIS. Here the declarant is the police officer and the statement was that the plaintiff suffered injuries when someone struck him in the head with a blunt object. There is an assertion, and plaintiff is offering the evidence to prove the truth of that assertion, so it would be hearsay unless it falls within an exception. In order to qualify as a statement made to obtain medical treatment, the statement does not have to be made by the patient, so **B** is incorrect. The manner in which the plaintiff sustained a head injury is pertinent to diagnosis and treatment, thus **C** is incorrect. There is no showing, however, that the police officer had any personal knowledge of how the plaintiff was injured. He might have seen the assault, but we have no basis for concluding that he did. He might have been repeating something that someone else told him, or he might have made a hasty assumption based on incomplete knowledge. The burden is on the party seeking to use a hearsay exception to provide the necessary foundation and here it is absent. Thus **D** is the correct answer and this evidence should be excluded. Choice **A** is incorrect.

d. Recorded Recollection   Rule 803(5) provides a hearsay exception for recorded recollections. We discussed this exception in Chapter 6, Witnesses and Impeachment.

e. Business Records   Rule 803(6) provides a hearsay exception for records of regularly conducted activity, generally known as "business records."

Rule 803(6)

(6) Records of a Regularly Conducted Activity. A record of an act, event, condition, opinion, or diagnosis if:

(A) the record was made at or near the time by—or from information transmitted by—someone with knowledge;

(B) the record was kept in the course of a regularly conducted activity of a business, organization, occupation, or calling, whether or not for profit;

(C) making the record was a regular practice of that activity;

(D) all these conditions are shown by the testimony of the custodian or another qualified witness, or by a certification that complies with Rule 902(11) or (12) or with a statute permitting certification; and

(E) the opponent does not show that the source of information or the method or circumstances of preparation indicate a lack of trustworthiness.

The exception for business records is one of the most commonly employed hearsay exceptions. The rule makes it unnecessary to call live witnesses to testify to the myriad facts that are routinely recorded by institutions on paper records or computer files. It eliminates the need to take people away from work to appear in court and allows for a more efficient presentation of facts. Because records routinely kept are usually more accurate than human memory, it also promotes accurate fact-finding.

To be admissible, records must be kept in the ordinary course of business, and it must be a regular practice to keep the type of record in question. A simple example is an inventory detailing the contents of a shipment delivered to a warehouse. Rather than calling a driver to testify what was on his truck on a particular day or calling the warehouseman to testify what he received from that driver on that day (something neither is likely to remember months later), we introduce the written inventory in evidence. The inventory is hearsay because it contains assertions about what the delivery contained, and we would be introducing it in evidence to prove the truth of those assertions. But it would be nonsensical to exclude it given that it is probably the best evidence of what the delivery contained. The rule requires that the record be kept in the ordinary course of business because a note or memo that is just made on one occasion does not have the reliability of records that are routinely kept.

The rule also requires that someone with personal knowledge of the information or someone who has obtained the information from someone with knowledge make the record. Because the record must be kept in the regular course of business, the person who makes the record also must have a business duty to do so. Records made by outsiders not part of the institution in question would not qualify.

The custodian of the records or another witness who is familiar with the record keeping practices of the institution can testify to the above foundational requirements. It is more common for institutions to send records to court with an appropriate certificate under Rule 902, and then it is not necessary to call a witness to establish the foundation.

The institution does not have to be a profit-making business for this hearsay exception to apply, but it must be some sort of business, organization, occupation, or calling. For example, one's personal checkbook or a hobbyist's records of her personal stamp collection would not qualify as a business record.

Business records frequently raise multiple hearsay issues. The document itself is hearsay if offered for its truth and if the author of the document reports statements by others and they are offered for their truth, we have multiple hearsay. The statements by others are not admissible unless they fall within another exception to the hearsay rule. Whenever there is any document, including business records, offered in evidence, you must be particularly watchful for multiple hearsay, and you must have a hearsay exception for each declarant.

To see how the business records exception works, let's consider this medical record, a common example of a business record:

Emergency Room Report

Name: *John Jones*
DOB: *12-5-80*
BP: *160/95*
Resp: *19*
Temp: *99.8*
Eyes: *PERL*

Exam: *Pt has 3 cm laceration over the right eye; swelling about the right mandible; strong odor of ETOH. Jackson, M.D.*

Hx: *Pt hit by car while crossing street in crosswalk. No LOC.*

Assume that this is a form, where the material in a regular font was printed on the form, and the material in italics was handwritten. Let's further assume that we have established that in this hospital the nurse records the information on the form, except for the "Exam" section and the drawing, which the doctor adds. Finally let's assume that the plaintiff in a personal injury case is offering the entire report for its truth.

The ER report was prepared in the ordinary course of business and it is routine practice to prepare such reports in the hospital. It was produced in response to a subpoena and came to court with an appropriate certificate under Rule 902, establishing its authenticity and the foundational requirements.

The nurse is the declarant for the sections she fills in, and she has a business duty to record this information. The nurse has personally observed some of the information she supplies: the blood pressure, respirations per minute, temperature, and with respect to the patient's eyes, "PERL" (pupils equal and react to light). The doctor is the declarant for the information she adds, and she has a business duty to record this information. The doctor has personally observed the facts she reports: the laceration, the swelling, and the strong odor of alcohol. She records the information in words and in a drawing, both of which constitute "statements" for purposes of the hearsay rule. Everything on the record that the nurse and doctor reported based on their personal observations is admissible as a business record.

The name, date of birth, and history are things the patient told the nurse. The nurse is the declarant as far as writing them on the record is concerned, and the patient is the declarant as far as stating the information to the nurse. This information raises a multiple hearsay problem. Insofar as the nurse is the declarant, her statements fall within the business records exception. To admit the information, however, we have to find an exception for the patient as a declarant. Here the exception would be statements made for the purpose of medical diagnosis or treatment. The patient tells the nurse his name, date of birth, how he got hurt, and the fact that he suffered no loss of consciousness in order to get treatment.

All of the information on the report is admissible, with one exception. The fact that the patient was in the crosswalk when he was hit by the car is not pertinent to diagnosis and treatment; it is relevant only with respect to who was at fault. Thus that information does not fall within the exception for statements made to obtain a medical diagnosis or treatment. So before this record would be admitted in evidence, we would have to redact the words "in crosswalk" from the report.

There is one final issue with respect to business records: trustworthiness. The opponent can object to a business record that would otherwise qualify for admissibility on the ground that the source of information or the method or circumstances of the preparation of the record indicate a lack of trustworthiness. The burden of establishing that the record is not trustworthy is on the opponent, as the Rule, amended in 2014, explicitly provides.

Courts take a variety of factors into account in assessing the trustworthiness of business records. If a record is made in anticipation of or with an eye to litigation, that undermines its trustworthiness. On the other hand, if the matter recorded is highly important to the business without regard to litigation, that adds to its trustworthiness. Other factors include whether the report was acted upon, whether there was any motive to falsify the information, whether the institution monitors inaccurate reporting, and whether the report is offered by or against the institution that prepared it. Reports of simple factual data are generally considered more trustworthy than opinions or conclusions in reports.

QUESTION 32. The defendant is on trial for the crime of bribing a public official to obtain a construction contract. The defendant has denied that he gave anything of value to the official. The prosecution has subpoenaed the sales records of a local jewelry store, which were produced with an appropriate certificate under Rule 902. The prosecution offers in evidence an invoice showing that the defendant charged a diamond tennis bracelet to his account and requested that it be shipped to the public official's home address. The defense objection to this exhibit should be:

A. Sustained, hearsay.
B. Sustained, the prosecution has not offered any records of the defendant.
C. Overruled, business records exception.
D. Overruled, statement by a party opponent.

ANALYSIS. The declarant is the employee of the jewelry store that wrote out the invoice in question. It contains the assertion that the defendant charged a tennis bracelet to his account and directed that it be shipped to the public official's home, and is offered to prove precisely that. The invoice is hearsay and inadmissible unless it falls within an exception.

Does it matter that this is a record from a third party? No, there is nothing that limits the business records that are admissible to the records of the parties in the case, thus **B** is incorrect. The invoice was made by someone with knowledge of the sale it records, was made in the ordinary course of business, and it was the regular practice of the store to make this type of record. The store employee does not have to rely on the customer's assertion of his name to identify him as the defendant, because he is billing the purchase to his account and must provide an account number. The store employee checks the identification of the customer. This is an ordinary example of the sort of document that is admissible under the business records exception. Thus **C** is the correct answer.

Is this a multiple hearsay problem? Is the defendant a second declarant who made a statement containing assertions at the time he placed the order? First, if he were it would not affect the admissibility of this record. The prosecution is offering the exhibit and the defendant is an opposing party, so any statements by the defendant would be admissible as statements by the opposing party. More fundamentally, when the defendant placed the order he was not making assertions, he was engaging in the *act* of ordering merchandise. "Please charge my account for the bracelet and send it to the following address . . ." is a verbal act, namely placing an order, which has independent legal significance much like language that constitutes an offer or acceptance during the making of a contract. Choice **D** is incorrect because the hearsay in this problem is the written invoice by the store employee, not the order by the defendant.

QUESTION 33. Plaintiff has sued the defendant grocery store after a tall display of cans fell on him, causing injuries. The files of the store contain a handwritten note from a worker, whose job includes stocking shelves, stating, "Boss, I know we don't usually put stuff like this in writing, but I think you should know I told my co-worker, Jerry, it was dangerous to stack the cans so high." Assume someone with knowledge identifies the handwriting. Plaintiff offers the note at trial. The defendant's objection should be:

A. Sustained, hearsay.
B. Overruled, not offered to prove truth of an assertion.
C. Overruled, business records exception.
D. Overruled, statement by a party opponent.

ANALYSIS. The declarant is the worker who wrote the note. The note contains an implied assertion that the cans were stacked too high. The plaintiff is offering the note to prove the truth of that assertion. Thus **B** is incorrect. The evidence is hearsay and would be inadmissible unless it falls within an exception. The note does not fall within the business records exception because it was not prepared in the ordinary course of business. This is clear from the fact that the worker states that he knows they do not usually put this type of thing in writing. Thus **C** is incorrect. The note is admissible, however, as a statement by a party opponent. The worker was employed by the grocery store and was making a statement about something within his scope of employment. Thus **D** is correct and **A** is incorrect.

QUESTION 34. Plaintiff has sued the defendant, a small independent software maker, for damages he sustained when the software he purchased from the defendant failed and erased substantial amounts of data from the plaintiff's computer. Plaintiff offers in evidence the defendant's records of software returns, which include the name of the customer, the date, and the reason the customer gave for the return. The records show that before the plaintiff made his purchase, thirty other customers had returned the same type of software, stating that it had failed and resulted in the deletion of data from their computers. Plaintiff offers this evidence both to prove that the software was defective, and to show that the defendant was on notice of the problem when he sold software to the plaintiff. The defendant's objection to the records should be:

A. Sustained, hearsay.
B. Overruled, business records exception.
C. Overruled, statement by a party opponent.
D. Overruled, with a limiting instruction that the evidence is only admissible to show that the defendant was aware of a potential problem with the software.

ANALYSIS. The declarant is the person who made the records of software returns, presumably either the defendant or one of his employees. The records contain assertions concerning the reason the software was returned and the plaintiff is offering the records both to prove the truth of those assertions (that the software was defective) and to prove that the defendant had notice of the potential problem. To prove the truth of the customers' assertions the records are hearsay; although merely to prove notice to the defendant they are not hearsay. Choice **A** is incorrect because it would not be proper to exclude the records altogether, given that they are admissible at least to prove notice of the problem to the defendant.

The material in the "reasons for return" section for the record does not fall within the business records exception because the person who supplied the information was not an employee of the business and had no business duty to report the information. Choice **B** is incorrect because the reasons the customers gave for returning the software are not admissible as business records of the defendant's business. Nor are they admissible as statements by a party opponent, the defendant, and thus **C** is incorrect as well. Although the records are statements by the defendant, they include statements by the customers. Whether we analyze the records as business records or statements by a party opponent, there is a multiple hearsay problem. There is no exception for the statements made by the customer declarants, and they cannot be admitted for their truth. The records can be admitted only to show that there were returns, and that the defendant was on notice that customers were claiming that there was a problem with the software. Thus **D** is the correct answer.

f. Public Records   Rule 803(8) makes three categories of public records admissible under a hearsay exception:

(8) Public Records.
A record or statement of a public office if:
    (A) it sets out:
        (i) the office's activities;
        (ii) a matter observed while under a legal duty to report, but not including, in a criminal case, a matter observed by law-enforcement personnel; or
        (iii) in a civil case or against the government in a criminal case, factual findings from a legally authorized investigation; and
    (B) the opponent does not show that the source of information or other circumstances indicate a lack of trustworthiness.

The first type of public record is a report of the office's activities. This is very straightforward and seldom results in significant disputes. For example, the passport office of the United States State Department issues passports to U.S. citizens for travel abroad. The records of the passport office could be introduced in order to prove that it issued a passport to a given person on a given date.

The second category is a record of an observation by a public official under a legal duty to make observations of that type. For example, the National Weather Service is an office within the U.S. Department of Commerce charged with reporting the amount of rainfall at various locations on a daily basis. We could introduce the records of the Weather Service in order to prove how much rain fell at a given location on a given day. The rule specifically excludes observations by law enforcement personnel in criminal cases. In practice, however, courts admit such evidence when it is offered against the government, but exclude it when offered against the defendant. One reason for the exclusion is that admitting such evidence against the defendant in a criminal case would be highly likely to violate the Confrontation Clause of the Sixth Amendment, because the defendant would not have an opportunity to cross-examine the maker of the record. We will discuss the Confrontation Clause in more detail in a later section of this chapter.

The third category admits factual findings from legally authorized investigations, but only in civil cases and against the government in criminal cases. Such evidence may not be admitted against the defendant in a criminal case, again principally due to Confrontation Clause concerns.

To illustrate the sort of evidence admissible under this category, let's look at the leading Supreme Court case on the subject, *Beech Aircraft Corp. v. Rainey*, 488 U.S. 153 (1988). Navy pilots were killed in a crash during a training exercise and the main question in the case was whether the crash was due to pilot error or equipment malfunction. A Navy JAG officer investigated the incident, came to some conclusions regarding those matters, and wrote a report. The Supreme Court decided that the opinions and conclusions in the report were admissible under the public records exception, 803(3)(A)(iii).

The Court declined to accept the argument of the opponent of this evidence that there is a distinction between "factual" findings and opinions and conclusions that require the drawing of inferences. The Court concluded that any line between "fact" and "opinion" is one of degree only and inevitably arbitrary. It found that the safeguards against the admission of unreliable evidence under this hearsay exception were (1) the necessity of factual investigation to make factual findings, and (2) the trustworthiness requirement in the rule.

Beech Aircraft means that a wide variety of government reports based on factual investigations are admissible in evidence. The author of a government report may rely on outside witnesses as sources of information. Moreover, the author of the report may make credibility determinations concerning those witnesses in reaching conclusions. The rule, however, only renders the report admissible in evidence; it does not require the fact finder to reach the same conclusions as the report.

Although the author of a report may rely on statements of witnesses in reaching his conclusions, such third party statements in reports constitute multiple hearsay and are not admissible unless they fall within another exception to the hearsay rule. If they do not, they must be redacted before the report is introduced in evidence. In other words, conclusions based on third party statements are admissible, but the statements themselves are not unless they fall within a hearsay exception.

The question of whether the report is trustworthy is for the opponent to raise and the opponent has the burden of proof on this issue, as the Rule, amended in 2014, explicitly provides. In determining trustworthiness, the judge should take into account whether the official who wrote the report had special skills or expertise, whether he or she had any bias, how soon the investigation took place relative to the events in question, and whether there were any hearings and how formal the hearings were. Here, as with business records, it is also important to consider whether the report was prepared with an awareness of possible litigation.

QUESTION 35. Plaintiff sued the defendant for injuries he suffered in an automobile accident. The plaintiff offers a report by the police officer who investigated the accident. The report contains this statement: "I arrived at the scene within a couple of minutes of the crash. The passenger in the defendant's vehicle was crying and bleeding and could not stop shaking. She stated, 'I thought I was going to die. You wouldn't believe how fast the defendant was driving when he blew through the red light.'" The plaintiff offers the report in evidence. The defendant's objection should be:

A. Sustained, hearsay.
B. Sustained, lack of personal knowledge.
C. Overruled, public report and excited utterance.
D. Overruled, public report and statement by a party opponent.

ANALYSIS. The police officer is a public official who is required by law to prepare reports of accidents that she investigates. To the extent the report contains her personal observations, it would be admissible as a public record. In this instance, however, the officer is quoting another person, so there is a multiple hearsay problem. The declarants are the officer as the author of the report and the passenger in the defendant's vehicle with respect to her statements. The officer as a declarant falls within the public records exception. The officer does not need personal knowledge of the accident to report what the passenger said, but only personal knowledge that she said it. Thus **B** is incorrect. We do need to find a hearsay exception for the passenger's statement because she makes an assertion and her statement is offered for its truth. She has just been in an accident and is still crying, bleeding, and shaking. Her statement is an excited utterance, and **C** is the correct answer. Choice **D** is incorrect, because although the declarant was a passenger in the defendant's vehicle, she is not a party to the suit.

QUESTION 36. A police officer found the deceased victim of an apparent homicide lying in a pool of blood on the sidewalk in front of a bar late at night. He conducted an investigation and wrote a report of his findings, as required by law. Among other things, the report states, "While I was taking photographs of the scene, a man approached who identified himself and said he lived in the neighborhood. He looked at the body and said the victim had probably been shot by some woman he made angry." The victim's estate has sued the defendant, a former girlfriend of the victim, for wrongful death. The plaintiff offers the police report in evidence. The defense objection should be:

A. Sustained, hearsay.

B. Sustained as to the statements by the witness, overruled with respect to the portions of the report based on the officer's observations and conclusions.

C. Overruled, public report and permissible lay opinion.

D. Overruled, public report and present sense impression.

ANALYSIS. The report itself is admissible under the public records exception because the author was a public official who conducted a factual investigation with legal authorization. Thus it would not be proper to exclude the entire report as hearsay and **A** is incorrect. The report of the statements by the witness constitutes multiple hearsay and for the statements to be admissible there must be hearsay exceptions for both the officer as a declarant and for the witness as a declarant. As we noted above, the officer as a declarant falls under the public records exception. Are the statements of the witness admissible as permissible lay opinion? As we saw in Chapter 7, for a lay opinion to be admissible it must be rationally based on perceptions by the witness. Here the witness did not observe anything that supports the conclusion that an angry woman killed the victim and so **C** is incorrect. Are the witness's statements admissible as a present sense impression? No, because the witness had no personal knowledge as to who caused the victim's death. Thus **D** is incorrect. The correct answer is **B**. Other parts of the report are admissible, but the statements of the witness must be redacted before it is admitted.

QUESTION 37. Plaintiff, the executor of decedent's estate, sued the defendant police officer for excessive use of force under the federal civil rights act. The officer had shot and killed the decedent during a riot. The main issue in the case was whether the officer's use of force was justified under all the circumstances. At trial the defendant officer offers a report prepared by a lieutenant in his department, following a factual investigation pursuant to state law. The lieutenant interviewed the available witnesses and examined the physical evidence. The report described in detail the factual circumstances under which the officer fired, and concluded that the officer's use of force was reasonable. What is the plaintiff's best argument to support his objection to the report's conclusion?

A. The report is hearsay not within any exception to the hearsay rule.
B. The lieutenant based his conclusion on hearsay statements by witnesses.
C. The lieutenant's conclusion was not a "factual finding," but an opinion based on inferences he drew.
D. The report is not trustworthy.

ANALYSIS. This hypothetical question parallels *Beech Aircraft* to a great extent. The report qualifies as a public record. A public official authored the report following a factual investigation authorized by law and it contains factual findings. Thus **A** is incorrect. Choice **B** is incorrect because public officials are entitled to speak with witnesses in conducting factual investigations and to base their conclusions in part on witness statements. *Beech Aircraft* specifically rejects the distinction between factual findings and opinions or conclusions, so **C** is incorrect. Although based on the limited facts provided we could not predict how a judge would rule, the plaintiff's best argument is **D**, that the report is not trustworthy. The lieutenant was undoubtedly aware that there might be litigation over the shooting; there is a possibility that he was biased in favor of the defendant, a member of his police department; and there was no hearing that supported the lieutenant's conclusions. Although a judge might find that the report was trustworthy enough to be admitted, these factors undermine trustworthiness in this case.

g. Vital Statistics   Rule 803(9) provides a specific exception for records of vital statistics.

> **(9) Public Records of Vital Statistics.**
> A record of a birth, death, or marriage, if reported to a public office in accordance with a legal duty.

Certain occupations and officials are required to report births, deaths, and marriages to public offices. The public records of such events are admissible under this exception.

h. Absence of Records   Sections (7) and (10) of Rule 803 provide a hearsay exception for the absence of records.

> **(7) Absence of a Record of a Regularly Conducted Activity.**
> Evidence that a matter is not included in a record described in paragraph (6) if:
>   **(A)** the evidence is admitted to prove that the matter did not occur or exist;
>   **(B)** a record was regularly kept for a matter of that kind; and
>   **(C)** the opponent does not show that the possible source of the information or other circumstances indicate a lack of trustworthiness.

> **(10) Absence of a Public Record.**
> Testimony—or a certification under Rule 902—that a diligent search failed to disclose a public record or statement if:
>   **(A)** the testimony or certification is admitted to prove that
>   **(i)** the record or statement does not exist; or
>   **(ii)** a matter did not occur or exist, if a public office regularly kept a record or statement for a matter of that kind; and
>   **(B)** in a criminal case, a prosecutor who intends to offer a certification provides written notice of that intent at least 14 days before trial, and the defendant does not object in writing within 7 days of receiving the notice—unless the court sets a different time for the notice or the objection.

These handy rules provide a method for proving the existence of a negative, that is, that something did not happen. If we would expect to find a record of a matter in business records or public records, because matters of that type were ordinarily recorded, the absence of a record provides a basis for concluding that the matter did not occur or exist. The proponent can show this either through testimony by the custodian of the records, or an appropriate certificate that no such record could be found under Rule 902.

For example, suppose the prosecution has charged the defendant in a criminal case with carrying a firearm without a license. To prove the absence of a license, the prosecutor could issue a subpoena to the licensing authority for any and all records of a firearms license issued to the defendant. If they could not find such a license, the agency could file a certificate with the court indicating that a due and diligent search was made for such a record and none was found.

In criminal cases the defendant would have a right under the Confrontation Clause of the Sixth Amendment to cross-examine the person who made the search. Hence the Rule was amended in 2013 to provide that where a prosecutor intends to offer a certificate rather than a live witness, the prosecution must give notice to the defendant and an opportunity for the defendant to object to proceeding by means of a certificate.

In 2014, Rule 803(7) was amended to clarify that with respect to the inference to be drawn due to the absence of business records under Rule 803(6), the burden of proof to show a lack of trustworthiness is on the opponent.

i. Ancient Documents   Rule 803(16) provides a hearsay exception for statements in ancient documents.

> **(16) Statements in Ancient Documents.**
> A statement in a document that was prepared before January 1, 1998, and whose authenticity is established.

Prior to 2014, ancient documents were defined as those that were at least twenty years old and whose authenticity was established. The Rule was amended to limit it to documents that were prepared before January 1, 1998. The purpose of the change was to render inadmissible unreliable electronically stored information, which has grown exponentially since 1998. Twenty-year-old hardcopy documents generated after 1998 may still be admissible, if shown to be reliable, under Rule 807.

j. Market Reports and Commercial Publications   Rule 803(17) provides a hearsay exception for the sort of data that business people routinely rely upon.

> **(17) Market Reports and Similar Commercial Publications.**
> Market quotations, lists, directories, or other compilations that are generally relied on by the public or by persons in particular occupations.

The rationale for this exception is that if the information is reliable enough for the business world, it is reliable enough for the courtroom.

k. Learned Treatises   Rule 803(18) provides a hearsay exception for the use of learned treatises.

> **(18) Statements in Learned Treatises, Periodicals, or Pamphlets.**
> A statement contained in a treatise, periodical, or pamphlet if:
>   (A) the statement is called to the attention of an expert witness on cross-examination or relied on by the expert on direct examination; and
>   (B) the publication is established as a reliable authority by the expert's admission or testimony, by another expert's testimony, or by judicial notice.
>   If admitted, the statement may be read into evidence but not received as an exhibit.

The declarant is the author of the treatise or publication in question and the proponent of the evidence is offering assertions in the treatise for their truth.

The proponent must establish that the treatise is a reliable authority through a stipulation by the parties, the testimony of an expert, or by asking the court to take judicial notice of its reliability. The proponent may use statements from the treatise either during the examination of his own expert, or on cross-examination of an opposing expert. The rule does not permit us to introduce the publication in question as an exhibit, however, but only to read the statements in question into evidence.

l. Reputation Concerning Character   We saw in Chapter 4 that when character evidence is admissible, ordinarily we may prove character only by offering opinion or reputation evidence. Rule 803(21) provides a hearsay exception for reputation evidence with respect to character.

> **(21) Reputation Concerning Character.**
> A reputation among a person's associates or in the community concerning the person's character.

Reputation evidence is what people in the community say about a person. Suppose a witness testifies, "I am familiar with the defendant's reputation in the community with respect to violence. He has a reputation as a very violent individual." The declarants are the people in the community who say that the defendant is violent. They made assertions about the person's character and we introduce reputation evidence to prove the truth of those assertions. Therefore reputation evidence is hearsay and it would be inadmissible unless there were an exception for it. This exception provides one.

m. Judgment of Conviction   Rule 803(22) provides a hearsay exception for a previous judgment of a felony conviction.

> **(22) Judgment of a Previous Conviction.**
> Evidence of a final judgment of conviction if:
>   (A) the judgment was entered after a trial or guilty plea, but not a nolo contendere plea;
>   (B) the conviction was for a crime punishable by death or by imprisonment for more than a year;
>   (C) the evidence is admitted to prove any fact essential to the judgment; and
>   (D) when offered by the prosecutor in a criminal case for a purpose other than impeachment, the judgment was against the defendant.
>   The pendency of an appeal may be shown but does not affect admissibility.

This is a very useful hearsay exception that promotes judicial economy. Suppose plaintiff sued defendant for wrongful death, alleging that defendant negligently caused an automobile accident that resulted in the death of plaintiff's decedent. Plaintiff has a judgment showing that the defendant was convicted of negligent homicide. This exception provides that the plaintiff may introduce the judgment to prove any fact that was essential to the judgment of conviction. The previous judgment is not conclusive proof of such facts, but it is admissible evidence of them. As a practical matter in many cases it would not be necessary to offer additional evidence, at least with respect to some of the matters in question.

Why is a hearsay exception necessary to introduce such evidence? The judgment of conviction is an out of court statement containing an assertion that the defendant was guilty. In essence, the jurors in the previous trial are the declarants. If we introduce the judgment to prove the truth of the assertion that the defendant was guilty, it is hearsay. Section (22) provides the exception for the admissibility of this hearsay.

Note that if the prosecution offers a judgment of conviction to prove facts in a criminal case the previous judgment must have been against the defendant in the present case.

n. Remaining Rule 803 Exceptions   The remaining Rule 803 exceptions are straightforward and do not require detailed explanations. We set forth the rules in question here.

(11) Records of Religious Organizations Concerning Personal or Family History.
A statement of birth, legitimacy, ancestry, marriage, divorce, death, relationship by blood or marriage, or similar facts of personal or family history, contained in a regularly kept record of a religious organization.

(12) Certificates of Marriage, Baptism, and Similar Ceremonies.
A statement of fact contained in a certificate:

(A) made by a person who is authorized by a religious organization or by law to perform the act certified;

(B) attesting that the person performed a marriage or similar ceremony or administered a sacrament; and

(C) purporting to have been issued at the time of the act or within a reasonable time after it.

(13) Family Records.
A statement of fact about personal or family history contained in a family record, such as a Bible, genealogy, chart, engraving on a ring, inscription on a portrait, or engraving on an urn or burial marker.

(14) Records of Documents That Affect an Interest in Property.
The record of a document that purports to establish or affect an interest in property if:

(A) the record is admitted to prove the content of the original recorded document, along with its signing and its delivery by each person who purports to have signed it;

(B) the record is kept in a public office; and

(C) a statute authorizes recording documents of that kind in that office.

(15) Statements in Documents That Affect an Interest in Property.
A statement contained in a document that purports to establish or affect an interest in property if the matter stated was relevant to the document's

purpose—unless later dealings with the property are inconsistent with the truth of the statement or the purport of the document.

(19) Reputation Concerning Personal or Family History.
A reputation among a person's family by blood, adoption, or marriage—or among a person's associates or in the community—concerning the person's birth, adoption, legitimacy, ancestry, marriage, divorce, death, relationship by blood, adoption, or marriage, or similar facts of personal or family history.

(20) Reputation Concerning Boundaries or General History.
A reputation in a community—arising before the controversy—concerning boundaries of land in the community or customs that affect the land, or concerning general historical events important to that community, state, or nation.

(23) Judgments Involving Personal, Family, or General History, or a Boundary.
A judgment that is admitted to prove a matter of personal, family, or general history, or boundaries, if the matter:
    (A) was essential to the judgment; and
    (B) could be proved by evidence of reputation.

4. Rule 804 Exceptions

a. Unavailability of Declarant's Live Testimony   Rule 804 provides five hearsay exceptions. The exceptions only apply when the declarant's live testimony is unavailable. The rule defines unavailability.

> **Rule 804. Hearsay Exceptions; Declarant Unavailable**
>
>   (a) Criteria for Being Unavailable. A declarant is considered to be unavailable as a witness if the declarant:
>
>   (1) is exempted from testifying about the subject matter of the declarant's statement because the court rules that a privilege applies;
>
>   (2) refuses to testify about the subject matter despite a court order to do so;
>
>   (3) testifies to not remembering the subject matter;
>
>   (4) cannot be present or testify at the trial or hearing because of death or a then-existing infirmity, physical illness, or mental illness; or
>
>   (5) is absent from the trial or hearing and the statement's proponent has not been able, by process or other reasonable means, to procure:
>
>   (A) the declarant's attendance, in the case of a hearsay exception under Rule 804(b)(1) or (6); or
>
>   (B) the declarant's attendance or testimony, in the case of a hearsay exception under Rule 804(b)(2), (3), or (4).
>
>   But this subdivision (a) does not apply if the statement's proponent procured or wrongfully caused the declarant's unavailability as a witness in order to prevent the declarant from attending or testifying.

The issue is whether live testimony from the witness is available. The proponent might not be able to obtain the presence of the witness because he is ill or infirm, dead, or cannot be located or served with a subpoena. The witness might be present, but his testimony might still be unavailable if the court rules the testimony is privileged, the witness refuses to testify, or the witness has no memory of the subject matter, as provided in the rule. If the proponent asserts that the witness cannot be found, or his appearance cannot be procured by subpoena, the proponent must establish that he made a good faith effort to locate the witness and obtain his attendance. If the proponent of the hearsay statement has procured or wrongfully caused the unavailability of the declarant's testimony, the court will not consider the testimony to be unavailable and the exceptions will not apply.

Note that unavailability itself is not a hearsay exception. The mere fact that a witness is not present or will not testify does not justify admitting his hearsay statements. Unavailability is a prerequisite to using the exceptions in Rule 804. To use the exceptions, the proponent must establish both unavailability and the individual requirements of the exception in question. Under Rule 104(a) the judge determines whether a witness is unavailable and whether the proponent has established the foundation for employing these hearsay exceptions.

b. Former Testimony   Rule 804(b)(1) provides a hearsay exception for previous testimony under specified conditions.

> (1) **Former Testimony.**
> Testimony that:
>   (A) was given as a witness at a trial, hearing, or lawful deposition, whether given during the current proceeding or a different one; and
>   (B) is now offered against a party who had—or, in a civil case, whose predecessor in interest had—an opportunity and similar motive to develop it by direct, cross-, or redirect examination.

When the testimony of a witness is not available at a trial or hearing, but the witness has testified at an earlier proceeding, the proponent may be able to offer the previous testimony. It does not matter whether the witness's previous testimony was in the same case or a different one. In a criminal case, what is essential is that the opponent must have had an opportunity and a similar motive to examine the witness at the prior proceeding. In a civil case, it is sufficient if the opponent's predecessor in interest had an opportunity and similar motive to examine the witness in the prior proceeding. Actual examination or cross-examination is not required. What is required is the opportunity to examine and a motive similar to the motive the opponent would have to develop the testimony in the present proceeding.

Suppose a criminal defendant was tried and convicted of robbery, then appealed and won a new trial. The victim of the robbery died while the appeal was pending. At the retrial on the robbery charge the victim is obviously unavailable. The prosecutor may read the transcript of the victim's testimony at the original trial to the jury in the retrial. The defendant had an opportunity to cross-examine the victim in the original trial, and given that the charge against him has not changed, his motive for developing the testimony will be the same in the retrial as it was in the original trial.

The former testimony exception applies to testimony given in another trial, a preliminary hearing, a motion hearing, other formal proceedings where examination and cross-examination are permitted, and depositions. The prosecution may never offer grand jury testimony against a criminal defendant, because the defendant never has an opportunity to cross-examine witnesses at a grand jury. Whether the defendant may offer grand jury testimony against the government will depend on whether the prosecution's motive to question the witness at the grand jury was the same as it would be at a later criminal trial.

When the prosecution offers former testimony against a criminal defendant, the defendant's right to an opportunity and similar motive to cross-examine the witness at the earlier proceeding is secured not only by the language of the rule, but also by the Confrontation Clause of the Sixth Amendment, discussed below. Courts have been generous in admitting testimony from preliminary hearings against a criminal defendant at trial, even though from a tactical perspective the motive to cross-examine at a preliminary hearing may be somewhat different than at trial.

In civil cases many courts have been generous in their reading of the "predecessor in interest" requirement. Such decisions have not limited the term to property interests, but have focused on whether the previous examination was conducted by someone with the same motive as the current party against whom the testimony is offered.

QUESTION 38. The defendant is on trial for motor vehicle homicide in the state superior court. He was previously tried in a lower court on the charge of improperly changing lanes during the same incident. A witness who saw the accident testified that the defendant changed lanes without signaling and collided with the decedent's vehicle. The defendant had an opportunity to cross-examine the witness at the lower court trial, but chose not to. The defendant was convicted and fined $500 on the motor vehicle violation. The prosecution cannot locate the witness at present, despite sending subpoenas to all his known addresses, checking the records of several state agencies, and having two investigators look for him during the two months prior to trial. The prosecution offers the witness's testimony from the earlier trial. The defense objection should be:

A. Overruled, former testimony exception.
B. Sustained, no one should be convicted of homicide in the absence of live witnesses to prove the case.
C. Sustained, prosecution has not made a sufficient showing that the witness is unavailable.
D. Sustained, the defendant did not have a similar motive to cross-examine the witness at the earlier trial.

ANALYSIS. The testimony from the previous trial is hearsay and inadmissible unless it falls within an exception. If an exception applies, however, the previous testimony would be admissible, despite the fact that defendant is on trial for homicide, a very serious charge. The rules of evidence do not change depending on the gravity of the case. Thus **B** is incorrect. To use the former testimony exception the prosecution must establish that the witness is unavailable. The evidence here demonstrates a good faith effort to locate the witness and the court should find the witness unavailable. Thus **C** is incorrect.

The first trial was for a motor vehicle offense that, standing alone, was not very serious as indicated by the fact that the court imposed a fine for the violation. With the far more serious homicide trial in the future, most defendants would not conduct a full cross-examination of the witness at the first trial and many would not question him at all at that point. The court should rule the previous testimony inadmissible because the defendant did not have a similar motive to cross-examine the witness at the earlier trial. Choice **D** is the correct answer and **A** is incorrect.

QUESTION 39. The defendant is on trial for bank robbery. It is the second trial, the first having ended in a mistrial due to a hung jury just one month ago. The prosecution would like to call the bank teller as a witness, to identify the defendant as the robber, but the teller cannot be found. The prosecutor has demonstrated to the court that he issued a subpoena to the teller's last known address and has had police officers look for him, all to no avail. Which of the following items of evidence will be admissible in lieu of live testimony from the teller?

A. The testimony of the teller from the first trial, where the defense lawyer failed to cross-examine him.
B. Testimony by a police officer that the teller identified the defendant at a line-up at the police station, where the defense lawyer was present.
C. The grand jury testimony of the teller.
D. A sworn affidavit from the teller identifying the defendant as the robber.

ANALYSIS. The prosecutor has made a sufficient showing of unavailability under Rule 804 to justify the use of former testimony. But first let's deal with the answers that do not constitute former testimony. As we discussed above, statements of identification of a person after perceiving him are treated as admissible and not hearsay under Rule 801(d)(1)(c). In order to use that rule, however, the declarant has to be present at the trial and subject to cross-examination. Because the teller is not present at the current trial, this rule cannot be invoked and thus **B** is incorrect. An affidavit executed outside of court constitutes hearsay and the fact that it is sworn does not make it admissible. Thus **D**

is incorrect. The grand jury testimony of the teller is former testimony. Neither the defendant nor his lawyer are allowed to be present at the grand jury, however, so the defendant had no opportunity to cross-examine the teller on that occasion. Thus **C** is incorrect. Choice **A** is the correct answer. Even though defense counsel did not cross-examine the teller at the first trial, he had an opportunity to do so and the motivation for the defendant to cross-examine was the same as it would be in the present trial. Actual cross-examination is not required, as long as the defendant had an opportunity and a similar motive to conduct cross-examination as he would have in the proceeding in which the former testimony is offered.

c. Dying Declarations   Rule 804(b)(2) recognizes a hearsay exception for certain statements made when the declarant believes that his death is imminent.

> **(2) Statement Under the Belief of Imminent Death.**
> In a prosecution for homicide or in a civil case, a statement that the declarant, while believing the declarant's death to be imminent, made about its cause or circumstances.

This exception is rarely employed. You probably have a better chance of seeing a question about it on the bar examination than you do of encountering it in practice. The exception applies only in civil cases and in homicide cases; it is not applicable in other criminal cases. It requires that the declarant believed his death to be imminent and that the statement was about the cause or circumstances of declarant's death. The declarant does not actually have to die, but the evidence must show that he believed he was going to die soon. Justice Cardozo wrote in a famous case, "There must be 'a settled hopeless expectation' that death is near at hand, and what is said must have been spoken in the hush of its impending presence."[6] The Supreme Court has indicated in dictum that dying declarations are not subject to the Confrontation Clause, because they were treated as an exception to the right of confrontation at common law.[7]

QUESTION 40. The declarant, a bank robber, was shot as he was leaving the bank. Near death on the street in front of the bank, with officers unable to stop the flow of blood, he whispered that he knew he was "done for." The declarant then tells the police that *A* is charged with a murder that he did not commit, that the declarant witnessed it, and that *B* was the killer. *A* is on trial for the murder in question and calls one of the officers to testify to what the declarant bank robber said. The prosecution's objection should be:

---

6. *Shepard v. United States*, 290 U.S. 96, 100 (1933).
7. *Crawford v. Washington*, 541 U.S. 36, 56, n.6 (2004).

A. Sustained, hearsay.
B. Overruled, hearsay should be admitted against the prosecution when it might keep an innocent person from going to prison.
C. Overruled, excited utterance.
D. Overruled, dying declaration.

ANALYSIS.   There is no exception to the hearsay rules specifically designed to protect criminal defendants (or anyone else). There is a residual hearsay exception that may under certain circumstances apply when no other exception applies, and we will discuss that below. Choice **B** is phrased far too broadly, however, and is incorrect. The declarant was just shot, which is a startling event, and he was no doubt still under the influence of that event. His statement, however, does not relate to the startling event and is not admissible as an excited utterance. Thus **C** is incorrect. There is a sufficient showing that the declarant believed his death was imminent—he knew he was "done for"—but his statement about the murder does not relate to the cause or circumstances of his own death. Therefore it does not qualify as a dying declaration. Choice **A** is the correct answer and **D** is incorrect.

d. Declarations Against Interest   Rule 804(b)(3) provides a hearsay exception for statements of an unavailable declarant that were against the declarant's penal or pecuniary interest when made.

> **(3) Statement Against Interest.**
> A statement that:
>   (A) a reasonable person in the declarant's position would have made only if the person believed it to be true because, when made, it was so contrary to the declarant's proprietary or pecuniary interest or had so great a tendency to invalidate the declarant's claim against someone else or to expose the declarant to civil or criminal liability; and
>   (B) is supported by corroborating circumstances that clearly indicate its trustworthiness, if it is offered in a criminal case as one that tends to expose the declarant to criminal liability.

Statements are admissible if they were so contrary to the declarant's penal or pecuniary interest that a reasonable person would not have made them unless they were true. The disadvantage must have been apparent to the declarant at the time the statement was made. The statement, "I just remembered I owe you a hundred dollars and I forgot to pay you back," is against the declarant's pecuniary interest. The statement, "The police have arrested Jones, but I'm the one who did that robbery," would be against the declarant's penal interest if it were said under circumstances where it might be repeated to the authorities.

   Not every statement in which the declarant admits some wrongdoing is a declaration against interest. For example, suppose the police arrested a member of a narcotics conspiracy. The officer interrogated the suspect and told him, "You could go to prison for twenty years if we charge you with trafficking. But if you cooperate with us and testify against your accomplices, we will recommend a suspended sentence." If the suspect then admitted his participation in the crime and spilled the beans on his co-conspirators, the statements would not be declarations against interest. Cooperating and making the statements served the declarant's interests, which undermines their reliability. Similarly, suppose an arrestee said to a police officer, "Okay, I participated in the robbery, but I didn't do the shooting—that was Smith." The statement was an effort to minimize the declarant's participation in the crime and shift the blame for the shooting to someone else. Depending on all the circumstances, such a statement may not be a declaration against interest.

If the declarant has made a long statement, only those portions of it that were against his interest when made are admissible. The parts of a lengthy narrative that were not against the declarant's interest would have to be redacted before the statement could be admitted.

Do not confuse statements by a party opponent, which are sometimes referred to as "admissions," with declarations against interest. Declarations against interest do not have to be made by parties to the litigation in which they are introduced, and usually are not statements by parties. Declarations against interest do not have to be offered against the declarant or his interest to be admissible. But declarations against interest must have been against the declarant's interest at the time they were made to be admissible. On the other hand, statements by a party opponent do not have to have been against the party's interest to be admissible, they simply must be offered by the opposing party.

Under part (B) of the rule, statements that were against the declarant's penal interest must be corroborated in order to be admissible. For example, if the defendant Jones is being tried for murder and he offers a statement by Smith admitting to the murder, corroboration is necessary for the statement to fall within this exception to the hearsay rule. The same is true when the prosecutor offers a declaration against interest on the ground it exposed the declarant to criminal liability.

QUESTION 41. Defendant is charged with arson of a church. His defense, is that another individual, Frank Firebug, set fire to the church, based solely on the testimony of a Witness. The Witness, who works with Firebug, will testify that Firebug told him that he set fire to the church.

The prosecutor's objection to the Witness's testimony should be:

A. Sustained, because there has been no corroboration of Firebug's statement.
B. Overruled, if defendant can show that Firebug is unavailable as a witness.

C. Overruled, declaration against interest exception.
D. Overruled, because Firebug's statement to the Witness was not made to a police officer.

ANALYSIS.   Firebug's statement is offered for the truth of the assertion that he set fire to the church and is hearsay. Mere unavailability of a witness is not sufficient to establish a hearsay exception. **B** is incorrect. Firebug's statement was a declaration against his penal interest. It is not necessary for such a statement to be made to a police officer to be admissible. Thus, **D** is incorrect. The rule provides, however, that statements against a declarant's penal interest must be corroborated to be admissible. Here there is no corroboration. Hence, **C** is incorrect and the correct answer is **A**.

QUESTION 42. Carmen was arrested for the kidnapping and murder of a child whose body had never been found. The police found her fingerprints in the child's bedroom following the abduction. The police told Carmen that she could avoid the death penalty if she would tell them where the body was. Carmen said she had delivered the child, still alive, to the defendant. The police later found some of the child's clothes in the defendant's home, but the child was never found. Carmen pleads the Fifth Amendment when the prosecutor calls her as a witness at the defendant's trial, and the prosecutor then calls a police officer as a witness to testify what Carmen told him. The defendant's objection should be:

A. Sustained, Carmen is not unavailable.
B. Sustained, hearsay.
C. Admissible, co-conspirator hearsay.
D. Admissible, declaration against interest.

ANALYSIS.   Carmen was the declarant and she made an assertion. The prosecutor is now offering her statement to prove the truth of the assertion and it would be inadmissible as hearsay unless it fell within an exception. It is not admissible as a statement by a co-conspirator because Carmen's participation in the conspiracy ended when she was arrested and began talking with the police. Thus **C** is incorrect. In order to qualify as a declaration against interest, the declarant's testimony must be unavailable at trial. Carmen is present, but her testimony is unavailable because she has asserted her Fifth Amendment rights. Thus **A** is incorrect. Does Carmen's statement qualify as a declaration against interest? There are probably sufficient facts in the case to meet the corroboration requirement, because of the child's clothing found at the defendant's home. Carmen's statement is not against her interest, however, because she made it to avoid the death penalty and to minimize her responsibility for the child's disappearance. She was attempting to serve her interests by talking with the police. Notice that under the facts presented, we really have no good reason to believe Carmen. Perhaps she killed the child and is simply trying to blame the defendant for the death. The statement is inadmissible hearsay. Thus **B** is correct, and **D** is incorrect.

QUESTION 43. *D* is on trial for the murder of *V*. He calls Amber Johnson as a witness. She would testify that her boyfriend Karl said to her before he died, "Baby, we've been together so long and shared so much, I know you ain't gonna rat me out. But I gotta tell you, it's tearing me apart that *D* is gonna go down for *V* when I'm the one who smoked him." *D* also has evidence that Karl's DNA was found in blood left at the crime scene, and another witness saw Karl's car leaving the scene shortly before the victim's body was discovered. How should the court rule on the prosecutor's objection to *D*'s offer of Amber's testimony?

A. Overruled, declaration against interest.
B. Overruled, dying declaration.
C. Sustained, hearsay.

ANALYSIS. The declarant is Karl and *D* is offering Karl's assertion that he killed *V* for its truth. The statement would be hearsay unless it fell within an exception. The fact pattern mentions that Karl died before trial, but there is nothing to suggest that he made the statement in question to Amber at a time when he thought his death was imminent. Therefore it does not qualify as a dying declaration and **B** is incorrect. There is sufficient corroboration for the statement to be admissible as a statement against penal interest. The question is whether the statement was against Karl's penal interest at the time he made it. Here it was not, because Karl did not expect it to be repeated to the authorities. He told Amber, "I know you ain't gonna rat me out." Because Karl did not expect the statement to expose him to criminal liability, it does not qualify as a declaration against interest. Thus **A** is incorrect and the correct answer is **C**.

e. Declarations of Pedigree Rule 804(B)(4) recognizes a hearsay exception for statements of person or family history. The exception is based on the likelihood that such statements are reliable. This exception is straightforward and does not require extended discussion.

(4) Statement of Personal or Family History.
A statement about:
(A) the declarant's own birth, adoption, legitimacy, ancestry, marriage, divorce, relationship by blood, adoption, or marriage, or similar facts of

personal or family history, even though the declarant had no way of acquiring personal knowledge about that fact; or

(B) another person concerning any of these facts, as well as death, if the declarant was related to the person by blood, adoption, or marriage or was so intimately associated with the person's family that the declarant's information is likely to be accurate.

f. Forfeiture by Wrongdoing   Rule 804(B)(6) provides that a party who wrongfully procures the unavailability of a declarant forfeits his ability to object to hearsay from that declarant.

> **(6) Statement Offered Against a Party That Wrongfully Caused the Declarant's Unavailability.**
> A statement offered against a party that wrongfully caused—or acquiesced in wrongfully causing—the declarant's unavailability as a witness, and did so intending that result.

Wrongfully procuring the unavailability of the declarant forfeits not only the party's hearsay objection to his out of court statements, but where the party is a criminal defendant, his Confrontation Clause objection as well. The rule applies where a party has murdered, threatened, or intimidated a witness, or committed a criminal act in order to procure the witness's unavailability. The party's conduct does not have to amount to a criminal act for the rule to apply; collusion with a witness to ensure that the witness will not appear at trial is sufficient as well. The rule would be triggered, for example, by evidence that a party facilitated a witness in taking a vacation to the Islands at the time of the party's trial.

For the rule to apply, the party must intend to procure the declarant's unavailability as a witness. If a party procures the declarant's unavailability for other reasons unconnected with his status as a witness, the rule does not apply. For example, hearsay from murder victims is not admissible against the defendant merely because the defendant is charged with killing the victim. For the forfeiture rule to apply, the defendant must have killed the victim to eliminate him or her as a witness. Once the intent to eliminate the person as a witness has been established, however, hearsay from the unavailable declarant is admissible in all trials against the party who procured his unavailability, not merely in the case in which the party intended to procure his unavailability.

QUESTION 44. The defendant came home from work early and found her husband in bed with another woman. Two days later, the police found the husband's body in a shallow grave in the backyard of their house. Two weeks before his death, the husband told his best friend Gary, "My wife told me if I cheated on her and she caught me, she would kill me." At the defendant's trial, the prosecutor calls Gary to testify about what the husband said. The defense objection should be:

A. Overruled, forfeiture by wrongdoing.
B. Overruled, dying declaration.
C. Overruled, declaration against interest.
D. Sustained, hearsay.

ANALYSIS.   This is a potential multiple hearsay problem, with the husband and the defendant wife as the two declarants. With respect to the wife as the declarant, her statement is not hearsay because the prosecutor is offering it against a party opponent, the defendant. To admit the statement, however, we would have to find a hearsay exception for the husband as a declarant. The prosecutor is offering the husband's assertion that his wife threatened to kill him for its truth, that is, that the wife really made the threat. Was it a dying declaration by the husband? No, because at the time he made the statement he did not believe that his death was imminent. Thus **B** is incorrect. Was the husband's statement a declaration against interest? He does not tell his best friend that he was cheating, but just that his wife threatened to kill him if he did. Repeating the threat by his wife was not against his penal or pecuniary interest. The statement was not a declaration against interest and **C** is incorrect. Finally, did the wife forfeit her hearsay objection and her Confrontation Clause right to cross-examine the husband by killing him? Whether she killed him remains to be proved, but even if she did, she did not do so to eliminate him as a witness. Forfeiture by wrongdoing does not apply here and **A** is incorrect. There is no hearsay exception for the husband's statement to Gary and it must be excluded. Choice **D** is the correct answer.

QUESTION 45. The defendant is charged with the murder of her husband. At the time of the murder, the wife and her husband were facing bank robbery charges. The husband was negotiating a deal with the prosecution to testify against his wife in exchange for immunity for himself. He did not show up for a court appearance one day and the police subsequently found his body in a quarry. Two days before the discovery of the body, the husband told his best friend Charlie, "My wife knows I'm meeting with the prosecutor. She told me that if I make a deal, I'd never live to testify." At the defendant wife's trial for murder, the prosecutor calls Charlie to testify to what the husband told him. The defense objection should be:

A. Sustained, hearsay.
B. Overruled, declaration against interest.
C. Overruled, forfeiture by wrongdoing.
D. Overruled, state of mind.

ANALYSIS. This is a potential multiple hearsay problem, with the wife and the husband as the declarants. As in the previous question, the prosecution is offering the wife's statement against her as a party opponent, and so her statement by itself is not hearsay. To admit it, however, there must be an exception for the husband's statement. Is it a declaration against interest? No, acknowledging that he is meeting with the prosecutor and that his wife might kill him for it is not against his penal or pecuniary interest. Meeting with the prosecutor might be against his interest in staying alive, but that does not qualify his statement that he is doing so as declaration against interest under the rule. Thus **B** is incorrect. Is the statement admissible under the state of mind exception? First, the husband's state of mind is not relevant in this homicide case. Second, his statement is not about his state of mind, but about the threat his wife made to him. He is asserting that an action happened in the past (his wife threatened him). It reflects his memory of what happened in the past, but proof of memory to prove the fact remembered is specifically excluded from the state of mind exception. Thus **D** is incorrect. Did the wife forfeit her hearsay objection and right to cross-examine under the Confrontation Clause because she killed her husband? In this case she did. She intended to eliminate him as a witness in the bank robbery case. That amounts to a forfeiture of her rights not only in the bank robbery case, but in this murder case as well. Choice **C** is the correct answer and **A** is incorrect.

5. Residual Hearsay Exception

Rule 807 provides a "catchall" exception for the trial judge to admit hearsay statements that do not fall within any of the recognized exceptions if the court determines the evidence is necessary and reliable.

> **Rule 807. Residual Exception**
> (a) In General. Under the following circumstances, a hearsay statement is not excluded by the rule against hearsay even if the statement is not specifically covered by a hearsay exception in Rule 803 or 804:
> (1) the statement has equivalent circumstantial guarantees of trustworthiness;
> (2) it is offered as evidence of a material fact;
> (3) it is more probative on the point for which it is offered than any other evidence that the proponent can obtain through reasonable efforts; and
> (4) admitting it will best serve the purposes of these rules and the interests of justice.
> (b) Notice. The statement is admissible only if, before the trial or hearing, the proponent gives an adverse party reasonable notice of the intent to offer the statement and its particulars, including the declarant's name and address, so that the party has a fair opportunity to meet it.

The requirement of necessity is established by the provision that the evidence must be "more probative on the point for which it is offered than any other evidence that the proponent can obtain through reasonable efforts." Reliability is established by the requirement that the evidence have "equivalent circumstantial guarantees of trustworthiness" as provided by the hearsay exceptions in Rules 803 and 804. Fairness requires that the opposing party have notice of the proponent's intention to invoke the exception.

The federal trial courts use the catchall exception infrequently, as Congress intended. It is difficult to summarize or categorize the factors that might persuade a court to employ this exception and the cases where it has been used tend to be sui generis.[8] The recognized exceptions take into account a large number of factors as demonstrating trustworthiness, such as spontaneity, the opportunities for a declarant to prevaricate, the motives of the declarant to speak truthfully or untruthfully, whether the circumstances were such that the declarant was able to perceive events accurately, the nature of what was at stake when the hearsay declaration was made, whether others were in a position to correct mistaken statements, whether statements were the result of some procedure or hearing, and whether there is or was an opportunity for the opponent to cross-examine the declarant, among others. With respect to necessity, courts focus on the diligence of the proponent in attempting to find other evidence to prove the point in question. Whether the proponent's efforts to find other evidence have been reasonable will depend in part on the importance of the point to be proven and the resources of the party in question.

For an example of the use of Rule 807, consider *United States v. Leal-Del Carmen*,[9] where the defendant was charged with alien smuggling. His defense was that he was one of the aliens being smuggled, and not one of the smugglers. When the border patrol agents interviewed the aliens (on videotape), three said that they had made travel arrangements with the defendant, but a fourth said that the defendant had not been "giving orders." The government kept the three who accused the defendant and deported the fourth before counsel had been assigned to represent the defendant. At trial the defendant offered the videotape of the exculpatory statement by the fourth alien but the trial judge excluded it. On appeal, with respect to the government's hearsay objection, the court held that the videotape was admissible under the catchall exception. As evidence of trustworthiness the court cited the fact that the statement was under oath, that the declarant made the statement voluntarily based on personal knowledge, and that presentation of the statement on videotape allowed

---

8. Probably the most common use has been for statements by child victims of abuse, where the child is unavailable or unable to testify. The cases have not established a general proposition that the catchall exception is always available in such cases. A variety of factors must be taken into account and there are many cases where the courts have rejected use of the catchall exception for child abuse victims.

9. *United States v. Leal-Del Carmen*, 697 F.3d 964 (9th Cir. 2012).

the jury to consider the demeanor of the witness, providing visual cues to assess her credibility.[10]

6. Confrontation Clause

The Sixth Amendment to the United States Constitution provides as follows, in pertinent part: "In all criminal prosecutions, the accused shall enjoy the right . . . to be confronted with the witnesses against him . . . " The Confrontation Clause applies only in criminal cases, and only with respect to witnesses against the defendant. The Confrontation Clause has no applicability to civil cases, and does not limit the evidence a criminal defendant can offer against the government.

Decisions of the Supreme Court establish that the right has three components: (1) the right to be present when a witness testifies against a criminal defendant; (2) the right to be in the view of the witness; and (3) the right to cross-examine the witness.

The right to be in the view of the witness is not absolute. The Supreme Court has held that in a child sexual abuse prosecution it was legitimate to permit a child witness to testify from another room by one-way closed circuit television, where the prosecution made a sufficient showing that testifying in the physical presence of the defendant would cause serious emotional suffering to the child.[11] Such exceptions are rare, and require a hearing and proof of the need for the procedure.

The most important right protected by the Confrontation Clause is the right to cross-examine witnesses against the defendant. The Supreme Court redefined the scope of this right in 2004 and several subsequent cases and there is still controversy concerning the contours of the right.[12] An exhaustive treatment of the doctrine and the issues concerning its application is beyond the scope of this Guide. We will focus on the main issues that the student of Evidence needs to understand.

When the prosecution offers hearsay evidence against a criminal defendant there are two questions that must be addressed. First, does the evidence fall within an exemption or exception to the hearsay rule? Second, would admission of the evidence violate the Confrontation Clause? The questions are related, but you must analyze them separately. Some evidence would be admissible under the hearsay rules, but not the Confrontation Clause; other evidence does not violate the Confrontation Clause, but is inadmissible under the hearsay rules.

---

10. As an alternative ground of admissibility, the court held that the evidence would have been admissible under Rule 804(b)(6), forfeiture by wrongdoing, because it was wrongful for the government to deport a witness with exculpatory information absent a knowing and intelligent waiver of his right to retain the witness by the defendant.

11. *Maryland v. Craig*, 497 U.S. 836 (1990).

12. See *Crawford v. Washington*, 541 U.S. 36 (2004), and its progeny.

The Confrontation Clause bars the introduction of "testimonial" hearsay against a criminal defendant unless the declarant is unavailable and the defendant had an opportunity to cross-examine the declarant. The Court has not spelled out a comprehensive definition of "testimonial" hearsay. It includes statements that are made for use in later criminal proceedings, such as affidavits that are prepared for use in Court; forensic reports; prior testimony from preliminary hearings, grand jury proceedings, and other trials; and statements made in response to police interrogation where the primary purpose of the interrogation is to establish or prove events potentially relevant to later criminal prosecution. Statements are not testimonial that are made in response to police interrogation to deal with an ongoing emergency that is threatening to a crime victim, the public, and/or the police.[13] The primary purpose inquiry is objective and takes into account when and where the interrogation took place, whether the encounter was formal or informal, and what purpose reasonable participants would have had for their statements and actions. A "911" call may be either testimonial or non-testimonial, depending on the circumstances. An encounter between the police and a declarant may begin as a response to an emergency, but then become testimonial once the emergency has been resolved.

If the police respond to a domestic disturbance and question the alleged victim to determine the extent of her injuries, the identity and current location of the person who assaulted her, and matters that might be pertinent to locating the assailant and terminating the threat that he poses to either the victim, the public, or the police, the victim's statements are likely to be held non-testimonial. On the other hand, once the alleged assailant is in custody, statements made in response to continuing questioning about the incident for the purpose of gathering evidence to use in court would be considered testimonial.

Where the prosecution introduces an out of court statement for a purpose other than proving the truth of the assertions in the statement, the Confrontation Clause is not implicated.

Forensic reports that are made for use in criminal proceedings are testimonial. The prosecution cannot introduce them in evidence without calling a witness with knowledge of the forensic procedures who can be cross-examined by the defendant. As of this writing, the case law is still developing with respect to the question of which laboratory or other personnel must be called as witnesses in connection with the introduction of forensic reports. In addition, there is ongoing controversy over the question of under what circumstances a substitute analyst may testify when the original analyst who performed a forensic test is unavailable.[14]

---

13. For what constitutes an ongoing emergency, see *Michigan v. Bryant*, 131 S. Ct. 1143 (2011).
14. See the various opinions from the badly splintered Court in *Williams v. Illinois*, 132 S. Ct. 2221 (2012).

A common problem in multi-defendant criminal cases arises when one or more of the co-defendants have made statements to the police but do not testify at trial. In the leading case, *Bruton v. United States,*[15] the Supreme Court held that it violated Bruton's Confrontation Clause rights for the prosecution to introduce the statement of a non-testifying co-defendant, even though the Court gave a limiting instruction that the jury could not consider the statement against Bruton. The statement was admissible against the co-defendant as a statement by a party opponent, but inadmissible against Bruton. The Court held that the likelihood that the jury could follow the limiting instruction was so slight that introduction of the statement violated Bruton's rights. In such situations, the prosecutor must decide whether to sever the cases and have separate trials, so that he can use the co-defendant's statement against him, or whether to have a joint trial and forego use of the statement altogether.

QUESTION 46. The plaintiff sued the defendant for setting fire to his building. An eyewitness to the fire testified in the grand jury investigating the fire as a criminal matter that he saw the defendant pouring something from a gasoline can through a window of the basement. At the civil trial, when the plaintiff called this person as a witness, he testified that he was at the scene of the fire, but did not see the defendant there. The plaintiff then offers the witness's statement to the grand jury. The defense objection should be:

A. Overruled, with a limiting instruction that the statement can be used for impeachment purposes only.
B. Overruled.
C. Sustained, violation of the defendant's Confrontation Clause rights.
D. Sustained, hearsay.

ANALYSIS. Let's begin with **C**, since this is the section about the Confrontation Clause. Choice **C** is incorrect because this is a civil case and the Confrontation Clause only applies in criminal cases. Even if this were a criminal case against the defendant, however, introducing the witness's statement to the grand jury would not violate his Confrontation Clause rights where the witness appears at trial and is subject to cross-examination then. A Confrontation Clause violation is cured by cross-examination, whether the cross-examination took place at the time the statement was originally made, or at the proceeding in which it is offered in evidence.

The grand jury testimony in this civil case is a prior inconsistent statement. The question is whether the plaintiff can only use it to impeach the witness under Rule 613, or whether the prior statement is admissible for its truth.

---

15. *Bruton v. United States,* 391 U.S. 123 (1968).

Under Rule 801(d)(1)(A), the statement is admissible for its truth because it was made under oath at a formal proceeding, the declarant is testifying in the current trial, and is subject to cross-examination concerning the statement. The correct answer is **B,** and **A** and **D** are incorrect.

QUESTION 47. Defendant is charged with stealing several high-definition television sets with Accomplice. After Accomplice was arrested, he made a tape-recorded statement to the police in which he admitted that he and Defendant took the televisions. Accomplice listened to the tape recording and signed a sworn affidavit that it was an accurate record of his statement and his recollection of the events. Accomplice died two days later of a heart attack.

If the prosecution offers the tape recording against Defendant at trial, the defense objection should be:

A. Sustained, admission of the tape would violate Defendant's rights under the Confrontation Clause.
B. Overruled, past recollection recorded exception.
C. Overruled, declaration against penal interest exception.
D. Overruled, dying declarations exception.

ANALYSIS.   Past recollection recorded is admissible only when the person who made the memorandum or report is on the stand and has a failure of recollection. The Accomplice is not on the witness stand, thus **B** is incorrect. It is unclear whether the statement was against Accomplice's penal interest. Most likely he was promised some sort of consideration for confessing and implicating the Defendant, in which event it would have been to his advantage to make the statement. In any event, the penal interest exception would satisfy only a hearsay exception, but not a Confrontation Clause objection. **C** is incorrect. There is no indication he was aware of his impending death at the time he made the statement, and it does not relate to the cause of his death. **D** is incorrect. The affidavit by the Accomplice was clearly prepared with the thought it would be used in a criminal proceeding and thus it was testimonial. Because the Defendant had no opportunity to cross-examine the Accomplice at any point, admission of the affidavit would violate his rights under the Confrontation Clause. **A** is correct.

QUESTION 48. In a conspiracy trial the government subpoenas from the telephone company and offers into evidence certified records showing that ten long-distance calls were made from defendant #1's home to the telephone number registered to defendant #2 during the time period in which the conspiracy was active. The defendants' objection to the records should be:

A. Sustained, relevance.
B. Sustained, hearsay.
C. Sustained, Confrontation Clause violation.
D. Overruled, business records exception.

ANALYSIS. The first question is whether this evidence is relevant. It tends to show that the defendants were in communication with each other, which makes it more likely that they were co-conspirators than it would be in the absence of any evidence that they had a relationship. Thus **A** is incorrect. The declarant is whoever entered the data into the records and the assertion is that calls were made between the numbers in question on the dates shown. These records are made in the ordinary course of business and it is the regular procedure of the telephone company to keep such records. They qualify as business records and are admissible against a hearsay exception, so **B** is incorrect. But does the admission of these records violate the defendants' Confrontation Clause rights? No, because the records do not constitute testimonial hearsay. The statements in the records were not made in the first instance to law enforcement personnel, did not result from police interrogation, and were not made in contemplation of their use in criminal proceedings. Business records made for ordinary business purposes, such as these, do not implicate the Confrontation Clause. Thus **C** is incorrect and the correct answer is **D**.

QUESTION 49. The Closer. The defendant David is on trial for the murder of Vanessa. The two were a couple until three months before Vanessa's death, when Vanessa began a new relationship with Jerry. The police found Vanessa dead in her living room, having been shot approximately two hours previously. The police found an unfinished, unmailed letter addressed to Jerry in Vanessa's handwriting, open on a table nearby, in which she wrote, "I'm sorry, I know this hurts you, but I'm going back to David." The prosecution's evidence established that Vanessa was shot at close range—within three feet based on powder burns in the area of the entrance wound. At trial the defendant David called Vanessa's mother as a witness. She testified she was familiar with her daughter's handwriting, and authenticated the letter as written by her. The defendant then called the officer who found the letter to the stand. He identified the exhibit proffered by the defense counsel as the letter he found and the defendant has offered the letter in evidence. How should the court rule on the prosecution's objection?

A. Sustained, the letter is hearsay.
B. Overruled.
C. Sustained, the state of mind of a homicide victim is not relevant in a murder case.

ANALYSIS.   This is an extremely difficult problem. Ordinarily I would use this problem as an essay question, because what is important is the reasoning you use to get to the right answer. Make sure you have thoroughly analyzed both the relevance and the hearsay issues before you read further.

The words in question are "I'm sorry, I know this hurts you, but I'm going back to David." The declarant is Vanessa and she makes two assertions: that she knows her letter will hurt Jerry, to whom it is addressed, and that she intends to go back to David. If the defendant is offering the letter to prove the truth of those assertions it would be hearsay and inadmissible unless it fell within an exception. In that event, **A** would be the correct answer.

What about the state of mind exception to the hearsay rule? Is **B** the correct answer? The words in question are assertions about Vanessa's state of mind—she knows her letter will hurt Jerry and she intends to go back to David. So far, so good, but evidence must be relevant to be admissible. A statement of intention could be relevant to prove the declarant later carried out the intention. Proof of intention can be some evidence of the happening of the act that was intended. But in the present case, Vanessa apparently had no opportunity to carry out the intention because she was killed. Apart from constituting evidence of future action, was her state of mind that she was willing to hurt Jerry and desirous of going back to David relevant? Ordinarily the state of mind of a homicide victim is not relevant in a murder case. As a general proposition, the statement in **C** is correct.

The state of mind or feelings of a homicide victim might be relevant under certain circumstances. If the killer were aware of the victim's state of mind and her state of mind provided him with a motive to kill her, then it would be relevant. The letter in question, however, was unfinished and unmailed.

We have been proceeding on the assumption that the defendant would be offering the letter to prove the truth of the assertions in it, which would make it hearsay. But is there another purpose for which the letter might be offered that could take it out of the hearsay rule? What if the statement in the letter is offered to prove the effect it had on the reader? "What reader?" you say—the letter was never mailed.

Now we have come by two different routes to the nub of the problem. The state of mind of the victim would be relevant if it were known to the killer and provided him with a motive to kill her. This is a conditional relevance problem under Rule 104(b). The relevance of the letter depends on whether a fact exists, namely if the killer read it. And the letter would not be hearsay if it were offered to prove the effect it had on the reader, which requires a reader.

Do you remember where the police found the letter? It was open on a table near the body. Vanessa was shot at close range. There is sufficient evidence to satisfy the jury by a preponderance of the evidence that the killer read the letter, which would make it relevant. That satisfies Rule 104(b) and the court should admit the letter, instructing the jury that it may not consider the letter unless the jury finds by a preponderance of the evidence that the killer did read it. Moreover, the defendant can argue that he is not offering the letter to prove the truth of its assertions, but only for the effect they would have had on the person who read them, namely the killer if the jury finds he did so. Both routes lead to the same result—the letter is admissible. If the jury concludes that the killer read it, it provides a powerful reason to believe that the killer was Jerry and to raise a reasonable doubt that it was David. The correct answer is **B**.

✴ Avery's Picks

1. Question 1   **E**
2. Question 2   **B**
3. Question 3   **B**
4. Question 4   **B**
5. Question 5   **C**
6. Question 6   **D**
7. Question 7   **D**
8. Question 8   **C**
9. Question 9   **A**
10. Question 10   **A**
11. Question 11   **C**
12. Question 12   **B**
13. Question 13   **C**
14. Question 14   **B**
15. Question 15   **A**
16. Question 16   **D**
17. Question 17   **D**
18. Question 18   **B**
19. Question 19   **D**
20. Question 20   **A**
21. Question 21   **B**
22. Question 22   **C**
23. Question 23   **D**
24. Question 24   **C**
25. Question 25   **D**
26. Question 26   **B**
27. Question 27   **D**
28. Question 28   **D**
29. Question 29   **C**
30. Question 30   **A**
31. Question 31   **D**
32. Question 32   **C**
33. Question 33   **D**
34. Question 34   **D**
35. Question 35   **C**
36. Question 36   **B**

37. Question 37   **D**
38. Question 38   **D**
39. Question 39   **A**
40. Question 40   **A**
41. Question 41   **A**
42. Question 42   **B**
43. Question 43   **C**
44. Question 44   **D**
45. Question 45   **C**
46. Question 46   **B**
47. Question 47   **A**
48. Question 48   **D**
49. Question 49   **B**

9

Authentication

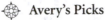
vidence is not admissible unless there has been a preliminary showing
that it is authentic. This is true whether the evidence is a document, a
photograph, an object, handwriting, or a voice. There must be a sufficient basis for concluding that the item offered in evidence is what the proponent claims it is. Merely because an item of evidence is authentic does not
mean it is admissible. It must satisfy all the other rules of evidence as well.

A. Authenticating Evidence

Rule 901(a) provides the basic rule with respect to authentication.

> **Rule 901. Authenticating or Identifying Evidence**
> **(a) In General.** To satisfy the requirement of authenticating or identify-
> ing an item of evidence, the proponent must produce evidence sufficient to
> support a finding that the item is what the proponent claims it is.

The trial judge makes the decision, under Rule 104(a), whether there has been
a sufficient foundation that a piece of evidence is authentic for it to be admitted. Ultimately it is up to the jury as the finder of fact to determine whether the
evidence is authentic. The judge must admit the evidence and submit it to the
jury for consideration as long as there is "evidence sufficient to support a finding" that the item is what it is claimed to be. That means sufficient evidence
for a reasonable jury to find, by a preponderance of the evidence, that the item
is authentic.

Any combination of direct and/or circumstantial evidence may serve as a basis for the court to find that a piece of evidence is authentic. Rule 901(b) provides a list of examples of how evidence may be authenticated.

(b) Examples. The following are examples only—not a complete list—of evidence that satisfies the requirement:

(1) Testimony of a Witness with Knowledge. Testimony that an item is what it is claimed to be.

(2) Nonexpert Opinion About Handwriting. A nonexpert's opinion that handwriting is genuine, based on a familiarity with it that was not acquired for the current litigation.

(3) Comparison by an Expert Witness or the Trier of Fact. A comparison with an authenticated specimen by an expert witness or the trier of fact.

(4) Distinctive Characteristics and the Like. The appearance, contents, substance, internal patterns, or other distinctive characteristics of the item, taken together with all the circumstances.

(5) Opinion About a Voice. An opinion identifying a person's voice—whether heard firsthand or through mechanical or electronic transmission or recording—based on hearing the voice at any time under circumstances that connect it with the alleged speaker.

(6) Evidence About a Telephone Conversation. For a telephone conversation, evidence that a call was made to the number assigned at the time to:

(A) a particular person, if circumstances, including self-identification, show that the person answering was the one called; or

(B) a particular business, if the call was made to a business and the call related to business reasonably transacted over the telephone.

(7) Evidence About Public Records. Evidence that:

(A) a document was recorded or filed in a public office as authorized by law; or

(B) a purported public record or statement is from the office where items of this kind are kept.

(8) Evidence About Ancient Documents or Data Compilations. For a document or data compilation, evidence that it:

(A) is in a condition that creates no suspicion about its authenticity;

(B) was in a place where, if authentic, it would likely be; and

(C) is at least 20 years old when offered.

(9) Evidence About a Process or System. Evidence describing a process or system and showing that it produces an accurate result.

(10) Methods Provided by a Statute or Rule. Any method of authentication or identification allowed by a federal statute or a rule prescribed by the Supreme Court.

Let's see what some of these examples look like in the courtroom. Notice in the examples below that the exhibits were marked for identification before they were shown to the witness. This is so it is clear from the record what item the lawyer and the witness are talking about. If the exhibit is not received in evidence, it does not get shown to the jury and does not go into the jury room during deliberations. It remains part of the court record, however. In the event of an appeal the rejected exhibits will be sent to the appellate court if a party is complaining of their exclusion from evidence.

Witness with Knowledge

Prosecutor:	Ms. Victim, showing you what has been marked as State's Ex. 10 for identification, can you tell us what this is?
Victim:	Yes, I can.
Prosecutor:	What is it?
Victim:	That's the ring that was stolen from my apartment last July.
Prosecutor:	How can you recognize it?
Victim:	It's been in my family for over one hundred years. It has a unique setting for the ruby, which is bordered by very small diamonds.
Prosecutor:	I offer this in evidence, your Honor.
Judge:	It may be received.

Distinctive Characteristics

Prosecutor:	Detective, showing you what has been marked as State's Ex. 5 for identification, can you tell us what this is?
Detective:	Yes, I can.
Prosecutor:	What is it?
Detective:	That is the revolver that I found at the crime scene.
Prosecutor:	How can you recognize it?
Detective:	When I took it into police custody, I scratched my initials in the butt of the gun. There they are—M.A.
Prosecutor:	I offer this in evidence, your Honor.
Judge:	It may be received.

Opinion About a Voice

Prosecutor:	Ms. Witness, have you ever spoken with the Defendant?
Witness:	Yes, I have spoken with the defendant on numerous occasions.
Prosecutor:	Were any of those occasions by telephone?
Witness:	Yes, we have spoken on the telephone.
Prosecutor:	How many times have you spoken with the Defendant on the telephone?
Witness:	Approximately fifty times.
Prosecutor:	Are you able to recognize the Defendant's voice when you speak to him on the telephone?
Witness:	Yes, easily.
Prosecutor:	Did you receive any telephone calls on Friday evening of last week?
Witness:	Yes.

Prosecutor:	Who called you?
Witness:	The Defendant.
Prosecutor:	What did he say?
Witness:	He said that if I testified against him in this trial he would hurt my children.

In this example, the threat against the witness would have no relevance unless it came from the defendant or someone else on his behalf. Authenticating the defendant's voice is thus essential for the conversation to be admissible.

The methods of authentication are simply logical and common sense ways of accomplishing the requirement of Rule 901(a): providing evidence that an item is what the proponent claims it is. A photograph is a common exhibit in trials. To authenticate the photograph it is not necessary to have the photographer testify, or to call someone from a photo lab who developed the picture. The issue is simply whether the photo actually depicts what it purports to depict. Anyone with knowledge of the subject matter of the photo may testify that it does. Here is an example.

Plaintiff's Lawyer:	Mr. Witness, were you present at the scene of the accident after the plaintiff's and the defendant's cars collided?
Witness:	Yes, I was.
Plaintiff's Lawyer:	What could you see?
Witness:	I could see the entire intersection, including the traffic control signals and the locations where both cars came to rest. I saw the debris from the accident scattered about the intersection.
Plaintiff's Lawyer:	Showing you what has been marked as Plaintiff's Exhibit three for identification, can you tell us what it is?
Witness:	It is a photo of the accident scene.
Plaintiff's Lawyer:	Does that photograph fairly and accurately depict the scene of the accident as you saw it in the moments after the collision?
Witness:	Yes.
Plaintiff's Lawyer:	I offer it, your Honor.
The Court:	It may be received.

An x-ray is a photograph, but it cannot be authenticated in the same way. It is an image of the inside of the body and usually there is no witness who could testify that it is a fair and accurate representation of what it depicts. Rule 901(b)(9) indicates that evidence can be authenticated by "describing a process or system and showing that it produces an accurate result." If we were introducing an x-ray for the first time, we could call an appropriate technician to explain the process to the judge and testify that it produces an accurate result. By now, however, x-ray technology is so commonplace that no one would raise the issue. The court would, in effect, be taking judicial notice of the process and its ability to produce accurate results.

Rule 901(b)(1) could also be used to authenticate the number from which an incoming call was dialed by having an appropriate witness explain how the process of identifying the incoming number works on a modern telephone.

Sometimes a relevant exhibit consists of fungible material. For example, one pile of white powder looks pretty much like another pile of white powder. How can the proponent establish that the material introduced into evidence is what the proponent claims it is? Under these circumstances the proponent uses chain of custody evidence to demonstrate the authenticity of the exhibit. For example, when white powder is seized in someone's home the police will put it into an evidence envelope with an identifying name or case number. The envelope will be logged into the police property room. When it is sent to the crime lab for analysis it will be logged out of the property room and into the lab. This process of documenting the movement and location of the item will continue until the exhibit is produced in court. An unbroken chain of custody is evidence that the powder produced in the courtroom is the same powder that was seized from the defendant's home. What if there is a break in the chain of custody because someone forgot to log an exhibit in or out? Usually a break in the chain of custody is not fatal to admissibility. Ordinarily a court will say the break goes to the weight of the evidence, not admissibility. However, if circumstances are suspicious enough to suggest evidence tampering, an incomplete chain of custody might result in the exclusion of evidence.

In today's world much authentication deals with electronically stored information. The technology is new, but the rules of authentication are the same. The proponent must offer sufficient evidence that the item in question is what he claims it is. For example, with respect to an email purportedly from X, it will be necessary to show that X was the author of the email in order to authenticate it. Evidence that the email includes X's name as the author or that the communication originated from a social networking site such as Facebook or MySpace that bore X's name would not be sufficient to authenticate the electronic communication as one authored by or sent by X. (Similarly, an incoming telephone call from an unknown caller cannot be authenticated as coming from X merely because the caller said his name was X.) Additional circumstantial evidence may be used to authenticate the email as coming from X, however. For example, evidence that the email was found on a computer that other evidence proved belonged to X, or for which X knew the passwords; evidence of the content of the email that might demonstrate that it came from X, for example, by including his picture, or by referring to information that one would expect X, but not many others, to know; evidence that X later appeared at a time and place that the email said he would; evidence that when an investigator who knew X's voice called the telephone number provided in the email, X answered; and the like. The question is simply whether the combination of direct and circumstantial evidence would be sufficient to convince the trier of fact by a preponderance of the evidence that the electronic information is what the proponent claims it is.

B. Self-Authenticating Evidence

Some exhibits are deemed self-authenticating, so that no testimony is required for their authenticity to be established. The exhibit itself includes information that establishes its authenticity, often a seal or certification. The self-authentication rules deal only with the issue of authentication. Demonstrating that an exhibit or document is authentic does not guarantee admissibility. It is essential to make sure the other rules of evidence have been complied with as well.

Rule 902 provides a list of self-authenticating items of evidence. They include:

- Domestic public documents under seal
- Domestic public documents signed and certified
- Certain foreign public documents
- Certified copies of public records
- Official publications issued by a public authority
- Newspapers and periodicals
- Trade inscriptions and the like
- Notarized documents
- Commercial paper and related documents
- Documents declared to be presumptively genuine under a federal statute
- Certified domestic business records
- Certified foreign business records
- Certified records generated by an electronic process or system[1]
- Certified data copied from an electronic device, storage medium, or file[2]

There are technical requirements that must be met with respect to several of the foregoing categories. You should review the rules in detail in order to make use of a particular category.

---

1. Added by the 2017 amendments to the FRE. The purpose of the amendments was to allow authentication of electronic evidence other than through the testimony of a foundation witness, by compliance with the provisions on business records in Rules 902 (11) and (12).

2. Added by the 2017 amendments to the FRE. The purpose of the amendments was to allow authentication of data copied from electronic evidence other than through the testimony of a foundation witness, by compliance with the provisions on business records in Rules 902 (11) and (12).

QUESTION 1. The Closer.   The defendant is charged with the theft of cash from a store where he used to work as a clerk. At the trial, the prosecutor seeks to offer in evidence through his former employer a handwritten letter stating, "I'm sorry I stole from you, but I needed the money for an operation. I will pay it back as soon as I can." The employer says that she became familiar with the defendant's handwriting when he was working for her and recognizes the signature on the letter as his. The defendant has denied that he wrote this letter and objects. The defendant's objection should be:

A. Sustained, because lay opinion testimony regarding handwriting identification is not admissible.

B. Sustained—unless the judge determines that the letter is authentic by a preponderance of the evidence.

C. Overruled, with an instruction to the jury that it is up to them to decide whether the letter is authentic.

D. Overruled—the court should hold the letter is authentic and instruct the jury that it must consider it to be authentic.

ANALYSIS.   Handwriting is one of the specific examples discussed in the rules. Rule 901(b) provides that a person who is not an expert may identify handwriting if he has familiarity with the author's handwriting that was not acquired for the purpose of litigation. Here the employer had such familiarity. Thus **A** is incorrect. The other choices require you to be clear about the burden of proof required to establish authenticity and the division of responsibilities between the judge and the jury. The judge does not make the ultimate decision about whether or not an item is authentic or genuine. The judge determines whether there is sufficient evidence to warrant admitting the item in evidence, but the jury makes the final decision about whether the item is authentic. Thus **D** is incorrect.

To admit the evidence the court must ask whether there is sufficient evidence for the jury to conclude by a preponderance of the evidence that the item is authentic. If there is, the judge admits the evidence. **B** is incorrect because the judge does not make a final decision on whether the item has been shown by a preponderance of the evidence to be authentic. The correct answer is **C**. If the jury believes the employer, there is enough evidence to conclude by a preponderance of the evidence that the defendant wrote the letter. So the judge will admit the letter into evidence. The jury, however, is free to decide that the employer is lying, or is mistaken, and to conclude that the defendant did not write this letter.

 Avery's Picks

1. Question 1   **C**

Contents of Writings, Recordings, and Photographs

CHAPTER OVERVIEW
A. When the Best Evidence Rule Applies
B. When the Best Evidence Rule Does Not Apply
C. The Preference for Originals
D. Secondary Evidence of Contents
E. Summaries
F. Proof of Contents Through Evidence from Opponent
✦ Avery's Picks

This chapter is about what is usually known as the "best evidence rule." The phrase "best evidence" is a misnomer. There is no rule that requires a party to offer the best evidence to prove something. What we do have is a rule that says when a party is attempting to prove the contents of a writing, recording, or photograph, there is a preference for the original. This is set forth in Rule 1002.

> **Rule 1002. Requirement of the Original**
> An original writing, recording, or photograph is required in order to prove its content unless these rules or a federal statute provides otherwise.

The terms "writing," "recording," and "photograph" are broadly defined in Rule 1001 to include any form and any content that one might imagine finding in a writing, recording, or photograph.[1] The preference for the original is intended to reduce the risk of fraud, forgery, or mistake when the contents of a writing, recording, or photograph are at issue.

---

1. In a copyright infringement action concerning the "Imperial Walkers" in the movie "The Empire Strikes Back," the court held that drawings of the creatures were "writings" within the meaning of Rule 1001(1) in *Seiler v. Lucasfilm, Ltd.*, 808 F.2d 1316 (9th Cir. 1986).

A.   When the Best Evidence Rule Applies

The best evidence rule applies *only* when a party is attempting to prove the contents of a writing, recording, or photograph. What you need to learn is how to determine when a party is trying to prove such content. There are two situations in which content is the issue. First, when litigation concerns a legally operative document the contents of the document must be proven. For example, if the litigation concerns the rights of the parties under a contract, a will, a mortgage, or a deed, it is necessary to prove the contents of the applicable document. Second, writings, recordings, and photographs may be introduced to prove events or conditions that are described or portrayed therein. Under those circumstances the party is using the contents of the writing, recording, or photograph to prove something about those events or conditions. If writings, recordings, or photographs are introduced for either of the foregoing purposes Rule 1002 requires the original unless there is an exception under the applicable rules or statutes.

Let's look at some examples. A supplier sues a buyer for failing to make payment for goods delivered. To prove the amount due the supplier wants to introduce a copy of the contract into evidence. Rule 1002 requires the original unless an exception applies. In a criminal case, the prosecution wants to prove that the defendant Jones was carrying a gun in a public place. To do so the prosecutor seeks to introduce into evidence a text from one person to another stating, "OMG, Jones just walked by with a gun." Rule 1002 requires the original of the text unless an exception applies. In a personal injury case the plaintiff wants to prove the extent of facial scarring she suffered by offering into evidence a photograph taken of her a month after the accident. Rule 1002 requires the original of the photograph unless an exception applies.

B.   When the Best Evidence Rule Does Not Apply

It is important to be able to see when the best evidence rule would not apply. Suppose in order to prove that the defendant Jones was carrying a gun in a public place the prosecutor called the witness who saw him. That witness later sent a text to the prosecutor describing what he saw. The opponent cannot successfully object to the witness's live testimony by arguing that the original of the text is required. The witness saw Jones with the gun and is competent to describe what he saw. The prosecutor in this instance is not trying to prove the content of a writing, but rather the happening of an event by calling a witness who saw it. Suppose a personal injury plaintiff offers to prove the extent of her facial scarring by describing the scars. The defendant cannot object on the ground that the original of a photograph of the plaintiff is required. The plaintiff is attempting to prove the contents of her face, so to speak, not the contents of a photograph of her face.

QUESTION 1. Plaintiff was in an automobile accident and was out of work for several weeks due to her injuries. At trial, she seeks to prove her lost wages by testifying to her weekly salary before the accident and multiplying it by the number of weeks she was forced to miss work. The defendant objects on best evidence grounds and argues that the payroll records from her employer are required to prove her lost wages. How should the court rule on the Defendant's objection?

A. Sustained.
B. Overruled.

ANALYSIS. The plaintiff is allowed to testify based on her personal knowledge of her pay rate and the amount of time she was out of work. The records are not required. Certainly introducing the original records as business records would be one way to prove what the plaintiff lost, but it is not the only way. **B** is the correct answer.

The foregoing examples demonstrate this proposition: where there is independent evidence of an event or condition, the fact that the event or condition is also described or portrayed in a writing, recording, or photograph does not support a best evidence objection to the independent evidence.

C.   The Preference for Originals

When the best evidence rule applies it requires the original of a writing, recording, or photograph unless an exception applies. Perhaps the most common exception recognized by the Federal Rules is when there is a "duplicate." Rule 1001(e) defines a duplicate:

> (e) A "duplicate" means a counterpart produced by a mechanical, photographic, chemical, electronic, or other equivalent process or technique that accurately reproduces the original.

As you can see, the definition of a "duplicate" is very broad. Duplicates are generally admissible to the same extent as originals, as provided in Rule 1003.

> **Rule 1003. Admissibility of Duplicates**
> A duplicate is admissible to the same extent as the original unless a genuine question is raised about the original's authenticity or the circumstances make it unfair to admit the duplicate.

Lacking evidence of unfairness or a genuine question about the authenticity of the original, a duplicate will be admissible. Photocopies are freely admissible in lieu of originals, unless such a question exists or in the rare instance where it might be unfair to use a photocopy.

D. Secondary Evidence of Contents

If a party is attempting to prove the content of a writing, recording, or photograph but does not have either an original or a duplicate, other secondary evidence of contents is admissible under a variety of circumstances, as set forth in Rule 1004.

> **Rule 1004. Admissibility of other Evidence of Content**
> An original is not required and other evidence of the content of a writing, recording, or photograph is admissible if:
> (a) all the originals are lost or destroyed, and not by the proponent acting in bad faith;
> (b) an original cannot be obtained by any available judicial process;
> (c) the party against whom the original would be offered had control of the original; was at that time put on notice, by pleadings or otherwise, that the original would be a subject of proof at the trial or hearing; and fails to produce it at the trial or hearing; or
> (d) the writing, recording, or photograph is not closely related to a controlling issue.

The other evidence of contents will usually be someone's memory of what the writing, recording, or photograph said or portrayed. Such evidence is admissible where the originals have been lost or destroyed other than by the proponent in bad faith. Secondary evidence is admissible where the original cannot be obtained through subpoena. If the opponent has the original and refuses to produce it, despite being on notice that it would be at issue at the trial, secondary evidence of contents by the proponent is admissible. If the writing, recording, or photograph relates to a collateral matter secondary evidence of contents is admissible. In addition, Rule 1005 provides that where the original is a public record the proponent can introduce a certified copy to prove the contents, or a copy that a witness testifies is correct after comparing it with the original.

E. Summaries

Sometimes a relevant document or set of documents is so voluminous that it is impractical to introduce the originals. Suppose plaintiff sues a major corporation for sex discrimination in employment. There might be hundreds of personnel files, containing thousands of pages of documents, required to establish a pattern of sex discrimination. It would be impractical and relatively meaningless to introduce the original files, since the jurors could hardly be expected to read them all. Rule 1006 deals with this situation.

> **RULE 1006. SUMMARIES TO PROVE CONTENT**
>
> The proponent may use a summary, chart, or calculation to prove the content of voluminous writings, recordings, or photographs that cannot be conveniently examined in court. The proponent must make the originals or duplicates available for examination or copying, or both, by other parties at a reasonable time and place. And the court may order the proponent to produce them in court.

The proponent can use a chart or summary instead of the original documents, so long as the opponent was given an opportunity to examine and copy the originals.

F.   Proof of Contents Through Evidence from Opponent

Finally, Rule 1007 provides that the proponent can prove the content of a writing, recording, or photograph through the testimony, deposition, or written statement of the opponent. Under those circumstances the proponent does not have to account for the absence of the original.

QUESTION 2. The Closer.   The defendant is on trial for murder. The prosecution alleged that she killed the victim because the victim stole the defendant's husband. A police officer would testify that he was in the defendant's house a week after the murder with a search warrant and that he seized a picture from the defendant's bedroom dresser drawer. The officer would testify that the picture shows the victim and the defendant's husband kissing. The defendant objects to the testimony. The court should:

A. Overrule the objection because the description of the picture is relevant on the issue of motive.
B. Overrule the objection because the best evidence rule does not apply to the case.
C. Sustain the objection unless the prosecution can provide a satisfactory explanation of why the original picture is missing.
D. Sustain the objection because the picture is not relevant.

ANALYSIS.   The basic question in any best evidence problem is whether the proponent is attempting to prove the contents of a writing, recording, or photograph. Here the prosecutor is trying to prove the contents of the photograph.

The prosecutor's theory is that the defendant had a photograph that showed her husband being unfaithful, which gave her a motive to kill him. Thus **B** is incorrect—the best evidence rule does apply to this case. Choices **A** and **D** address the issue of relevance. The contents of the picture are clearly relevant. The fact that the defendant had such a picture makes it more likely that she killed her husband than if she had no such evidence of infidelity. Thus **D** is incorrect. Choice **A** is also incorrect, because a description of the picture is not admissible simply because it is relevant. The best evidence rule must also be satisfied. The correct answer is **C**. The officer's memory of what the picture contained is not admissible unless the prosecution can show that the original was lost or destroyed through no bad faith of the government.

 # Avery's Picks

1. Question 1   **B**
2. Question 2   **C**

Index